TV's American Dream

TV's American Dream

US Television after the Great Recession

Barbara Selznick

BLOOMSBURY ACADEMIC

NEW YORK • LONDON • OXFORD • NEW DELHI • SYDNEY

BLOOMSBURY ACADEMIC
Bloomsbury Publishing Inc
1385 Broadway, New York, NY 10018, USA
50 Bedford Square, London, WC1B 3DP, UK
29 Earlsfort Terrace, Dublin 2, Ireland

BLOOMSBURY, BLOOMSBURY ACADEMIC and the Diana logo are trademarks of
Bloomsbury Publishing Plc

First published in the United States of America 2025

Cover design: Eleanor Rose
Cover illustration © Tithi Luadthong / Alamy

Library of Congress Cataloging-in-Publication Data
Names: Selznick, Barbara J., 1970- author.
Title: TV's American dream: U.S. television after the Great Recession / Barbara Selznick.
Description: New York: Bloomsbury Academic, 2025. |
Includes bibliographical references and index.
Identifiers: LCCN 2024028784 (print) | LCCN 2024028785 (ebook) |
ISBN 9781501389689 (paperback) | ISBN 9781501389696 (hardback) |
ISBN 9781501389672 (ebook) | ISBN 9781501389665 (pdf)
Subjects: LCSH: Television programs–United States–History–21st century. |
American Dream on television. | Global Financial Crisis, 2008-2009–Influence.
Classification: LCC PN1992.3.U5 S355 2025 (print) | LCC PN1992.3.U5 (ebook) |
DDC 302.23/450973–dc23/eng/20240828
LC record available at https://lccn.loc.gov/2024028784
LC ebook record available at https://lccn.loc.gov/2024028785

ISBN: HB: 978-1-5013-8969-6
PB: 978-1-5013-8968-9
ePDF: 978-1-5013-8966-5
eBook: 978-1-5013-8967-2

Typeset by Deanta Global Publishing Services, Chennai, India

To find out more about our authors and books visit www.bloomsbury.com
and sign up for our newsletters.

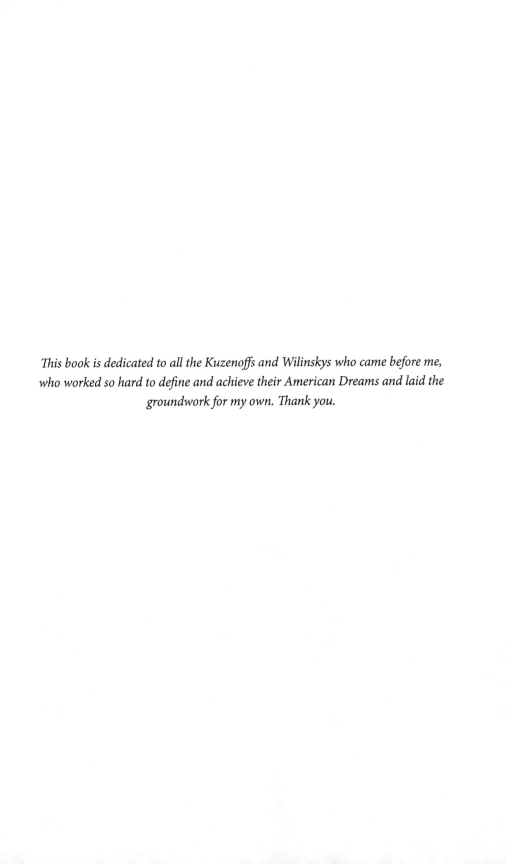

This book is dedicated to all the Kuzenoffs and Wilinskys who came before me, who worked so hard to define and achieve their American Dreams and laid the groundwork for my own. Thank you.

Contents

Acknowledgments   viii

Introduction: Introducing the Dream: Everything Changes   1
1   Franchising the Dream: Tentpole Television   15
2   Believing the Dream: Network Rebranding   57
3   Transgressing the Dream: Signature Comedies   93
4   Rerunning the Dream: Television Syndication   135
Conclusion: Holding on to the Dream: Everything Changes   173

Works Cited   177
Index   201

Acknowledgments

The world, and my world, has changed in countless ways since the start of this project. It has been a challenging few years, full of both celebration and loss. Many people provided the support—emotional, intellectual, physical—that allowed me to complete this book.

The folks at Bloomsbury were champions of this project from the beginning. Katie Gallof Houck and Stephanie Grace-Petinos were both patient with me and persistent on my behalf. I'd also like to thank the anonymous readers for their insightful comments and helpful suggestions.

My colleagues in the School of Theatre, Film and Television at the University of Arizona continue to inspire me and broaden my perspective. I want to especially thank my film and television colleagues: Jacob Bricca, Anna Cooper, Mary Beth Haralovich, Nicole Koschmann Yuri Makino, Orquidea Morales, Michael Mulcahy, Shane Riches, Brad Schauer, Beverly Seckinger, Lisanne Skyler, and Cody Young. I appreciate their hard work, humor, and friendship in the midst of so much chaos. Brant Pope also provided much-needed support and inspiration. My students continually shape my thinking on all things media related, offering me a range of viewpoints from the Millennial and Gen Z television audiences. Their ideas inform my thinking by challenging my academic framework and pushing back against my Gen X assumptions.

Many friends, colleagues, and scholars, too many to list here, bolstered me through some difficult times, encouraged me to keep researching and writing, and, whether they know it or not, informed my thinking. I can, without a single doubt, say that I would never have finished this without the guidance and inspiration of Karla Fuller and Julie Sandor. Their generosity with their time and discerning brain power was invaluable and much valued. Thank you, thank you, thank you. An extra special thanks to Julie for her gentle (and, when necessary, not-so-gentle) editing in the final stages of the project.

There was much that was lost while I worked on this book amid a global pandemic but, for me, the personal losses that came after were the most difficult. Knowing, without a single reservation, that my mother would have been so very proud of this accomplishment is one of the best gifts she could have given me. I like to imagine that she and my dad are off somewhere still laughing over the fact that I get to watch television as a job. Navigating her loss (and a seemingly endless estate process) was made bearable by the support of my family, who also gave me plenty to celebrate. Thank you to Steven and Katherine and their beautiful children and grandchildren for providing much-needed respite (and great vacations). Elyn and Mark did considerable heavy lifting (often literally) so that I could keep working. It's an honor to be Betty's daughter alongside Elyn, whose reminders that "we've got this" became the soundtrack moving me forward. My husband, Sanford, is unendingly understanding, strong, and inspirational. I appreciate that he explains computery space science to me as if I can understand it, and he (sometimes) laughs at my jokes. He watches so much television with me and cooks me great food; I especially enjoy the food. I'm amazed when I think about all the changes my children went through while I worked on this manuscript. Throughout, Lily and Ellis were encouraging and understanding; they asked about my work, and (mostly) respected my writing time even while they were trying to navigate high school from home and eventually their own university lives. They are ridiculously impressive people— definitely a net-plus for my life and for the world. I think my kids would be upset with me if I didn't acknowledge our dogs, who really do deserve to be thanked. Dogs are wonderful. Maya was the best of the best dogs and I miss her, I'm thankful that Milo has stopped eating my shoes, and I admire that Timmy doesn't realize that he's the size of a big cat.

This book is about the depiction of the American Dream on television in the face of crisis and change. As I researched and wrote, one thing that became clear is how fortunate I am in this life. In the face of my personal crises and changes, I have people to lift me up and talk me down—and I am grateful for the opportunity to publicly acknowledge how lucky I am to have them.

Introduction

Introducing the Dream: Everything Changes

Like so many concepts that live in the realm of the mythic, the idea of the American Dream began before it was named. The term "American Dream" entered common usage in John Truslow Adams's 1931 book *The Epic of America*. Adams describes how

> the American dream that has lured tens of millions of all nations to our shores in the past century has not been a dream of merely material plenty, though that has doubtless counted heavily. It has been much more than that. It has been a dream of being able to grow to fullest development as man and woman, unhampered by the barriers which had slowly been erected in older civilizations, unrepressed by social orders. (1931, 405)

This picture of the American Dream offers opportunity not only, or even primarily, for the accumulation of possessions but for unimpeded personal growth and freedom. Adams proposes that, unlike in other countries, in America anyone can succeed, anyone can become whoever they want to be. Writing during the Great Depression, Adams found hope for Americans not in the material goods that many could no longer afford, but in the promise of self-reinvention and the hope of upward mobility. Adams demonstrates that the concept of the American Dream has and continues to adjust and adapt to changes in the US political, economic, social, and cultural contexts. The Great Recession of the early 2000s and its complicated aftermath offered yet another opportunity for questions and transformations.

While Adams may have popularized the phrase, the idea of the American Dream existed well before this in popular imagination, for example, theorized by Alexis De Tocqueville in the 1830s (*Democracy in America*) and discussed by Walter Lippmann in 1914 (*Drift and Mastery: An Attempt to Diagnose the Current Unrest*). The creed consistently transforms and adapts to changes in the US political, economic, social, and cultural contexts. Jim Cullen, in *The American Dream: A Short History of an Idea That Shaped a Nation*, examines how the roots of the Dream were established by the Puritans as they set out to create a new world that offered the potential that "things—religious and otherwise—could be different" (2006, 15). The Dream was reconfigured with the expansion of the United States across the west, emphasizing individualism as a means of achieving a Dream centered on personal autonomy. Industrialization, the Great Depression, the rise of credit-culture after the Second World War, and so on. all reshaped the structure and function of an American Dream that is both shared and personal; that is imagined to be available to everyone but needs to be earned; that is a source of communal connection and reliant on individual effort; that is always possible but, at the same time, always out of reach; that is "largely an illusion but is a very useful and valuable one" (Samuel 2012, 171).

In all cases, the American Dream, at its heart, is an imagining of what is possible for people to achieve in the United States at a given point in time. The finish line of the American Dream is forever a moving target. Is it freedom—religious freedom, freedom to control one's own destiny, freedom to work where and when one wants? Is it upward mobility—in terms of socioeconomic class, education, at work, or for one's children? Is it measured by consumption—a home, a car, an iPhone? The idea of the American Dream has meant all these things at different times and at the same time. As will be discussed below and in the following chapters, these conceptualizations are undergirded by certain values and ideals including that all Americans have equal opportunity to achieve the Dream, that achievement of the Dream rests on a person's individual merits rather than a hereditary claim, that, regardless of one's past, the Dream's achievement is always possible through hard work and skill. The interpretation of these values, the weight that they're given, and the ways that they're defined vary at given points in time, shaped by historical context and their potential usefulness. Because the American Dream is also very useful. As Jennifer Hochschild explains, "the American dream is an impressive ideology. It has for centuries lured people to America and moved them around within it, and it has kept them striving in horrible conditions against impossible odds" (1996, 25).

Hegemonic ideas about the American Dream are shaped by and reflected in popular culture. This book explores what television programming can tell us about how the American Dream shifted in the aftermath of the 2007–9 Great Recession. Television is a particularly interesting medium to examine at this time because, just as the economy and social systems were being rocked by the recession, the US television industry was undergoing its own fundamental transformations. These shifts impacted not only television's industrial and economic operations but also how industrial players appealed to audiences. Changes in technologies, modes of viewing, distribution patterns, and economic models all prompted innovative business strategies. *TV's American Dream* connects the impact of the Great Recession with changes in the television industry to explore how television programs of the post-Recession period contributed to the construction of the myth of the American Dream. To lay the groundwork, this introduction will (very) briefly review ideas that will be further fleshed out within the book's chapters: conceptions of the American Dream and the impact of the Great Recession, changes within the television industry, and the potential television has as a popular medium to shape our understanding of the American Dream.

A Myth of Contradictions: The American Dream

The American Dream has been the subject of many books and articles, both academic and popular. Much of this work illustrates how the term and the values associated with it have changed over time. The core beliefs of the Dream took shape very early in the founding of the United States. These ideals, at times contradictory, are both a prescription of what is required to achieve the Dream and a promise to those who follow its rules. For all the ways that they fail those who believe, the American Dream and its underlying tenets must be recognized as ideals (or delusions). Yet, these values form the bedrock of much of US society and, when probed, unsettle the very foundation of how Americans see themselves and their nation.

Cullen's excellent history attributes the basis of the Dream to the Puritans, demonstrating the fundamental importance of freedom within the concept of the Dream. As Cullen notes, the Puritans defined religious freedom differently than we do today (2006, 21–2), but it was still a search for freedom, for themselves and, importantly, for their children (2006, 16). Additionally, the Puritans believed that individuals were responsible for their actions (even as their fates were predetermined by God) and, as a result, "Agency, in turn, lies at the very core of the American Dream, the bedrock premise upon which all else depends" (Cullen 2006, 10). Julie Levinson demonstrates the continued focus on individual responsibility in the contemporary Dream, writing in 2012 that the American Dream paints us as "active subjects rather than compliant objects of our personal destinies" (2012, 21).

Even while foregrounding personal responsibility, the Puritans stressed the importance of community. John Winthrop, in his famous 1630 speech "A Model of Christian Charity" in which he explains how America will be "as a city upon a hill," said, "We must delight in each other, make others' condition our own, rejoice together, mourn together, labor and suffer together, always having before our eyes our commission and community in the work, our community as members of the same body" (Cullen 2006, 23). Cullen notes that the American Dream "still straddles—perhaps it's more accurate to say it *blurs*—the tension between one and many, a tension we still all too often fail to recognize" (2006, 32). Furthermore, Hochschild observes that regardless of the individualism inherent in the Dream, Americans are often offended by people who are only concerned about themselves (1996, 24). The Puritans, then, introduced a conflict between individualism and social responsibility that continues to complicate the American Dream.

The Founding Fathers relied on individualism as a basis for success and achievement, turning away from the British aristocracy's use of inherited titles as a determinant of opportunity. Instead, the United States would be shaped as a meritocracy in which "individuals get ahead and earn rewards in direct proportion to their individual efforts and abilities" (McNamee and Miller 2018, 2). The early establishment of a "natural aristocracy" differed from our current understanding of meritocracy because it overtly limited the potential for leadership to certain populations (White men), yet it was revolutionary in its untethering of potential from heredity (Cullen 2006, 53). The Civil War, under the guidance of Abraham Lincoln, promoted the notion of success through merit by suggesting some level of equality should also be at play, even if this conceptualization of equality still heavily favored White people. Lincoln challenged America "to afford, all, an unfettered start, and a fair chance, in the race of life" (Cullen 2006, 96). Cullen argues Lincoln's interest in emancipation at least partially rested in his concern that White Americans would be psychologically hampered by the refusal to recognize all people as equal (2006, 86). The American Dream could then rest on the (deceptive) idea that all US citizens have equal access to the Dream and an equal opportunity to reach it. With this misconception in place, lack of merit could be used to justify why some fail to achieve the Dream.

Industrialization and the Roaring Twenties established consumerism and materialism as a means of determining a person's value, thus making the accumulation of wealth and individual achievement a goal of the Dream, an aspiration soon crushed by the Great Depression. Franklin Delano Roosevelt and his New Deal refocused the American Dream on community responsibility (Samuel 2012, 20), encouraging Americans to support the government's implementation of (and use of tax dollars for) programs that would create opportunities for people to pursue their greater potential (White and Hanson 2011, 4). Nevertheless, materialism became tied to success and happiness, signaling the achievement of the Dream.

These values that lay the basis for the American Dream—freedom, individualism, social responsibility, materialism, equality—were established early on in US history and are repeatedly redefined and reordered. After the Second World War, consumerism took hold, with notions of success focusing on wealth over communal responsibility (Levinson 2012, 15–16). As part of the fight against communism, consumerism was seen as a means by which to both mark one's individuality and one's belonging. Material purchases, demonstrating upward mobility, evidenced the attainment of the American Dream (Turnock 2007, 148). The growth of the credit industry also made consumer purchases available to more people regardless of class, allowing greater numbers of Americans to feel as though they had achieved the Dream. Education took on special importance as Americans vied for coveted white-collar jobs (Samuel 2012, 67). And, as (White) Americans moved to the suburbs, home and car ownership came to represent the attainment of the postwar American Dream serving not simply as a display of socioeconomic status but confirming the ultimate achievement of autonomy and freedom.

Lawrence Samuel writes, however, "Some social critics were not happy to see the American Dream turned into a ticky-tacky house filled with the latest appliances" (2012, 57). The materialistic Dream chased by the "organization men" of the middle class was opposed by some in the 1960s who instead defined the Dream around more spiritual values of "happiness and contentment" (Samuel 2012, 59) or worked to expand the Dream to more Americans. The civil rights movements of the 1960s saw people previously excluded by the Dream (particularly Black Americans and women) fighting for inclusion. As Roderick Bush and Melanie Bush observe, "The very idea of the American Dream in a society where the racialized, gendered, and classed lower orders believed that they were all entitled to such a dream became a destabilizing force" (2015, 25). The equal rights movements of the 1960s and 1970s both opened up questions about equality within the Dream and jump-started the New Right of the 1960s composed of groups threatened by the prospects of a more equitable and inclusive system.

The economic and social turmoil of the 1970s, a period in which the American Dream was "downsized" (Samuel 2012, 104), ushered in a neoliberal mindset under the leadership of Ronald Reagan in the 1980s. With a focus on the individualistic American Dream, Reagan proposed an "Economic Bill of Rights," which offered Americans four freedoms: the freedom to work, the freedom to enjoy the fruits of one's labor, the freedom to own and control property, and the freedom to participate in a free market (Jillson 2016, 228–9). Reagan's devotion to the unregulated marketplace celebrated individual economic achievements and inhibited the vision of a government and a citizenry that shared responsibility for creating equal and fair opportunities for all Americans to achieve the Dream. Although in ensuing years, the presidency would be held by both Republicans and Democrats, they continued to promote a neoliberal ideology dedicated to personal responsibility. In the 1990s, Bill Clinton, for example, expanded deregulatory policies and advanced principles of the "ownership society" in which autonomous hard work and personal responsibility were promoted as the means to achieve the Dream (Jillson 2016, 237).

The Dream under Pressure: The Great Recession

The Great Recession shook the foundation of the neoliberal American Dream as the assumptions, expectations, and practices of the economy failed, thus serving as a catalyst for at least a discursive reconsideration of the American Dream. As is well documented, the recession was the immediate result of a crash within the housing market. Certainly, earlier problems within the US economy troubled notions of the Dream. Well before the Great Recession, deregulation (particularly of banks), globalization, a growing wealth gap, the rising national debt (in part created by wars in Iraq and Afghanistan) and consumer debt (stemming from a reliance on credit), the increasing costs of education, and so on. contributed to Americans in the 1990s and early 2000s "losing faith in the American Dream or whatever it was they believe the American Dream to be" (Kamp 2009). Several of these economic changes fueled the recession as "the combination of deregulation and individualism as a way of life led to the rise of a new breed of financial, corporate managers focused on their own short-term profits as the guiding principle of their increasingly risky decisions" (Castells, Caraça and Cardoso 2012, 2).

In great numbers, Americans lost their homes or found themselves underwater on their mortgages, saw their stock-based retirement funds shrink, and lost their jobs as businesses downsized and closed. Median family income reportedly fell by 71 percent between 2000 and 2013 (Jillson 2016, 226). Triggered by the housing crisis and the overextension of consumer credit, the Great Recession could be seen as a symbol of the failure of the American Dream. If, as Cal Jillson argues, the path to the American Dream is imagined to be education, good character, hard work, and "a little luck" (2016, 6), the path appeared to be blocked for many who experienced a lack of luck as their lives were torn apart by those trying to push the boundaries of their own fulfillment. The desire for homeownership—and the greed of those willing to exploit this desire—created conditions in which the illusion of the Dream began to crumble. While the middle class suffered, "at the heart of the events that triggered the crises . . . there was the 'complacence of the elites' managing the economy" (Castells, Caraça and Cardoso 2012, 2). The meritocratic nature of the United States was questioned by both the working and middle classes' use of credit to "live beyond their means" and the upper classes' readiness to write and implement policies that encouraged this for personal gain.

As the economy began a slow recovery in 2009, the government pumped a great deal of money into failing industries and, over time, unemployment rates declined, wages increased, household net worth began to rebuild, and home prices and sales increased. Yet tensions and anxieties about the future continued throughout and after the recovery and impacted the ideologies that structure the American Dream. David Kamp observed in 2009, "What needs to change is our expectation of what the dream promises and our understanding of what the vague and promiscuously used term, 'the American Dream,' is really supposed to mean" (2009). The American Dream, or at least what people said about the American Dream, in the wake of the Great Recession shifted. Many of these changes seemed to rest on the rising inequality in the United States. Not only did the wealth gap reach "record high levels" (Fry and Kochhar 2014), but more attention was also being paid to the inequity within the educational system, which left residents of poorer neighborhoods with weaker tax bases from which to draw education funding (Perrucci and Perrucci 2009, 42). During the recovery, scholars noted and the Occupy Movement protested a growing sense that the government was controlled by and, therefore, benefited the wealthy (H. Smith 2012, 412). As John White writes, "Double-digit unemployment—coupled with a widespread feeling that the federal government was helping big shots rather than ordinary citizens gave way to a sense that the American Dream had shrunk" (2011, 43).

The optimism that generally surrounded the American Dream was hampered by this growing sense of inequality and the stagnation of upward mobility. The belief that "one could realize the fruits of one's aspirations through applied intelligence and effort" (Cullen 2006, 61) had previously allowed for continued hope. But the sense that increasing one's class status was becoming more difficult developed well before the Great Recession, and only intensified afterward. According to a Pew study, "a December 2015 survey found that 49% of Americans said they felt they were falling behind the cost of living, while 42% said they were staying about even; only 7% said they thought their family income was going up faster than the cost of living" (Tyson 2016). Optimism was further undermined by apparent cracks in the meritocracy. During and after the Great Recession, there were not many opportunities to prove one's merit, regardless of innate talent or willingness to work hard. Unemployment was high and wages were low. Christopher Ellis observes in 2017 that Americans believed both that people are given the opportunity to succeed but also that people are wealthy because of "circumstances from birth" (2017, 57). Moreover, white-collar workers increasingly lost their jobs. Barbara Ehrenreich writes, "If anyone can testify credibly to the disappearance of the American dream, it is the white-collar unemployed—the people who 'played by the rule,' 'did everything right,' and still end up in ruin" (2005, 237).

The instability experienced across classes tested traditional loyalties, leading some upper-middle-class, white-collar workers, who had been aligned with the upper classes, to rethink their allegiance and recognize inequalities built into the social structures. These questions supported a shift away from individual consumption and a greater focus on spiritual and communal ideals. Americans increasingly sought a happiness and fulfillment that could be attained by focusing on others. John White and Sandra Hanson found that in a 2008 survey, the Dream, though still encompassing economic facets, was "broadened to include a greater sense of personal well-being and quality-of-life issues" (2011, 10). While the Tea Party continued to promote the importance of individual responsibility by cutting/eliminating safety net programs in the supposed pursuit of fiscal responsibility (H. Smith 2012, 344), Barack Obama was elected president with rhetoric that implored social responsibility. As progressivism was embraced by growing numbers of Americans, people saw Obama's election as "an opportunity to shift our thinking away from the more material elements of the American

Dream (new house, car, clothes) to the more spiritual or simply nonmaterial, such as cleaner environment, health care for all, a turn away from militarism, and so forth" (D'Antonio 2011, 136).

The post-Recession recovery, however, under the leadership of President Obama, did not resolve existing apprehensions. Manuel Castells et al. explain, "unemployment remained close to a double-digit level, while the fiscal crisis spread in local and state governments. Social spending cuts and layoffs in both private and public sectors fueled resentment. . . . The fiscal crisis became a time bomb, while the social safety net shrank in the midst of the greater need" (2012, 8). The ideals undergirding the Dream—freedom, individualism, materialism, optimism, equality, social responsibility, meritocracy, and so on—were negotiated in people's daily lives and in the popular culture they consumed.

As will be discussed throughout this book, this insecurity seriously impacted the Millennial generation—here defined as those born between 1981 and 1996 (Dimock 2017)—at the same time that they were becoming an important group of consumers and the most sought-after television audience in the United States. In general, studies of Millennials in the post-Recession period acknowledge that "what they all have in common is the knowledge that the recession has in some way shattered the world they thought they knew" (Jayson 2009). Before the Great Recession, this generation had been seen as a very optimistic group of young Americans who were heavily supported by their families (Jayson 2009). As a cohort, Millennials' faith and trust were rocked by the economic crisis fueled by institutional and personal greed in which younger Americans were "hit especially hard" (Schoon and Mortimer 2017, 1). Millennials lost a great deal of faith in governmental and social institutions as well as the American Dream (Schoon and Mortimer 2017, 2).

Instead of rejecting the American Dream, Millennials, as will be discussed, reconfigured it. They navigated the dichotomies that unfolded including those between individualism and social responsibility, optimism for and anxiety about the future, the desire for both material goods and spiritual happiness, and faith in the meritocracy and a recognition of social inequities. Ingrid Schoon and Jeylan Mortimer found, "The way young people are responding to the recession might both affect, and reflect, how they cope with the crisis. They show growing distrust in social institutions and the economy—but also assign increasing importance to supporting others" (2017, 4). Millennials appeared to transform some of their anxiety and cynicism into a strange kind of optimism. For example, Millennials' "heightened social consciences" (A. Smith 2018, 449) translated into an enthusiasm for solving the world's problems (Stein 2015, 8). Yet, the confidence displayed by Millennials was tinged with an awareness of what was lost. As one Millennial told Sharon Jayson, "I can't have what I wanted, so I'm going to more or less settle. . . . However, I think that sparks creativity. We will have people who are going to rise to the occasion and look for creative solutions" (Jayson 2009).

The hopes and concerns voiced by Millennials reflected an essential destabilization of an American Dream burdened by the trauma of economic anxiety. Television became a companion for people and their fears. Bambi Haggins writes, "As the most widely accessible American medium, television is the loom upon which the thread of Dream mythology is woven—often imperceptibly—into the fabric of American culture" (1999, 23). Yet, even as people turned to television for clarification and comfort, the medium itself was undergoing its own upheaval that, like the American Dream and the Great Recession, had been set in motion decades earlier.

The Promise and Threat of Abundance: The Television Industry

Although the Great Recession coincided with the development of streaming television, significant changes within the industry began with economic, political, and technological shifts that gained traction in the 1980s and 1990s. The growth of cable, satellite, and computer technologies increased the number of television channels. An industry that was once ruled by three major networks was awash with television channels competing for viewers through cable, satellite, video on demand, broadband, and so on. Technologies such as VHS, digital cable, DVDs, DVRs, the internet, and mobile phones increased the number of distribution windows for television shows. Producers of both mainstream programs and those with niche audiences found additional opportunities to recoup production costs. Simultaneously, these new individualized windows decreased the value of traditional syndication markets by reducing exclusivity. The changing windows structure, in fact, contributed to the 2007 Writer's Guild of America strike, in which writers asked for residuals from DVDs and other new media sales to offset the reduced money they were getting from syndication. The resulting economic environment proved somewhat confusing for media companies. In 2004, Lee Gomes wrote in *The Wall Street Journal* that television was in the process of "media-disintermediation" in which the industry was "getting rid of the middleman, and right now, cable and satellite companies are middlemen because TV is whatever they say it is. But what if you could connect directly to, say, 'The West Wing' without Comcast? Without, even, NBC?" (Gomes 2004, B1). Gomes questions the ability of the gatekeepers to actually guard the gate as viewers and media makers turned to the internet.

The effort to maintain control within this changing environment was eased by the media deregulation that allowed production companies and distribution channels to converge under the umbrellas of a small number of media corporations. Conglomeration consolidated broadcast and cable networks with the major production and distribution companies as well as with formerly independent producers and distributors and internet operators. So, although audiences were presented with more television networks and new ways to watch television shows, fewer companies determined which shows got access to these new distribution channels. At the same time, new ways to watch television ushered in additional content. Cable networks sought to draw audiences with original programming and, in the 2010s, streaming platforms like Netflix and Amazon began producing original series. Streaming platforms also made it easier for viewers to access international programming, creating even more competition for US content. Furthermore, other technologies such as video games and social media platforms led viewers away from television programming, dividing the potential television audience among even more activities. The television industry, therefore, competed for smaller audiences apportioned among more leisure options.

Within this context of the fragmented audience, as Simone Murray demonstrates regarding film, television audiences continued to insist on high production values despite the decline in ratings numbers and the associated advertising rates to support these production costs (2005, 420). In response, businesses within the television industry strategized about how to best appeal to viewers and draw in audiences. For example, some media conglomerates recreated the mass audience, using different branches of the company to appeal to a variety of audiences, by "'tiering' a wide range of niche taste cultures within the same corporate-semiotic family or umbrella" (Caldwell 2006, 124). Others focused on targeting audiences who would form loyal champions to support not only the television programs but also the ancillary products and secondary distribution windows that contribute to profits, establishing "multiple revenue streams to maintain budgets and remain competitive" (Lotz 2007, 128). Media companies increasingly recognized that profits could be made by aggregating smaller, but loyal, audiences to support individual television programs, television networks, or media conglomerates.

In the 2010s, the young, tech-savvy Millennials were at the heart of this competition for loyal audiences with broadcast networks, cable channels, and the growing over-the-top (OTT) streaming and internet platforms strategizing ways to appeal to this valuable demographic group. The older programming strategy that focused on "least objectionable programming" (LOP) to amass a broad audience was not likely to create shows with strong viewer loyalty (McDowell and Batten 2005, 5). People still watched LOP content but were unlikely to actively seek it out in alternative distribution windows. Much attention was paid to the content that created "buzz," which would allow a network to "set itself apart in a crowded TV environment" (Haley 2004, 12a). Content, and control of this content, grew increasingly important as "the commercial priority amongst global media players has gravitated from a desire to control access to a desire to control high-profile content" (S. Murray 2005, 418). The need to reach viewers resulted in many changes to television distribution and television programming. To speak to audiences who were still reeling from the Great Recession, television creators found ways to calm nerves and acknowledge concerns, mostly without ever mentioning the anxiety and fear simmering beneath the surface of the American Dream.

Toward a Critical Media Industries Studies: Methodology

Each chapter in this book will highlight a strategy used within the television industry to navigate the post-Recession corporate and sociocultural context. While none of these strategies were necessarily new to the mid-2010s, they each took on a function at this time to facilitate television's usefulness for Americans traumatized by the economic breakdown. Central to the argument is that the programming created in this environment, like all television content, speaks to its audiences and contributes to popular perceptions of their world. The chapters combine a media industries methodology that situates media products within their industrial and economic contexts and the cultural forum model that views television as a platform for social conversation. A media economics approach to media industries posits that "media industries possess a number of distinctive economic characteristics, and an understanding of these characteristics can provide useful insights into a wide range of dimension of the behavior of media industries and their audiences/consumers" (Napoli 2009, 168). According to the cultural forum model

> the conflicts we see in television drama, embedded in familiar and nonthreatening frames, are conflicts ongoing in American social experience and cultural history. In a few cases we might see strong perspectives that argue for the absolute correctness of one point of view or another. But for the most part the rhetoric of television drama is a rhetoric of discussion. (Newcomb and Hirsch 1983, 49)

Television programs, then, may not speak overtly about the American Dream, but would depict certain images of contentment, success, freedom, and equality that inform how it was understood.

The goal of this interdisciplinarity is to work toward what Douglas Kellner describes as a critical media industries studies that "can help individuals become aware of the connection between media and forces of domination and resistance, and can help make audiences more critical and informed consumers and producers of their culture" (2009, 105). The production companies and distribution platforms examined in these chapters are analyzed for their positionality in relation to the industrial pressures of the post-Recession period. And the television series derived by these industrial players initiate specific discussions that appeal to particular audiences. As a result, the programs—the culture created—inscribe and reinscribe stories about the American Dream, reinforcing some values and ideals, while potentially questioning others.

As people struggled with angst and economic uncertainty after the Great Recession, television offered ways to come to terms with the wavering sense of hope for the future that many find in the American Dream. What then, can we learn from looking at this period when we are years out from the mid-2010s? Undoubtedly, understanding the past to make sense of the present provides insight into the development of the television industry. The business of television continues to change along with the ways that people understand and make use of the medium (if it can still be thought of as a medium). Looking at how television is shaped by moments of stress provides insight into what television is now and how it will continue to develop. Most particularly, this project hopes to offer an awareness of the ways that the television industry and television content are impacted by their sociocultural environment, how they are influenced by audiences and their concerns. The notion of the American Dream is foundational for this research, teasing out ideas about how we know and think about this mythical promise and what opportunities can be found in television to shape fundamental ideas about who we are as a nation. This project views the mid-2010s as an inflection point for US society and for television when social, cultural, economic, technological, and industrial factors intersect to offer a critical moment that tells us not only about television but about the hopes and fears of people chasing the American Dream.

To these ends, Chapter 1, "Franchising the Dream," examines the creation of tentpole television by looking at two televisual outings of the very popular DC and Marvel superhero franchises: *Arrow* and *Daredevil*. This chapter focuses on how these franchise entries were utilized by their production companies and distributors to expand their audiences through stories that centered on the Dream's values of individualism and social responsibility as well as autonomy and freedom. Chapter 2, "Believing the Dream," concentrates on the post-Recession rebranding of two popular cable networks, Hallmark Channel and USA Network. Looking at the industrial reasons for the rebrandings, the chapter considers how these networks relied on, reflected, and revised notions of optimism and hope for the future, foundational tenets of the American Dream, to appeal to audiences. Chapter 3, "Transgressing the Dream," explores the use of signature comedies to attract attention to distribution platforms. Through the case studies of *Unbreakable Kimmy Schmidt* and *Atlanta*, this chapter investigates how these series utilize comedy centered on marginalized groups to question the illusion of equity underlying the meritocracy and reimagine what it takes to be meritorious in the face of precarity. Finally, Chapter 4, "Rerunning the Dream," analyzes how media libraries and second-cycle shows can be mobilized to appeal to anxious audiences. *Friends* and *The Office* demonstrate that a nostalgic vision of security, community, and work/life balance, provided reassuring visions of a pre-Recession American Dream.

While each chapter primarily focuses on the first season of each series, please consider this a spoiler alert. Storylines from all seasons are discussed and major plotlines may be revealed. Thus is the nature of writing about television in the current social/industrial environment.

1

Franchising the Dream: Tentpole Television

The American Dream, upended by the Great Recession, retrenched to traditional ideas about economic security while also being renegotiated by Americans devastated by economic precarity. One of the central questions about the American Dream deliberated by Millennials centered on its promise: Did the Dream offer individual achievement or was it a social contract that extended possibility to all? This push-pull between personal gain and social responsibility was central to this generation and played out in the cultural narratives it embraced.

The Millennial generation—who in 2008 were between twelve and twenty-seven years old (Dimock 2017)—spanned an age range that was an important target audience for popular culture such as television programming. During this time, older Millennials faced struggles to find employment and pay off debt while younger Millennials managed the childhood trauma of living with parents who lost their homes and jobs. Changes within the industry, such as the rise of streaming services, the growing amount of original content, and adjustments in viewer behavior and attitudes, all contributed to how these viewers were pursued. One strategy that proved successful, if unreliably so, was the focus on buzz-generating programming that would build loyalty with viewers, pull audiences across platforms, and generate lucrative franchises. This type of content, known as tentpole television, was often designed around themes and narratives expected to attract the attention of the desired Millennial viewers.

Superhero narratives gained notable popularity in the years following the recession. Although the concept of the American Dream can be read into most US media productions, US-based superhero narratives, with their focus on American exceptionalism, have a particular connection with the myth (Dittmer 2013, 10). Superheroes with extraordinary abilities—regardless of whether they gain their skills through hard work, genetic mutation, or alien intervention—

epitomize the physical and moral qualities expected from those who will achieve the American Dream. Not only are they remarkably strong, due to biological or technological enhancements, but they display the penchant for hard work, discipline, and courage admired within the US meritocracy. Even more than that, however, the lone superhero represents the foundational belief that responsibility rests within each individual for their own success and their achievement of the American Dream.[1] A core belief of the Dream is that we are "masters of our own fate." We "go our own way" and "do our own thing." For Americans, "it all comes down to the individual" (McNamee and Miller 2018, 4). And each person has the freedom, the power, and the responsibility to control their choices and their futures. Even when heroes act within a group, such as the Justice League or the Avengers, superhero narratives are ultimately about personal responsibility. Freedom, then, is seen as a right that Americans have, but individuals are responsible for protecting and marshalling their freedom to achieve the Dream.

This chapter will examine how the industrial impetus toward tentpole television interacted with Millennials' shifting expectations and ideals after the Great Recession to shape representations of the American Dream in these superhero narratives. The superhero genre demonstrates the balance of individual and community responsibility within the Dream that spoke to the coveted Millennial viewers in the 2010s. And tentpole television offered an advantageous industrial channel for these narratives. This chapter will examine two examples of tentpole superhero series, *Arrow* (CW 2012–20) and *Daredevil* (Netflix 2015–18), that offered particular, and often problematic, representations of the American Dream. As this chapter will demonstrate, in response to their industrial pressures, each of these shows told different stories about the Dream's balance between the individual and the community.

Controlling the Dream: Superheroes and Agency

Where the materialistic myth involves a concept of freedom that emphasizes the freedom to do as one pleases, the moralistic myth tends toward the idea of freedom that stresses the freedom to be as one conceives himself.

Fisher 1973, 161

The demand that superheroes become "masters of their own fate" fills a void in modern society in which, according to Umberto Eco, "man becomes a number in the realm of the organization which has usurped his decision-making role, he has no means of production and is thus deprived of his power to decide" (2005, 146). Superheroes, Eco argues, offer a myth that demonstrates the potential to break free of the drudgery of industrial society and take control of one's own life. In this context, we can understand superheroes as embodiments of agency, which, according to Jim Cullen, "lies at the very core of the American Dream" (2006, 10). If, as the Dream promises, fulfillment and achievement is dependent on individual action, not inheritance, wealth, or lineage, then the superhero displays the autonomy to take charge of this individual potential to become "someone different, someone better" (Brooker 2013, 12).

Telling stories about gaining and mobilizing individual agency, superhero narratives are shaped by and, in turn, contribute to discourses about the balance of personal happiness and social responsibility within the American Dream. Underlying this is the concept of merit, since the notion of autonomy and how it is best used is tied to those who display particular positive qualities. Although the concept of merit, discussed in greater detail in Chapter 3, changes meaning both historically and culturally, at its core, it is the idea that to earn the Dream, individuals must embody particular traits that promote success. Merit cannot be inherited or purchased. It can be innate or learned, but it must be based on individual qualities that yield either meritorious actions or meritorious results (Sen 2000, 8). At different times and for different audiences, superhero narratives balance these elements in distinct ways, though in all cases, they confirm that even those extraordinary abilities that are inherited (such as Superman's abilities or Thor's strengths) require individual effort and discipline and must be continuously nurtured.

The agency displayed by superheroes goes beyond their power for self-improvement and their cultivation of innate and learned skills. Superheroes also model the freedom to determine their future goals by defining their own American Dream. In the Preface to his book *The Epic of America*, James Truslow Adams describes the "American dream of a better, richer, and happier life for all our citizens of every rank" (1931, viii). Cullen notes that the ambiguity in the American Dream rests in the variable ideas about what makes for a "better, richer, and happier life" (2006, 7). Distinctions can be made between the materialistic and the moralistic understanding of the American Dream with one focusing more on wealth and objects and the other on happiness and contentment. Additionally, some definitions of the American Dream clearly emphasize individual achievement, while others highlight the Dream's communal aspects. Foregrounding the social responsibility that undergirds the Dream, Barack Obama said during his first presidential campaign, "What makes us one American family is that we have to stand up and fight for each other's dreams. . . . It's time to reaffirm that fundamental belief—I am my brother's keeper, I am my sister's keeper—through our politics, our policies, and in our daily lives" (Cullen 2017, 23). Walter Fisher examines the benefits and drawbacks of these different visions of the Dream, discussing the materialistic myth as one that focuses on individual achievement through hard work and the moralistic myth as focusing on "charity, compassion, and true regard for the dignity and worth of each and every individual" (1973, 161). Fisher goes on to tie these myths of the dream to structures of freedom and autonomy writing, "Where the materialistic myth involves a concept of freedom that emphasizes the freedom *to do* as one pleases, the moralistic myth tends toward the idea of freedom that stresses the freedom *to be* as one conceives himself" (1973, 161).

Superheroes often, though not exclusively, adopt the moralistic and communal vision of the American Dream and, in doing so, emphasize their autonomy to find a "better, richer and happier life" not in their own personal pleasure but in their decision to conceive of themselves as good people who serve society. Superheroes see their freedom as intertwined with community responsibility (Cullen 2006, 22). Drawing on what seems like a New Deal inspired vision of the American Dream, superheroes promote the four freedoms espoused by Franklin Roosevelt: freedom of speech, freedom of worship, freedom from want, and freedom from fear (Cullen 2006, 57). Focusing their unique skills on the last two of these freedoms, superheroes seek to assure a level of equality for all Americans to guarantee them the opportunities and conditions necessary to pursue their American Dream, free of want and fear.[2] Roosevelt's notion of the American Dream, although considered by some to be materialistic in its focus on economic security, also emphasized the nation's responsibility to all of its citizens.[3] Superheroes, however, suggest that these two ideals are in line with each other as they exercise the freedom to surrender their own traditional vision of the American Dream—their personal safety, comfort, community, family, or home—to help others.

This focus on finding their American Dream, their future happiness, in the protection of their fellow citizens is often the key to distinguishing the heroes from the villains in superhero narratives. While heroes attempt to salvage equality and fairness for those weaker than themselves (which is pretty much all "regular" people), villains generally subscribe to the ideology that underlies all types of inequality in the United States: those with power are more meritorious and worthy than those without it (Bush and Bush 2015, 95). Because of this, villains within superhero narratives, from the Joker in the Dark Knight trilogy to Thanos in *The Avengers*, often use the discourse of the American Dream to oppress others. Superhero narratives, then, to some (and differing) extents, define their American Dream in a very Puritanical way that rests on the freedom to serve a higher order with the ultimate goal of making the world a better place. And, in doing so, these stories create distinct discourses around the relationship between individual freedom and community responsibility within the Dream. The heavy burden carried by superheroes when choosing to serve their community is evident with characters such as Captain America or Spider-Man in the Marvel movies being required to forsake romantic love in order to save the world.[4]

The ways that fictional superheroes balance individual interests and community responsibility shift over time, reflecting social and economic changes that impact conceptualizations of what it means to be "free" to pursue the Dream. Roosevelt's abovementioned freedoms from want and fear, according to Cullen, did not find favor with some people, "particularly those whose American Dreams were premised on acquiring as much as possible without having to share it with anyone else" (2006, 57). Resultingly, Harry Truman replaced these two freedoms with "freedom of enterprise" (Cullen 2006, 58). Additionally, in the 1980s, the discourse of freedom was taken up by economic conservatives to promote emancipation from regulation and taxation (Cullen 2006, 107). Similarly, and often interrelatedly, the idea of societal obligations changed in meaning and prominence. Milton Friedman's 1962 *Capitalism and Freedom* bemoaned the integration of freedom and social responsibility, writing, "Few trends could so thoroughly undermine the very foundations of our free society as the acceptance by corporate officials of a social responsibility other than to make as much money for their stockholders as possible" (1962, 133). And, in the 2000s, freedom was intertwined with the idea of the ownership society, which, among other reforms, unsuccessfully sought to privatize Social Security to provide individuals with the "freedom" to control their "economic destinies and not expect employers or the federal government to provide a safety net" (H. Smith 2012, 89). The strengthening of neoliberal ideologies since the 1980s impacted how people conceived of society's responsibilities to help others achieve the Dream (H. Smith 2012, 62).

Courting Millennial Viewers: Tentpole Television

The dream is really about day-to-day control of your life.

Kadlec 2014

The definition and weight given to these values of the American Dream again transformed in the wake of the 2008 recession. Television industry insiders struggled to understand how younger Americans, those sought as viewers for the shows discussed in this chapter, adjusted their perspectives to navigate the changing world. Powered by Barack Obama's audacity of hope, Millennials remained optimistic about the American Dream but redefined it to fit the world in which their parents lost their homes and their jobs while they incurred unprecedented student debts and faced high unemployment. As discussed in more detail in the next chapter, Jill Sinha notes the inconsistency between the Millennials' continued optimism and their expectation "to be 'worse off'" than their parents" (2017, 14). Millennials, recognizing that they would probably not reach the economic status of their parents, focused on happiness, work-life balance, and the significance of love and friendship (Sinha 2017, 18).

Freedom became an important value that allowed Millennials to reshape the American Dream in ways they could both understand and attain. A 2009 *USA Today* article quoted an adolescent psychologist discussing how the recession impacted Millennials: "They talk more about having autonomy and freedom, and in so doing, not being as enslaved to material goals that they perceived their parents being caught up in" (Jayson 2009, 1A). *Time* reported in 2014 that travel and self-employment were important for Millennials, for whom "the dream is really about day-to-day control of your life" (Kadlec 2014). The desire for freedom, perhaps not coincidentally, meshed with the economic environment faced by this generation as they entered the workforce. Although seen as financially cautious and risk averse, Millennials, who perhaps could not find steady jobs anyway, expressed a greater interest in working for themselves (Rudin and McBreen 2017). According to many reports, Millennials also delayed getting married, having children, and buying homes. While these trends connected to the generation's focus on autonomy (sometimes ungenerously described as narcissism), others noted that the expressed interest in travel over family-building and self-employment over a nine-to-five job also reflected the economic necessities of the time. Dan Kadlec writes, "A true American Dream has to feel attainable, and many Millennials aren't feeling they can attain much more than a day-to-day lifestyle that suits them" (2014). At the same time, however, Millennials' sense of agency may have been limited by their increasing reliance on their parents. A study by Bank of America/*USA Today* from 2015, noted that 36 percent of adult Millennials reported getting "a lot" of financial assistance from their parents. This dependence on their parents, only one of the consequences of the socioeconomic fallout from the irresponsibility (and criminality) of older generations, continued to limit Millennials' autonomy and freedom as they made choices prescribed by the world passed down to them (Bank of America/USA Today 2015).

Finding a way to regain a sense of agency and redefine the American Dream often led to the rejection of the values and priorities of their elders. Additionally, in the wake of the recession, the US middle class began to realign its loyalties away from the upper class to the working class. Losing faith in the upper-class strategies to ensure its security, the middle class moved to support social welfare programs (such as public health care) generally associated with the working class, but upon which the middle class increasingly relied. As Stephen Shapiro explains, "These policies benefit the laboring class, but they also give the middle class a safety net as well in times when aspirational individualism has seemed to fail" (2016, 194). To this end, Millennials made the American Dream more attainable by refocusing their priorities away from materialistic goods and toward social welfare, both as a revisioning of the Dream and as a way of supporting potentially needed programs. Sinha advised Millennials that "Participating more fully in, and re-creating vibrant, interdependent, and empowered civil society starts with accepting responsibility to care for one another as an integral part of community" (2017, 27).

The needs of the community may also have become more apparent to Millennials who were increasingly both connected to a global society through technology, and, through their living arrangements, enmeshed within local communities. As Millennials turned away from home buying—either for financial reasons or because they didn't want the responsibility—they moved to urban areas where they rented apartments. As city-dwellers, Millennials existed within an ecosystem in which they were physically closer to their neighbors and felt a greater social attachment to them. In a *Time* article analyzing this trend, Ellen Dunham-Jones, a professor of architecture and urban design at Georgia Tech, explains, "Unlike their parents, who calculated their worth in terms of square feet, ultimately inventing the McMansion, this generation is more interested in the amenities of the city itself: great public spaces, walkability, diverse people and activities with which they can participate" (Frizell 2014).

Redefining the American Dream away from "stuff" and toward community-building contributed to Millennials in the post-Recession period, finding a sense of autonomy that differentiated them from the failures of their parents and justified a Dream that they could both believe in and achieve.

Additionally, as Millennials considered the needs of the community, they tended to be much more inclusive and tolerant, focused on equality and fairness. As the most racially diverse generation in US history, Millennials held more progressive political viewers. A 2014 Pew Research report found that "white Millennials, while less liberal than the non-whites of their generation, are more liberal than the whites in older generations" (Pew Research Center 2014). Problematically, however, Millennials were raised on the concept of colorblindness, encouraged not to "see" race or discuss it. As Kristen Warner explains, "racial colorblindness is the ideological politically correct default lens we use to make everyone the same" (2015, 2). Colorblindness allows for a guilt-free embracing of many of the values behind the traditional American Dream since the decision not to "see race" means that people are only achieving (or not achieving) based on their own, individual merits. This approach, Warner notes, could be "better understood as a means of marginalizing and undermining the experiences of minorities in American society" (2015, 25). The goal of making the American Dream accessible for *all* Americans, while important for Millennials, entailed celebrating diversity without acknowledging the distinct experiences of diverse groups or the systemic discrimination they faced.

As this discussion demonstrates, the American Dream shifted for television's desired viewers. The recession impacted the potential of the Dream and resulted in a rethinking and rebalancing of its promise of freedom and its expectation of social responsibility. Furthermore, viewers were more likely to align and sympathize with the working class rather than the upper class who seemed to have abandoned them to high unemployment and student debt. And the Millennial audiences conceived of diversity in ways that helped to assuage concerns about inequities within the meritocracy.

While redefining their own needs, platforms like The CW and Netflix, as well as the companies that produced their programming, searched for ways to attract Millennials to shows that would not only generate high viewership but also increase viewer loyalty across programs and platforms. Tentpole television offered one means of meeting audience and industrial demands. The entertainment industries have used the concept of the tentpole in myriad ways.[5] On television, the term originally referred to shows around which the night's schedule was built in order to bolster new shows or programs that had not yet found their audience (McGee 1979, 27).[6] In the early 2000s, the changing television ecosystem called for a different type of tentpole. As streaming television developed, OTT television provided notable competition, requiring that traditional broadcast and cable networks work even harder to stand out. At the same time, in the interests of economizing and synergy, they had to wring as much as possible from their existing intellectual property. Even before the 2010s and the rise of streaming platforms, growing conglomeration and competition initiated a wave of television franchises stemming from shows such as *Law & Order* (NBC, 1990–2010; 2021–present) and *CSI* (CBS, 2000–15). New expectations of tentpole programs, however, demanded more than could be provided by a new franchise installment. For this, television networks turned to content with greater potential to enmesh viewers in a platform brand. They had to anchor one night's television schedule, gain the attention of Millennial viewers, and also draw audiences over a number of different nights, and even, a number of different viewing platforms.

To this end, tentpoles since the 2010s have served three functions. First, in addition to garnering a large audience, they must generate anticipation to help bring new viewers to the platform. Tentpoles need to achieve both buzz and high ratings so that they establish a talked-about brand and, like traditional tentpole shows, draw audiences to other content on the platform simply by bringing in viewers. Second, tentpoles work within the corporate family to give rise to other content hopefully by starting or revitalizing a media franchise. Finally, tentpoles must be able to move across, and move viewers across, multiple platforms. As television programs are increasingly untethered from the networks on which they air, shows need to draw fans to rewatch on other platforms or gain new viewers when they shift platforms.

As production companies and distribution platforms consider future shows, then, they look for what attracts and increases audiences, generates franchises, and moves successfully across platforms while maintaining or building viewership. The remainder of this chapter will explore how industrial pressures combined with the shifting conceptualizations of the post-Recession American Dream to shape representations in two tentpole programs aimed at the valuable Millennial audience—*Arrow* and *Daredevil*. Focusing on the first seasons of each show will demonstrate that differing industrial expectations determined how *Arrow* and *Daredevil* responded to and helped to constitute the Millennial revision of the American Dream in the context of economic inequality.

Saving the Dream for the Undeserving Poor: *Arrow*

Oliver Queen was up to Robin Hood-esque shenanigans and foiling wealth inequality years before phrases such as "the 1%" or "Occupy Wall Street" grabbed headlines.

Truitt 2012, 1D

It can't be saved because the people there don't want it to be saved.

"Sacrifice"

In 2012, The CW premiered *Arrow*, a one-hour drama based on the DC Comics character created in 1941, intending to introduce an addictive tentpole series that appealed to a wide range of viewers across distribution formats. *Arrow's* labyrinthine narrative begins as rich, young, White, playboy Oliver Queen, presumed dead when his yacht disappeared at sea, is rescued from a seemingly deserted island. In flashbacks, however, we see that, after his boating accident, Oliver is washed up on a remote island and enmeshed in a set of adventures that lead to his transformation into a disciplined survivor, a powerful fighter, and a highly trained archer (as well as, somehow, a high-ranking member of the Russian mob). Intercutting the past and the present, the first season examines both Oliver's time on the island and his return to his family after being rescued.

Oliver sets out, at least in the first season, to save his city from malicious operators who generally take the form of evil global capitalists. He is given this task by his father, Robert Queen, who, like Oliver survives the shipwreck but kills himself (and another crew member) to ensure Oliver's survival. Before killing himself, Robert implores Oliver "You can survive this. Make it home. Make it better. Right my wrongs. But you gotta live through this first" ("Pilot"). To undo Robert's damage to Starling City, Oliver must foil the nefarious plot subtly termed The Undertaking, a scheme to rid the city of crime by leveling the city's poor neighborhood ("The Glades").[7] The plan is, effectively, to eliminate crime by killing the poor people.

In his superhero guise, Oliver is nicknamed The Hood, and the police deem him a dangerous vigilante who, according to producer Andrew Kreisberg,[8] "As part of his evolution as a hero, the character will move from revenge to redemption" (Stanley 2012, C10). *Arrow*, in its depiction of Oliver's developing agency and the use he makes of various types of freedom, offers post-Recession Millennial viewers a timely consideration of the American Dream within a city that is being literally ravaged by economic inequality. Ultimately, what we see, however, is that *Arrow* does not take full advantage of the opportunity to question and revise the American Dream as, in order to fulfill its industrial expectations, it centers questions of agency and autonomy on the wealthy, White, male lead while eliding the possibility of the American Dream for those he protects.

Produced by DC Entertainment (along with Warner Bros. Television and Berlanti Productions), for The CW, *Arrow* was created as a tentpole program to benefit several players within the entertainment industry. Warner Bros., as the owner of DC Comics (DC Entertainment's parent company) and co-owner of The CW (with CBS, Inc.), had the most to gain from the show's success. Through DC Entertainment, formed in 2009, Warner Bros. planned to move DC Comics content across Warner Bros.' divisions. DC Entertainment recognized that a program such as *Arrow* could build a franchise of shows by "testing" and spinning off new characters into their own shows (Thielman 2014, 10). This potential played out in the second season of *Arrow* when the character of Barry Allen, The Flash, was introduced and then reappeared in 2014 with his own show. *Arrow* offered the opportunity to create a cycle of shows centered on characters less well-known than the DC juggernauts Batman and Superman. These characters would operate outside of the cinematic universe that DC was building and serve a different audience than the darker films.

The plan for a franchise ultimately resulted in the creation of numerous shows for The CW that eventually included *The Flash* (2014–23), *Supergirl* (2015–21), *Black Lightening* (2018–21), *Legends of Tomorrow* (2016–22), and *Batwoman* (2019–22). Like the Marvel Cinematic Universe, the DC shows exist in the same universe and interact with each other, a fact that was highlighted by yearly crossover story arcs that integrated many of the characters from the different shows. Interestingly, while the DC television programs merged into a cohesive universe, they were disconnected from past DC shows and the DC films. This separation between the television and film universes allowed the shows to build a franchise without the pressure of fitting in with the storylines and pre-production planning of the DC films. Additionally, viewers didn't have to be existing fans of the films, thereby attracting a new audience to the DC universe through The CW.[9] That these shows were often referred to by fans as the "Arrowverse" (a name complicated by *Arrow* ending in 2020 while the other shows continued) demonstrates the central position that *Arrow* played as the tentpole for this franchise.

Warner Bros. viewed The CW as a strong platform through which to find new viewers for its DC content. *Arrow*'s placement on The CW rather than another broadcast or cable network (for example, DC's *Gotham* aired on Fox), signified DC's attempt to reach The CW's younger, female-skewed audience. As Charles Joseph explains, "Warner Bros. Entertainment Group was interested in tapping into the power of fandoms, influencers, ecommerce and social media of viewers who were watching Millennial centric television programming on the CW network" (2018, 28).

While Warner Bros. hoped that *Arrow* would open up inroads to young influencers, The CW saw the same show as a means to broaden that audience, an impetus that came from its CBS co-owner.[10] The CW acted as the network affiliate for several of CBS's owned and operated stations (at the time of The CW's sale to Nexstar in 2022, eight of CBS's twenty-nine owned and operated stations were CW affiliates). In its role as a station owner, CBS had a vested interest in pushing The CW to move beyond its niche of young viewers (primarily women). The push to expand The CW's audience came from station affiliates, including those owned by CBS. While the younger, more female audience worked well for some aspects of the television business (such as merchandising and repeat viewing), broadcast stations emphasized their need for additional advertisers. As the audience for The CW diversified by adding both older and more male viewers, the network and its affiliates found new advertisers such as quick-serve restaurants and financial service businesses (Lafayette 2014, 16). Furthermore, affiliates wanted an older and larger audience to provide a stronger viewer base for the stations' late local news (Holloway 2014, 15; Malone 2014, 17). So, affiliates encouraged The CW to move away from its image as the "Gossip Girl Network" (Holloway 2014, 15) and bring back the male audience that had declined since the end of *Smallville* in 2011 (Martin 2014). *Arrow* was a series that could potentially meet the demands of both of The CW's parent companies by bringing in a fresh audience for Warner Bros. content and broadening the network's audience for the CBS affiliates. At the 2012 upfronts, The CW's relatively new president Mark Pedowitz announced The CW's upcoming "transformative season" (Rose 2012) that would increase the range of viewers for the network (Holloway 2014, 13).

And *Arrow* did expand The CW's audience, bringing in a more gender balanced and older Millennial viewership (Joseph 2018, 33). For older audiences, promotion of the program repeatedly described the show as being "more" than a regular superhero show, appealing to the older viewers' growing interests in more complex, darker programs. Thom Sherman, The CW's Development head described *Arrow* as "provocative and sophisticated and edgy" (Reid 2012). Adult themes were used to appeal to a more mature audience. Producer Kreisberg noted that the show will explore "the consequences of taking the law into your own hands" (Stanley 2012, C10). To appeal to men, the show was promoted by CW President Mark Pedowitz as a "bold, edge-of-your-seat action show" (Heldenfels 2012) and a crime thriller (Stanley 2012, C10). And, as a nod to the increased diversity of the Millennial audience and its expectations of inclusion, the series created characters of color who hadn't first appeared in the comics. Most notably, as will be discussed below, the series added John Diggle, an African American Army veteran initially hired as Oliver's bodyguard who eventually becomes his crime-fighting assistant and confidant.

Arrow's success at broadening the audience was borne out in ratings and research numbers. In 2014, *Arrow*'s audience was 53 percent male and 47 percent female (Holloway 2014, 14). This gave *Arrow* the second highest male audience on The CW, second only to *The Flash*, which had a 59 percent male audience. *Arrow* and *The Flash* worked together to increase the male viewership of the network and, it was also assumed, the average viewer age. In the 2011–12, audience research showed that The CW's audience was 29.6 percent men with a median age of 36.8. In the 2014 season, these numbers showed more gender balance with a 39.2 percent male viewership with a median age of 41.7 (Holloway 2014, 12).

While the show attracted older males, to maintain its young female viewers, *Arrow*'s executive producer Marc Guggenheim maintained that the show was not "just" a crime thriller: "there's a strong emotional center. It's not all about the action adventure" (Stanley 2012, C10). The show does, in fact, highlight relationships—familial, friendship, and romantic. Additionally, reviewers, producers, and fans, all observe the show's blatant attempt to use sex appeal by taking many opportunities to present star Stephen Amell without a shirt. Almost every review of the first episode mentions Amell's abs and his frequent scenes of shirtless exercise. Even the show's co-creator and executive producer Greg Berlanti highlights the balance the show was trying to create by referring to Amell's body, saying, "There was the boy in me that loved comic books, who loved some of those scenes in that for the superhero-ness, and then there was the person in me who didn't mind having a hot guy doing the salmon ladder" (Reisman 2016). Joseph discusses how *Arrow*, then, increased The CW's demographic range but still upheld the network's brand and core audience, writing, "Putting superheroes front and center has allowed the network to enjoy renewed success through fan and critically acclaimed series while expanding its audience base, but without distorting its DNA" (2018, 43).

As we have seen so far, then, as a tentpole, *Arrow* garnered attention and brought in new viewers for both The CW and DC. It was also set up to ignite a franchise that would benefit its production companies and distribution platform. Furthermore, it was expected that *Arrow*, as television content, would successfully move across platforms to the benefit of all involved, allowing The CW to use content to "partner with and empower influencers" (Joseph 2018, 28). As The CW entered the second decade of the new millennium, it, like other traditional television networks, looked for ways to profit from the growing digital environment. When Pedowitz took over at the helm of The CW in 2011, he highlighted the importance of expanding into the digital marketplace (Holloway 2014, 13; Rose 2012) and creating an "active digital community" (Cochran and Winchell 2017, 202). In response, The CW moved away from only thinking about digital engagement as being about social media, but, introducing the new slogan "TV Now," emphasizing the network's ability to provide viewers with content on demand. Episodes were put up on The CW's own streaming service, CWTV, the day after they aired so that viewers didn't fall behind. Pedowitz also made deals with Hulu and Netflix, with in-season episodes going on Hulu for a limited time and full seasons going to Netflix after the season finale, allowing viewers to catch up before joining the live viewing either the next week or for the new season (Grossman 2011, 30). *Arrow* was expected to work well with the new viewing patterns emerging in the streaming television environment.

Arrow's strength as a tentpole resided in its abilities to meet the demands of its corporate sponsors by bringing together a range of loyal viewers across multiple platforms. It also had the potential to speak to Millennials' contemporary interests and concerns. One advertising executive observed that *Arrow* was a strong choice for The CW's attempt to appeal to its Millennial audience because, as a comic book character, "Oliver Queen was up to Robin Hood-esque shenanigans and foiling wealth inequality years before phrases such as 'the 1%' or 'Occupy Wall Street' grabbed headlines" (Truitt 2012, 1D). Industry insiders recognized that *Arrow* "could be understood as the representation of a populist desire to make a corrupt elite pay for what they have done, in a context where the political and legal system seem powerless to do so" (Pineda and Jimenez-Varea 2017, 16). Of course, within *Arrow*, the power to save the city, the freedom and agency to become a better person, still rests within an attractive, heavily muscled, rich, White character who tries to save the underclass.

As a CW show that used emotional, relationship drama to balance out the action of the show, *Arrow* foregrounds the process by which Oliver himself is saved through his realization of mental and physical freedom. In flashbacks we are shown the "before" and "after" versions of Oliver Queen that demonstrate his personal growth into someone with merit. Before his yacht is destroyed, Oliver is a spoiled, rich, immoral playboy who could have stepped straight out of CW's own *Gossip Girl*, embodying an image of the American Dream from the 1980s or 1990s that celebrated superficiality and materialism. Although Oliver appears to be having fun, we are clearly shown that his life is empty and unsatisfying; he is not a useful member of society. Perry Dantzler writes that before his time on the island, "Oliver makes decisions without regard for other people's safety or happiness, intent on defining his own pleasure" (2017, 37). Trapped on the island, however, Oliver not only learns how to survive through fighting but also develops significant meritorious traits like determination, responsibility, resilience, loyalty, and kindness. Through Oliver's constraints—he is both generally unable to get off the island and, often, literally, physically imprisoned—he finds his inner strength and his autonomy. The suggestion that hardships make people stronger is central to US ideology. Sarah Banet-Weiser observes that an ad campaign for Levi's spun the Great Recession as a moment for working class men to rebuild America "organized around a conventional and hegemonic set of normative values, such as competitiveness, adventurousness, stoicism, willpower, independence, honor, authenticity, and persistence" (2014, 91). *Arrow* similarly depicts Oliver's time on the island as an opportunity for him to separate from his past self and become a better, more meritorious person. The physical hardships become, like the recession, the difficulty needed to instigate growth.

Importantly, *Arrow* implies that Oliver's merits are not only learned on the island but are actually innate; the physical and emotional difficulties of the island unleash the true merits that always, already, existed within him. He learned necessary skills on the island, mostly with the help of "othered" Asian characters such as Yao Fei and his daughter Shado, whose depictions are disturbingly reminiscent of the Orientalism delineated by Edward Said, but the will and discipline to survive on the island as well as the loyalty and responsibility to protect others were already within Oliver. He tells his ex-girlfriend Laurel, "Those five years didn't change me. They scraped away all the things I wasn't and revealed the person I always was, which is the person . . . that's who you always saw" ("Sacrifice"). Oliver's true constraints were his wealth and privilege. The baggage of the Queen family, Oliver's inheritance, covered up his true merits of resilience, loyalty, discipline, and the ability to self-sacrifice.

The show, however, glosses over the fact that Oliver's life-advantages also provide him with the resources to "become someone else; something else" (words spoken in Oliver's voice-over introduction to each episode). This spirit of reinvention, along with the autonomy to transform oneself, rests on the exceptional freedom that Oliver Queen has as a man of privilege. For example, Oliver builds a nightclub in an abandoned Queen steel factory in The Glades to create a cover for an underground base. In addition to funding the cost of opening a club, Oliver also easily outfits this base with computers, ammunition, gadgets, and workout equipment. Oliver also has easy access to important people and places. And his physical strength comes from the care of his body (his workouts). Although his time on the island may have unearthed his innate meritorious qualities, the ability to activate them once he returns to society is silently enabled by his inherited resources.

In many ways, the dual messaging about autonomy mirrors that surrounding the American Dream. On the one hand, the overt claim is that anyone can reinvent themselves if they have the "right stuff"—some of these skills are learned and some are innate, but none require an inheritance or are determined by past success or failure. In other words, just like entrepreneurial capitalism, the American Dream asserts that hard work will lead to success. On the other hand, an unspoken but often acknowledged reality of the Dream that is discussed in greater detail in Chapter 3 is that the ability to act on one's merits is frequently limited to those who have access to and can draw on the benefits of family background and past successes. Oliver "must depend wholly on his billionaire status to maintain his alternate crime-fighting persona and pay for his arsenal of technological gadgets, vehicles and costumes" (Hassler-Forest 2012, 147). Therefore, as Dan Hassler-Forest observes, like Batman and Iron Man, *Arrow's* "superpower may indeed be defined as Capital" (2012, 147). Even Oliver's skill at adapting (to the island, to The Glades, to his rich bachelor lifestyle, to the Russian mob), which Lisa Perdiago argues "is the foundation of the series" (2017, 24), is associated with those in the upper class who have the competencies and resources to move between cultural strata (Peterson and Kern 1996). This is a skill that is reserved for Oliver, who can reinvent himself to adjust to the shifting realities of his life.

Oliver's freedom to move between worlds also means that the series shifts between glamorized depiction of Oliver's wealthy lifestyle and dreary images of the poverty and the underworld. *Arrow* features large, extravagant homes (the Queen mansion was filmed at the Hatley Castle in British Columbia), high-rise office buildings with floor to ceiling windows, fast and expensive cars, and well-coiffed people at black-tie events. The high-key lighting, and polished images used for these scenes contrast with the grainy and gray camera work on the island and the sinister shadows that paint The Glades. Scenes in The Glades take place in abandoned factories and dangerous streets, depicting it as a dark, run-down, and treacherous place. The first time Oliver goes to The Glades, the muted colors highlight the cold of the streets. Oliver walks past two people wearing dirty, mismatched clothing, warming themselves by a trash can fire, and piles of garbage near an abandoned building before reaching the chain-link fence with a "condemned" sign that is protecting the old factory. So, while the narrative may center on the dangers of income inequality, the images of the show favor privilege, reaffirming the comforts of the materialistic American Dream (Figure 1).

As will be further discussed in Chapter 3, the various lifestyles shown in *Arrow*, demonstrate how, like its Millennial viewers, the show negotiated the contradiction between hope and cynicism regarding the American Dream. The hopeful nature of the show is reaffirmed in its celebration of the freedom of reinvention, the potential for the autonomy to become someone better. At the same time, however, the show acknowledges the limitations placed on Oliver's agency. Just as Millennials found themselves struggling to create an American Dream in an economy ravaged by the greed and neglect of older generations, Oliver also grapples with a future shaped by his parents and their co-conspirators.

Figure 1 Oliver walks past people warming themselves by a trash can fire in The Glades in "The Pilot." *Arrow* © Warner Bros. Entertainment 2012–20.

Oliver is burdened by his father's dying wish, and, despite his growing agency, many of Oliver's decisions are determined by the guilt he inherits from his father.

The emphasis placed on Oliver's relationship with his father, a focus of many superhero narratives, is one of several father/son relationships that trigger the negotiation of individual autonomy and social responsibility within *Arrow*.[11] Fathers, the show suggests, bind their sons to particular ideas about the promises of the American Dream.[12] Oliver's best friend Tommy is more tragically impacted by his father's vision of the Dream. Tommy is the son of Malcolm Merlyn, the man behind The Undertaking. The two developed a fraught relationship when Malcolm's wife/Tommy's mother was killed in a random attack in The Glades. After his wife's murder, Malcolm withdrew from Tommy, nurturing a hatred for the people in The Glades.[13] Tommy grows to resent his father, especially after being financially cutoff. Forced to earn a living, Tommy actually thrives both as the manager of Oliver's club and as a romantic partner to Laurel. Once independent of his family connections, this rich, White man with cultural capital and privileged connections, appears to be achieving the American Dream. The show frequently uses Tommy's struggle for independence to generate drama and he is, ultimately, deemed expendable when he is killed during The Undertaking while trying to save Laurel. Although we later learn that over 500 people in The Glades also died, *Arrow* shifts viewers' emotional connection away from the poor people killed (none of whom are characters we know) to focus on Tommy—a handsome, White, wealthy character—whose attempt to redeem himself in pursuit of the American Dream is destroyed by his own father's twisted view of social responsibility.

In Malcolm's mind, the poor people in The Glades are responsible for crime and need to be destroyed in order to "save the city." Malcolm is never quite clear about who he is saving the city for, other than the wealthy elites. Malcolm, however, like Oliver, is working within a framework of public service. He simply blames the "wrong" people for the city's problems and offers an ominous solution that kills the American Dream even for the deserving such as Tommy. Malcolm's disturbing views are set against Oliver's more noble conceptions of how to save Starling City: "Malcolm wants to destroy The Glades, while Oliver wants to improve the district and worries about its people. Malcolm targets the poor and Oliver targets the rich. Malcolm works with an elite group of wealthy co-conspirators, while Oliver operates with a tiny group of non-elites, mostly underground" (Pineda and Jimenez-Varea 2017, 157). Importantly, Oliver's drive to serve the city by rooting out corruption among the wealthy does not necessarily stem from his own desires and dreams, but it's a task given to him by his father. Once Oliver develops his own community, bringing Diggle and Felicity Smoak onto his crime-fighting team, he is encouraged to think outside of his list and to go after street criminals (often people from The Glades who are either greedy or misguided in their attempts at revenge/justice). At this point, Oliver begins to truly assert his own autonomy while still mobilizing this freedom to choose who to help/serve. And, in all cases, the help that Oliver gives others is grounded in a sense of paternalism as he acts as the one person who knows who deserves help and how to help them.

Both Oliver Queen and his alter ego, the Hood, experience a freedom not available to most others within Starling City in terms of agency and the freedom to move through the city. Even Diggle and Felicity aren't granted this autonomy, tied to Oliver figuratively, as they mainly focus on the bad guys that he chooses, and literally, Diggle in his cover as Oliver's driver/bodyguard and Felicity as the computer expert who works from the base under Oliver's club. The privileges given to Oliver underscore the show's focus on White, male freedom. *Arrow's* characters of different gender, races, and ethnicities primarily offer a gesture to inclusion. Warner notes in her analysis of The CW's *Vampire Diaries* (2009–17) that within The CW shows:

> The worldviews of the characters must reflect the ideals and beliefs of this millennial demographic. This translates into sanitized versions of feminism underpinning female protagonist representation, as well as the downplay of class as a prohibitive factor for an individual's success in framing these stories. Intersecting with those characteristics is the required ideal that exists both in the real and fiction world concerning the paradoxical multicultural/post-racial society in which racial colorblindness is the standard way of seeing others. (2015, 101)

In a show designed to appeal to "colorblind" Millennial viewers, the inclusion of women and people of color is primarily a superficial way to symbolize equality while systemic discrimination (based on race, ethnicity, gender, sexuality, or economic class) is rarely discussed as part of the process of saving the city. Diggle, on occasion, does mention issues of race, such as when he voices concerns about Oliver trying to be "the white knight swooping in to save the disenfranchised" by gentrifying The Glades with his club ("Lone Gunman") or when, after donning a hoodie to buy drugs so that Oliver can analyze them, he snidely remarks, "the Person of Color has successfully purchased your drugs" ("Unfinished Business").

These concerns, however, are rarely given any weight, nor do they contribute to the main narrative. Asian characters fare particularly poorly in this first season of *Arrow* as they are mainly either depicted as members of the triad or as characters particularly lacking in agency, whose destinies lay in the hands of other (White) characters. For example, as noted above, although Yao Fei and his daughter Shado teach Oliver to survive on the island, their fates are repeatedly determined by Oliver who chooses to save them or sacrifice them.[14] As Rodney Thomas observes, "Black and Asian lives are eliminated on *Arrow* so that the whites in power can maintain their façade of protecting a civilized society—by any means necessary" (2017, 172). Autonomy, then, which marks Oliver as an idealized representation of the (White, privileged) American Dream, separates him from those around him and those he uses that freedom to serve. He is from the city, but not of the city, and he is certainly not of The Glades.

In fact, the people in The Glades are rarely represented at all within *Arrow*. And, when they are, their depictions tend to support Malcolm's concerns. Residents of The Glades are mainly portrayed as thieves, drug addicts, drug dealers, and looters. When The Undertaking begins in the season's last episode, panic ensues within The Glades and we are shown people pushing each other to escape, walking through the streets with baseball bats, and looting stores after throwing trash cans through their windows (though the show does seem to avoid racializing the mob, if only by avoiding clear facial close-ups). As Laurel, one of the few main characters who as a legal aid lawyer regularly interacts with people in The Glades, watches her office building collapse, two ominous people pass by in the dark background, one carrying a bat and the other a box. Roy Harper, a character from The Glades who is introduced as a thief, is perhaps one of the few exceptions. Roy's criminality is shown to be based on necessity. Additionally, Roy is changed by an encounter with The Hood that spurs him to want to help people, which he does during The Undertaking, as he prevents two people from brutally robbing an old man and aids a bus full of trapped passengers. Roy is set apart from others in The Glades by an association with the Hood that inspires him to be a better person. Despite Oliver's claims that the poverty and crime in The Glades are a "symptom" of the abuses by the wealthy, and the clear positioning of Malcolm as evil, the show's portrayals leave room to question whether people in The Glades are truly worthy of help—whether they deserve access to the American Dream or would even be able to take advantage of it. We wonder whether we should agree with Malcolm's assessment that The Glades "can't be saved because the people there don't want it to be saved"

("Sacrifice"). Good people within The Glades, with the exception of Roy, are not granted agency; if we see them at all, it's as an abused mob, frightened victims, or vulnerable targets. We are not asked, as viewers, to identify with people in The Glades but merely recognize that they shouldn't be killed. The public that Oliver is saving, then, is an abstraction that is utilized to confirm Oliver's heroism as he pushes away his family, friends, and loved ones to save people who may not even warrant saving.[15]

What we see throughout the first season of *Arrow* is Oliver thriving under the burden given to him by his father. By utilizing the agency afforded to him by his innate merits (and, without overt acknowledgment, his pedigree), Oliver wrestles to balance the rewards he wants to claim for his own American Dream with the need to serve an undeserving society as the Hood. In its focus on Oliver and its glamorizing of wealth, *Arrow* raises fundamental questions about the balance between freedom and social responsibility in the American Dream. Oliver freely gives up his own quest for the Dream to right his father's wrongs and save the city, but we never quite see the value of what is being saved. We see Oliver alienate his family, navigate several failed romantic relationships, watch his best friend die, and repeatedly put his life in danger to protect others. But what remains unclear is what is gained by Oliver's sacrifice of his own personal "better, richer and happier life." The limited success of The Undertaking, ending on a tragic note, serves as an effective cliffhanger to draw viewers back to the second season. Not only did The Hood fail and the city crumble, but the potential of the American Dream—seen in Tommy—is destroyed in this process.

Arrow's role as a tentpole for a broadcast network shaped its representation of the American Dream. In keeping with The CW brand and the desire to produce a "must see" drama with twenty-three episodes to appeal to a broad (yet young) audience, it highlights romantic drama and action designed to draw viewers into a DC franchise.[16] The superhero narrative aims to attract Millennials grappling with the middle-class promise of the American Dream. At the same time, the show locates the abilities to pursue the Dream within a young, White, attractive, upper-class man who can mobilize the freedom and autonomy to become "something more." Moreover, the superficial inclusion of diversity eases concerns about equity that may problematize the notion of individual opportunity. *Arrow* celebrates the community responsibility inherent in the moralistic American Dream by acknowledging the precarity and oppression caused by income inequality while still glamorizing the consumerism that undergirds the materialistic Dream. In the process, as meritorious people (the rich and middle class) exercise their freedom to save the poor, *Arrow* questions whether those being protected deserve the sacrifices others are making for them.

Saving the Dream with/for the Working Class, One Punch at a Time: *Daredevil*

What really makes people . . . heroes is not that they have heightened senses, it's not that they have law degrees; just that they're willing to do it. They're not turning away; they're going to save these people's lives, even if that's just quality of life.

Cornet 2015

The martyrs, the saints, the saviors . . . they all end up bloody and alone.
"The Path of the Righteous"

The industrial expectations for *Arrow*, as a broadcast television show on The CW, differed from those for *Daredevil*, which premiered on Netflix. On paper, the two series shared many similarities: both were used to start franchises, strove for a Millennial audience, and were promoted as dark and gritty. Narrative and stylistic similarities exist as well: they each center on a morally ambiguous vigilante battling to "save his city," feature villains who also make claims about trying to make the city better (by sacrificing poor people and buying up real estate), utilize flashbacks to provide insight into the characters, highlight father/son relationships, and include a best friend who is upset upon discovering the hero's secret identity. Nevertheless, the specific industrial goals of Marvel and Netflix resulted in a vastly different depiction of the American Dream.

Marvel's *Daredevil* premiered on Netflix in 2015, with the entire season of thirteen episodes released in fifty countries. The program, one of five Marvel series announced for distribution on Netflix, focuses on the characters of Matthew Murdock, a blind attorney-by-day and crime-fighter-by-night, created for Marvel Comics in 1964. Its story would contribute to the larger narrative of the upcoming *The Defenders* series that would bring together four Marvel/Netflix characters but could stand alone. And, unlike *Arrow*'s first season, it offered a strong sense of narrative closure since there were no initial plans for a second season.

Blinded in a childhood accident, Matt is orphaned when his father is killed by mobsters for refusing to throw a boxing match. While living in a Catholic orphanage in Hell's Kitchen, Matt is befriended by a mysterious man who trains him to use his greatly enhanced remaining senses to navigate the world around him and to fight. As in *Arrow*, much of this backstory is told through flashbacks. In the present, Matt is an attorney who, with his law school friend Foggy, eschews a cushy job at a prestigious law firm to start a small practice in Hell's Kitchen to help the people among whom he was raised. At night, dressed in all black, Matt uses his acquired fighting skills to combat the criminal elements that overtook Hell's Kitchen in the wake of "the Incident" (the fight for New York seen in *The Avengers* [2012]).

The first season of *Daredevil* tells the story of how Matt's work as an attorney and his nighttime activities as a vigilante lead him, and those helping him, to uncover and attempt to stop the crime syndicate run by Wilson Fisk. Fisk's vague plan to help the city rests on his desire for power and the assumption that if he is in control of crime, things will be "better." Matt attempts to take down Fisk both as a lawyer and as a vigilante, often questioning which method is more effective. Much of the work in unraveling Fisk's connection to the crime syndicate is done by Foggy Nelson, Matt's friend and law partner, Karen Page, a client saved by Matt and Foggy who becomes their secretary, and Ben Urich, an investigative reporter persuaded by Karen to look into a series of connected crimes. Matt is also helped by nurse Claire Temple, who fixes his broken body (and serves as a love interest), as the show continuously reminds us that Matt is just a man who is repeatedly left bloody after his fights, and, to a lesser extent, by police sergeant Brett Mahoney, an honest New York City police officer.

The inclusion of and the strength given to these additional characters points to one of the primary ways that *Daredevil* questions mainstream depictions of the American Dream. These characters and others—not *only* the titular superhero— demonstrate that people across class strata work to achieve and then mobilize their autonomy in defining their own American Dream. *Daredevil* also relies on the problematic portrayal of diversity appreciated by Millennials; although the primary characters of Matt, Foggy, and Karen are all White, as will be discussed below, Ben, Claire, and Brett are people of color who in many ways also offer the superficial depiction of diversity seen in *Arrow*. Additionally, *Daredevil* proposes a significant rethinking of the materialistic American Dream focused on class mobility. The industrial opportunities that encourage these more progressive representations, however, also serve to replace the materialistic American Dream with a questionable moralistic myth grounded in violence.

This 2015 version was not *Daredevil*'s first live-action adaptation. Before even the failed 2003 film starring Ben Affleck, the character appeared in the 1989

TV movie *The Trial of the Incredible Hulk* on NBC, which was intended as a backdoor pilot for a Daredevil series that never came to fruition (Blumberg 2016, 123).[17] Since then, Marvel's status significantly increased, with Disney buying the company for $4 billion in 2009 and growing its film output into a movie franchise unprecedented in scope and box office returns (Jurgensen 2015, D1). The return of *Daredevil* to television was announced in 2013 when Marvel Television struck a deal with Netflix for the distribution of five series: *Daredevil, Jessica Jones* (2015–19), *Luke Cage* (2016–18), *Iron Fist* (2017–18), and *The Defenders* (2017), in which the four characters would form an Avengers-like team. Netflix reportedly paid Marvel $200 million for sixty hours of programming without seeing a pilot—or any footage at all (Spangler 2014; Jurgensen, 2015, D1). At the time of the announcement, Marvel had one show on television, *Marvel's Agents of S.H.I.E.L.D.*, which aired on the Disney-owned ABC network. The deal with Netflix—for five series with no pilot—was beyond the norm of anything that would be considered by a traditional broadcast or cable network (Itzkoff, Netflix Builds 2015, C1). Netflix, however, was interested in the "street level" Marvel heroes that were not being utilized in the Marvel films, seeing these potentially darker characters as a perfect fit to match Netflix's edgy content for more mature audiences (even though they would eventually end up in a section of Disney+ requiring parental approval).

Marvel's and Netflix's goals in the creation of *Daredevil* and the other series were advantageously aligned. Each company had a vested interest in trying to elevate the established, and to some extent culturally devalued, superhero genre as the basis for the formation of a television tentpole. As Michael Newman and Elana Levine discuss, the attempt to legitimize television encouraged viewers to distinguish themselves through their programs of choice and created space for "highbrow" viewers who didn't want to be associated with traditional television and the mass audience (2012, 3). To attract even more viewers, production and distribution companies recognized the effectiveness of drawing on familiar genres and "upgrading" them. Cecilia Lima et al explain that these shows "make use of the genres that are already part of the repertoire of the audience to create original content, bringing forth products that show the most important elements and aesthetics of TV series (especially cable TV)" (2015, 251). Both Netflix and Marvel could benefit from offering audiences something familiar but different: Netflix by retaining existing subscribers and drawing in new (and international) viewers and Marvel by building upon its audience for an already established superhero franchise through existing intellectual property.

By the time *Daredevil* premiered on Netflix in 2015, seven US television shows featured superheroes. *Arrow* and *The Flash* were doing well by CW standards (which meant low ratings but strong male audiences) and *Gotham* on Fox was considered mildly successful with a 2.0 rating in the 18–49 demographic (Baysinger, With Netflix 2015, 7). But on ABC, *Agents of S.H.I.E.L.D.*'s ratings had declined since its first season and the new Marvel show, *Agent Carter* was not attracting the expected audience. NBC's DC-based *Constantine* (2014–15) was on its way to being cancelled and CW's *iZombie* (2015–19) had just premiered (Baysinger, With Netflix 2015, 7). Despite the lackluster performance of Marvel's ABC shows, *Daredevil* generated a great deal of excitement demonstrating the potential, like all tentpole television series, to expand audiences for Marvel and Netflix, generate a franchise (as well as expand on the existing Marvel Universe), and move viewers across platforms.

For Marvel, the series on Netflix offered a means of exploiting existing source material to bring new audiences to the Marvel Universe. Joseph Loeb, Executive Vice President of Marvel Television, got the idea for the Netflix shows after watching the big battle scene in *The Avengers*. He explained, "The Avengers are here to save the universe and the street level heroes are here to save the neighborhood" (Baysinger, With Netflix 2015, 8). These series integrated into the MCU but with a different—"street level"—perspective, that appealed to a more mature audience (Radosinska 2017, 26). Writing in *The Wall Street Journal*, John Jurgensen observed that "'Daredevil' and the other gritty shows on deck with Netflix give the studio a way to diversify. They're targeting an audience that prizes R-rated action and horror, while still playing in the same fictional world of the glossier Marvel properties" (2015, D1). Capitalizing on Netflix's lack of content regulations and its Millennial audience looking for "edgy" content, Marvel sought viewers who were older than those drawn to the family-centric PG-13-rated films but younger than the broadcast viewers attracted to ABC content (Baysinger, With Netflix 2015, 8).

The process of modifying the superhero show for more mature, selective viewers involved several different strategies. Centering on a more "human" superhero, *Daredevil* featured a dark tone, in both style and theme, and a great deal of violence that presented a crime story that was "more Sin City than Agents of S.H.I.E.L.D." (Lackner 2015, A9). Additionally, demonstrating what Newman and Levine call the "most ubiquitous legitimating strategy" (2012, 5), much of the publicity surrounding *Daredevil* connected the series to the cinematic art form. *Daredevil* was celebrated as a film-like, cohesive narrative with a deliberate vision. The short-form nature of the thirteen-episode program, the narrative that wraps up the story arc at the end of the season (but still leaves room for additional seasons), and the ability to binge watch contributed to creating a discourse that associated *Daredevil* with a cinematic experience. Additionally, in a move unusual for television, the same cinematographer (Matthew J. Lloyd) worked on all the episodes, furthering the ideas of a consistent vision for the series (Pagello 2017, 738). Joe Quesada, Marvel Entertainment's chief creative officer, said, "We can sit there and look at 13 episodes and plan it out as a very large movie. It makes seeing the big picture a little bit easier" (J. Hughes 2014). Promotion of the series' stars foregrounded their high-end acting credentials. Charlie Cox was noted for his work in the acclaimed HBO series *Boardwalk Empire* (2010–14) rather than his starring role in the 2007 fantasy film *Stardust* (2007) and Vincent D'Onofrio was described by Loeb as an actor with "gravitas and versatility" (McCarthy 2014). Furthermore, the show's creators frequently cited the New American Cinema films *The French Connection* (1971) and *Taxi Driver* (1976) as inspirations for the look and feel of the program. One critic observed that "one of the noticeably different aspects of *Daredevil* is just how 'un-Marvel' the series looked" (Baysinger, With Netflix 2015, 8). While the Marvel movies feature glossy, high-rise buildings hovering over a bustling New York City and expensive special effects, *Daredevil* focuses on the small, everyday neighborhood of Hell's Kitchen (made out to be much grimier and more dangerous than its current reality), avoiding CGI and instead utilizing long takes and a slow pace to build realism. Showrunner Steven DeKnight asserts, "We wanted to be grounded, gritty, as realistic as we could portray" (Alloway 2014). This involved shooting the show in New York City, with dark lighting, run-down sets, and a portrayal of violence that included "broken bones and spilled blood" (Truitt 2015, 3D). According to Terence McSweeney, "*Daredevil* is by far the most explicitly violent entrant in the entirety of the MCU" (2018, 224).

The representation of violence, with images of the hero bloody, bruised, and in pain, contributes to a complex characterization that ties Matt to other antiheroes seen on "quality" television. Viewers are encouraged to connect to Matt as a human being, not a superhero with extraordinary powers. DeKnight explains that "in every aspect he's a man that's just pushed himself to the limits" (Alloway 2014). To appeal to adult viewers, Matt is shown to be morally questionable, and the series interrogates the concepts of right and wrong. As we see Matt torture criminals to get information, the series probes the possibility that Matt enjoys hurting people, and that he is as much like the villainous Fisk as he is different than him. Discussing his character, Cox notes, "Murdock is a walking contradiction: He's a lawyer by day and a vigilante by night. He's a committed Catholic on the one hand, and at the same time, he's playing God" (Sacks 2015, 3). DeKnight describes Matt as "one of the most morally grey of the heroes" (Alloway 2014). This conflicting characterization led to comparisons between *Daredevil* and some of the more critically acclaimed complex dramas that successfully attracted adult viewers. Sarah Smith suggested that *Daredevil* could "elevate" the superhero story like *True Detective* (HBO, 2014–present) did for the crime procedural (2015, A10). Jurgensen compared Matt's moral struggle to those of Tony Soprano and Walter White (2015, D1), and a headline in *The Capital Times* (Madison) proposed that "Netflix's '*Daredevil*' Might Just Be 'The Wire' of Superhero Shows" (R. Thomas 2015, 3).

The discourse of legitimization that surrounded *Daredevil* allowed Marvel to expand the reach of its franchise so that the brand penetrated more people on multiple platforms. Although discussing *Agents of S.H.I.E.L.D.* and *Agent Carter*, Sarah Hughes's observations also apply equally to *Daredevil*: "The TV series can reference the movies and the movies can speak to the TV series" (2014). This synergy most directly benefited Marvel, which owned the production companies for the series, the film franchise to which the series were tied, and the original comic book material. In addition, the series opened new opportunities for Marvel merchandise sales, a significant component of Disney profits that further drives brand loyalty. Tony Lisanti notes that Disney Consumer Products was "slowly building the Avengers franchise character by character into a dominant year-round boys' brand that also has the potential to expand beyond its core audience" (2013, 122). One of Disney Consumer Products' most important goals was to target the missing 18–34-year-olds (Lisanti 2013, 124). Although there was limited transmedia expansion for *Daredevil*, Disney Consumer Products instituted the Marvel Knight Merchandising Program that emphasized "sophisticated and edgy" fashion at companies like Hot Topic, Forever 21, and Under Armor as well as a small line of collectibles for teens and adults (Glaser 2015). While limited in comparison to the merchandising for the Marvel films, this campaign would help tie older, Millennial consumers to the Marvel brand.

Marvel's foray into television expanded after *Daredevil* succeeded as a strong tentpole to usher in a new iteration of the MCU franchise. Marvel and Netflix moved forward with all the originally planned series as well as a *Daredevil* spin-off *The Punisher* (2017–19) and additional seasons for *Daredevil*, *Jessica Jones*, and *Luke Cage*. Marvel also introduced new programs on a range of platforms. In

2017, Marvel had thirteen shows at some stage of development or production.[18] According to Netflix, Marvel's television approach seemed to be working to bring new viewers to the Marvel franchise. In 2017, the platform reported that one in eight viewers of Marvel's Netflix shows were new to comic-based content (Truitt 2017).

This extension of Marvel's reach to include viewers drawn to the "grittier, adult fare" with "themes rooted in heavier subjects like faith and trauma" also fit well with Netflix's mid-2010s strategies (Baugher 2020). Netflix, in the second decade of the new millennium, secured its role as a television platform and demonstrated the potential of streaming as a distribution model. Although it had successfully made deals with many media companies for the second-cycle streaming rights for their television content, Netflix understood that these same companies would soon develop their own streaming platforms. In 2011 Netflix's CEO Reed Hastings explained that he saw HBO becoming more "Netflix-like" with its HBO Go on-demand service (Learmonth 2011). Additionally, the growth of Hulu and Amazon Prime Video resulted in a competitive market that increased fees for second-cycle series and necessitated the construction of a unique brand (Bookman 2014). To that end, Netflix in 2013, began distributing original, first-run content. Although some of the initial "originals," such as *Lilyhammer* (Netflix, 2012–14), were, and still are, first available on other platforms in other countries, Netflix quickly commissioned its own content to allow for greater control.

In these early years, all original programming on Netflix needed to be tentpole content that would both build a brand for the platform and bring in subscribers. Previously, Netflix's brand primarily relied on its services—allowing viewers to choose what to watch and when to watch it—to "brand itself as disruptive, youthful, individualistic, techy, and capable of satisfying immediate viewer desire" (Havens 2018, 327). In 2014, as Timothy Havens explains, Netflix rebranded in a way that also relied on programming to create this image (2018, 327–8). Programming, furthermore, was intended to expand the Netflix audience. Ted Sarandos, Netflix's Chief Content Officer explained in 2015,

> Netflix was born on the Internet, so our demographic was younger and more male when we were beginning, [but] it's far more mainstream today. So you really are covering all demographics trying to find programming that people love and attach to in a way that leads to retention and creates a brand halo for Netflix as well. We really are trying to program something for everyone. (Multicultural Content Goes Multiplatform 2016, 13)

To that end, after its initial success with *House of Cards* (Netflix, 2013–18) and *Orange Is the New Black* (Netflix, 2013–19), Netflix began a partnership with Dreamworks animation for children's programming. It also developed the very expensive (and unsuccessful) *Marco Polo* (Netflix, 2014–16) with the Weinstein Brothers and the science fiction series *Sense8* (Netflix, 2015–18) from sci-fi icons the Wachowskis and J. Michael Straczynski (Kulikowski 2014). The Marvel series were part of this expansion, helping to both retain the core Netflix viewership of young men but also bring a new audience of more mainstream Marvel fans. *Daredevil* balanced Netflix's interest in the "instant name recognition and built in audience" that comes from superhero shows (Mudhar 2014) with a focus on diverse "nonconventional heroes—really grounded, not capes and cod pieces" (Itzkoff, Netflix Builds 2015, C1).

Netflix further expected the Marvel series to reinforce the platform's global expansion. As Kevin McDonald outlines, Netflix began its international drive in 2010 and by 2014 was available in Canada, Latin America, UK, Ireland, and most of Continental Europe (2016, 212). This growth, put pressure on Netflix both in terms of the financial investment required and the need for content. Netflix commissioned content for which it owned the international rights and that would also appeal to global audiences. Based on the dominance of Marvel films at the global box office, Netflix gambled that the series could have the same level of international popularity. Discussing the Marvel deal, Sarandos explains, "We were taking what I thought was a pretty measured bet on someone with a great track record of serving a very discriminating fan base" (Itzkoff, Netflix Builds 2015, C1). Consequently, *Daredevil*, as mentioned above, was released simultaneously in fifty countries (Moylan, California Streaming 2015).

The show proved successful with national and international audiences both in creating buzz and attracting viewers. Eric Pallotta, Netflix's Social Media Director noted that the "pre-launch chatter for *Daredevil* has been bigger on social media than it has been for any of Netflix's other original programs" (Moylan, California Streaming 2015). Hastings, in a letter to stockholders, mentioned the positive reaction to *Daredevil* (and other Netflix originals) as a reason for the higher-than-projected subscriber increase both domestically and overseas that instigated a jump in Netflix stock a week after *Daredevil*'s release (M. Murphy 2015; Bond 2015). Initial research demonstrated that *Daredevil* had strong viewership on Netflix. Additionally, according to Luth Research, 10.7 percent of subscribers in the United States watched at least one episode of

Daredevil in the first eleven days of its release, making it one of the most watched shows on the platform (Wallenstein 2015).

Although the sample used by Luth was limited, this preliminary finding demonstrates that *Daredevil* succeeded as tentpole television, capturing the young, male, international audience, as well as many other viewers, for Netflix and Marvel, drawing attention to and excitement for the upcoming television franchise, and encouraging new viewers to the films and Marvel merchandise. By exploiting the market for dark and complex content, both Marvel and Netflix used *Daredevil* as a tentpole to expand the audience for the existing franchise, create a new television universe, and encourage audiences to immerse themselves in both the Marvel and Netflix brands. To do this, *Daredevil* capitalized on Marvel's potential for a darker, more complicated vision of the American Dream.

As with *Arrow*, and all televisual representations, the industrial motivations that shaped *Daredevil* intersected with the shifting ideals of its target audience. As discussed above, the Millennial audience was reconfiguring its socioeconomic allegiance away from the upper class and toward the working class. According to Shapiro, the television programs created for Millennials reflected this realignment, including some series that went beyond just depicting the struggles of the working class. These programs encouraged a stronger connection between the classes by representing middle-class characters who reject upper-class ideals and values in favor of an affiliation with the working class (S. Shapiro 2016, 196–7). Furthermore, Shapiro observes that the melding of prestige drama and mainstream genre (such as superhero shows) was particularly ideal for representing this shifting allegiance of the middle class:

> The return by middle-class audiences to the generic narratives associated with lowbrow taste within the safety of high-production, subscription television can be now seen as itself an indicative feature of the ongoing rearrangement of the composition of class alliances. This change of perspective is less a matter of "downward identification," where the viewer is asked to imaginatively "be" the working-class, than one where the professional-managerial viewer's watching allows for an expression about the loss of faith with the American Dream and beginning the process of imagining how alignment with a lower class might function. (2016, 196)

The "lowbrow" superhero genre was ideal for portraying a narrative that questioned class by recreating the genre as prestige television speaking to the concerns of Millennials rethinking the state of the American Dream. In approaching these themes within the parameters of the Netflix brand image, *Daredevil* offers viewers moments of extreme violence, complex moral questions (centered on Matt's Catholic upbringing), and a shifting identification that ties us not only to the superhero but to a range of other characters, including the villain.

Matt's struggle for autonomy pushes at the boundaries of meritorious respectability. Unlike Oliver Queen, his good qualities were apparent from a young age. In the series' opening scene, Matt loses his sight when he saves an old man from getting hit by a car. In flashbacks, we see him as a resourceful, intelligent, loyal, and brave child. Matt's many positive qualities—from his intelligence to his resilience to his secret ability to navigate the physical world—set him well on his way toward achieving the traditional American Dream. He grows up to be a handsome, likable, religious, ethical, law school graduate. Matt, along with Foggy, rejects the well-paying world of corporate law for the freedom to help people from the old neighborhood.

Interestingly, the independence that Matt attains on this path leads him away from the traditional values associated with the Dream. Matt develops his autonomy as the Devil of Hell's Kitchen or The Man in Black (both names given to the vigilante by the press) as he runs around the city fighting crime and saving the innocent. *Arrow* demonstrates how Oliver becomes meritorious and worthy of the American Dream, through his acceptance of the skills and responsibilities required for being The Hood. In *Daredevil*, however, becoming a vigilante frees Matt to let his devil out, a devil that is only checked by his innate goodness and his religion. To this end, rather than bolstering the American Dream, *Daredevil* questions its foundations, suggesting that striving for the upper-class ideal of a home, a family, and a well-paying job, may not lead to a "better, richer, and happier life" or to social justice.

It's the series' villain, Fisk, who embodies the materialistic American Dream, encouraging a critique of these values. Rising from a working-class background, Fisk's determination and intelligence allow him to succeed. Fisk even espouses some of the ideals of the Dream with lines such as "Problems are just opportunities that haven't presented themselves" ("Condemned"). He wields the myth of the American Dream, creating a false history for himself and establishing a media image that generates trust in him. As Fisk becomes the ideal of the materialistic American Dream, *Daredevil*'s viewers (unlike most of the diegetic public) recognize this package as a sham. The traditional American Dream is seen to rest in a brutal and dangerous man who lacks the merit to make him deserving but has still attains wealth and power.

As they integrate their pasts with their presents, both Matt and Fisk demonstrate the pressures faced by class straddlers. As explained by Matthew Pustz in his discussion of Spider-Man, class straddlers are people who experience class mobility; they are born into the working class but move up into the middle or even upper class (2006, 74). Once Fisk achieved his goal of upward mobility, however, he turned his back on the working class, telling his art dealer girlfriend Vanessa that his goal is to make the city better for people like her, which he does by exploiting the community from which he came. Matt, on the other hand, uses his straddler position to shift his alignment within the class hierarchy. As a lawyer, he embodies the aspirations of the middle-class American Dream, but as a vigilante he demonstrates a form of street justice and violence that connects him with his working-class father who, when boxing, would "let the devil out" ("Into the Ring"). Matt must integrate his middle-class and working-class allegiances, grappling with living the life of a lone soldier fighting injustice or the life of a caring law partner with friends.

The two characters who best recognize Matt's predicament are Claire and his priest, Father Lantom. Each counsels Matt about the dangers he is facing by taking on the Daredevil persona. Claire, taking an individualistic perspective, warns Matt that he will be unhappy, reminding him "The martyrs, the saints, the saviors . . . they all end up bloody and alone" ("The Path of the Righteous"). Demonstrating similar concerns, Father Lantom, however, focuses on Matt's responsibility to the community: "When good people do bad things the entire community is tainted" ("Speak of the Devil"). Matt, then, in exercising his freedom and constructing his own American Dream, is focused less on weighing his individual happiness against his social responsibility and more on the best way to align this Dream with both his middle-class sense of justice and his inherited urge to unleash the devil in him. He must decide how to "be the man this city needs" in a way that will also allow him to sleep at night ("World on Fire").

This embracing of complex personal and moral decisions is tied to *Daredevil*'s position as a prestige genre series trying to reach a mature audience. *Daredevil* utilizes tropes of the superhero narrative (such as a secret identity, supervillain, and the transformed orphan), but complicates many of the underlying issues. Diegetically, The Man in Black is seen by his New York community at different times as both a savior and a dangerous killer. To the viewers, he appears as a hero but one with very human frailties, both physically and morally. Matt's body gets broken and bruised, he wrestles with questions of sin, and cries when he feels alone. In its questioning of toxic masculinity, embodied most clearly in Fisk's father, which denies men many human attributes, *Daredevil* underscores Matt's humanity as a strength that saves him from being a killer.[19]

Because of his vulnerability, Daredevil "protects the city by demonstrating his weaknesses to stand in for the social precarity of the people who live within it" (Vernon and Gustafson 2020, 149). And, at the same time, Matt is bolstered by the strengths and abilities of these non-superheroes he is fighting to help. Writing about the show, Roth Cornet observes, "Daredevil is the lead, and certainly the central superhero in the series, but the people surrounding him are equally compelling and as likely to make dangerously courageous choices— and with far less skill to back them up. That—and *Daredevil's* sometimes murky morality—opens up an interesting conversation about what it means to be a hero" (2015). As Cornet and others note, the "supporting" characters in *Daredevil* are given the opportunity to display autonomy when they choose to be courageous rather than afraid, when they make difficult choices that threaten their lives. Deborah Ann Woll, who played Karen Page, explained, "What really makes people like Matt, and Foggy, and Karen heroes is not that they have heightened senses, it's not that they have law degrees; just that they're willing to do it. They're not turning away; they're going to save these people's lives, even if that's just quality of life" (Cornet 2015). *Daredevil* offers us "regular" people who have the freedom to determine their path to the American Dream. In this case, Foggy (a lawyer), Karen (a secretary), Claire (a nurse), Ben (a reporter), and Elena Cardenas (an ad-hoc community organizer) make the choice that is usually only reserved for the superhero in these narratives—to find their own happiness in the moralistic American Dream by conceiving of themselves as those who help others.

Additionally, the people being helped, those who are in danger of being squeezed out of the American Dream, are strong and active individuals. Throughout the season, characters from the underclass demonstrate more strength of character than those of the upper classes. The series establishes the humanity within New York's Hell's Kitchen, creating a narrative for the city in which people foster community. Sitting in Josie's, a local dive bar, swathed in darkness, Karen tells Foggy how scared she is of the city since a man was murdered in her apartment and another tried to kill her. Karen is framed, unsettlingly, in a medium close-up with a shaky camera as she confesses her fears. To reassure her, Foggy focuses on the goodness of the people of New York, pointing out other patrons in the bar, all of whom are White men coded as working class: one large, tattooed man playing pool who is the head of a biker gang also organizes the food drive every Thanksgiving; another large man with tattoos in a cutoff shirt, sitting in a booth drinking a beer is married to the woman who works at the dry cleaners around the corner from their office; and a third, who Foggy admits really is a criminal, is also "turning it around," and trying to get his kid into a good day care. Like Foggy, *Daredevil* asks us to look past appearances and see the humanity in ordinary, working-class people. In another instance, Santino, a young Latino, finds a bloody Daredevil passed out in a dumpster. Going against a media stereotype that might have had him try to rob Daredevil or at least look under the mask, Santino rushes to find Claire, the nurse who lives in the building (who also chooses to help Matt). Most notably, Foggy, Matt, and Karen take the case of Elena Cardenas, an older, Guatemalan, Spanish-speaking woman, who lives in a rent-controlled building in Hell's Kitchen. The building owner (controlled by Fisk) is trying to clear out the tenants so it can be given to and razed by the Yakuza (for reasons that are explained in *The Defenders*). Mrs. Cardenas and some of her neighbors refuse the buyout offer because they simply want to stay in their homes. The result is a series of problems in the building such as a lack of heat, hot water, and gas. Instead of caving to the demands of Fisk's global capital consortium, Mrs. Cardenas and her neighbors work together, sharing essential resources. Mrs. Cardenas and her neighbors are regular people willing to fight to keep their homes and maintain their community, both staples of their American Dream. Mitch Murray, observing the power that *Daredevil* offers to its non-super characters, writes, "In this representation of a collective, a kind of superpower can be understood to manifest in the real world" (2017, 47). In this way, *Daredevil* works against the critique that superhero narratives disempower viewers by encouraging them to wait for salvation by exceptional heroes rather than fight to create and protect their own dreams.

In addition to portraying strong people fighting for the American Dream, *Daredevil* examines the pressures they face in this process. The inclusion of the housing conflict faced by Mrs. Cardenas and her neighbors is only one way that *Daredevil* asks viewers to consider the stresses being put on the American Dream for the middle and working classes. The price of real estate in New York is raised repeatedly in relation to the quality of Matt and Foggy's law offices, Matt's apartment, and Mrs. Cardenas's attempt to hold on to her rent-controlled apartment. Gentrification is a major force behind Fisk's plan to make the city "better." Additionally, the third episode of the season,

"Rabbit in a Snowstorm" spends a surprisingly long amount of screen time examining Ben's attempts to get insurance for his ill wife's hospital stay. Ben and a sympathetic hospital administrator sit in a cramped, cluttered office as he explains why she should support his appeal to the insurance company. The camera's placement at chair level on either side of the desk keeps viewers positioned in the room as Ben argues his case. The episode spends almost two minutes solely on the insurance issue (which only tangentially comes up later in relation to the show's overall narrative), and then another minute showing Ben's reaction both in a close-up outside of the administrator's office and as he sits with his sleeping wife. The episode makes certain that we see the human toll of the problems with the US health care system that affect middle-class professionals, underscoring *Daredevil*'s alignment of this character with a significant welfare issue.

Certainly, *Daredevil* does not depict all of the underclass as strong and deserving. The season features gun runners, drug dealers, thieves, and drug addicts who are clearly participants in the demise of the American Dream in Hell's Kitchen. Furthermore, while *Arrow* demonstrates sympathy for some of these characters, suggesting that drug addiction and robbery, for example, are the result of a desperation initiated by the greed of the upper class, *Daredevil* offers no such understanding. If there can be resilient and morally upright working-class people chasing the American Dream, then, *Daredevil* proposes that those who choose a different path are doing so by choice and deserve to be violently punished. As part of the series' appeal to a global and mature audience, *Daredevil* foregrounds this violence to mark it as prestige and to speak in an international language. Bloody and gory depictions are also enabled by Netflix existing outside of Federal Communications Commision regulations. The series features numerous scenes of The Man in Black beating petty criminals to stop crime or gain information and elaborately choreographed fight sequences (Figure 2). One of the most stylistically celebrated scenes of the season is a three-minute-long take of *Daredevil* moving through rooms off a long hallway beating up characters who are holding a young boy hostage ("Cut Man"). The show often revels in the violence. And, although the justification for and morality of violence appears to be a major theme within the show—Matt discusses this with his priest, as well as Claire and Foggy—the series ultimately sides with violence as it is used to protect the working classes from upper-class oppression. Alyssa Rosenberg writes that the show doesn't do much "to convince me that *Daredevil* has thought very much about the anti-heroic nature of a moral philosophy

Figure 2 The Devil of Hell's Kitchen violently interrogates a man who abducted a child in "The Cut Man." *Daredevil* © Walt Disney Co. 2015–18.

where the most noble thing a parent or a lawyer can do is to hit someone very, very hard" (Daredevil the Wrong Hero for Out Times? 2015, D2). While the show makes efforts, then, to depict the working class with agency and sympathy, the need to legitimate the series for older Millennial audiences limited its exploration of the moral ambiguity of violence to conversation rather than practice. The American Dream, and its realignment with working-class values, the show suggests is found in Matt's freedom to pursue vigilante justice through barely contained violence.

Another impact of the prestige status of the series is its descent into cynicism and despair at given moments. By killing significant and likable characters (as well as many insignificant and unlikable characters), the series maintains its reputation as a serious drama. Notably, two "good" characters who are killed are people of color: African American journalist, Ben, is killed by Fisk for getting too close to his true backstory, and Mrs. Cardenas is killed as a plot device both for viewers (to show us how truly heinous Fisk is) and diegetically (Fisk kills her to enrage The Man in Black). As discussed previously, these are also the two characters through whom social problems, housing, and health insurance, are examined. Unlike the references to social issues, which demonstrate middle-class alignment with the working class, the deaths of these characters directly drive (White) character development and action. Mrs. Cardenas's death causes Matt, Karen, and Foggy to question the legal methods by which they are trying to take down Fisk. A drunk Foggy tells Karen, "We were gunna help the people that we grew up with. Give them the same shot as the big boys, like Fisk. It's all bullshit" ("Speak of the Devil"). Matt, meanwhile, takes to the streets, beating up petty criminals until he finds the man who killed Mrs. Cardenas. Ben's murder sparks a similar crisis of faith in the justice system. The last episode of the season, opens with Ben's funeral presented in slow motion with soulful music and track-in medium close-ups of the main characters as well as Ben's wife, sitting in a wheelchair. Karen expresses her guilt at pulling Ben into the investigation, only to be absolved by his wife. Matt, on the other hand, is further plunged into guilt for his failure to stop Fisk in any way possible. These characters of color are robbed of their American Dreams, and while their deaths are the results of the decisions they made, it's impossible to ignore that narratively, these deaths still serve the plotlines focused on the younger, White characters. In the same way that Black and Asian characters are killed in *Arrow* so that White characters can protect civilized society, Ben's and Mrs. Cardenas's deaths are used to justify Matt's turn toward violence to protect his city.

The series, however, does not end in despair but on an optimistic note. Fisk and many of his compatriots are in custody, and Matt, Foggy, and Karen reunite outside their office building to put up the sign for the firm of Nelson and Murdock. They stand on the street in New York, as people walk both behind them and in the foreground, laughing at the new name the newspapers created for the Devil of Hell's Kitchen: Daredevil. After Foggy leaves, Karen and Matt acknowledge that, although Fisk is in jail, it doesn't bring back the people who have been killed or undo things that have been done. Matt suggests that all they can do is "move forward. Together." As he and Karen walk into the building, the camera cuts to a position from across the street and tracks back (literally the opposite of moving forward), providing a long shot of the building with a trash can, a trash bag, and a fire hydrant in the foreground. This shot situates Karen and Matt within their working class, somewhat dirty city. They are the young, White, middle class who have chosen to live within the working-class community, to help them fight for their American Dream. After briefly showing us Fisk in jail, the last shots of the series, underscore the idea that it is not enough to serve justice through the law. Rather, Matt, in his new, red, iconic Daredevil costume stands on a rooftop high above the city, hears a scream, takes out his weapons, and runs to help. The city still needs a vigilante/superhero and Matt wants to live this life. As the tentpole series in the Marvel/Netflix franchise, *Daredevil* introduces tension between middle-class respectability and working-class action that is repeated in all the later series. This theme shapes the series' depiction of the moralistic American Dream grounded in working-class values (questionably defined), appealing to Millennial viewers grappling with their own expectations and fears.

Conclusion

As we have seen, both *Arrow* and *Daredevil* served as important tentpole series. The expectations that they would attract Millennial audiences and draw in new viewers to their respective DC and Marvel franchises led to the production of narratives that had many similarities including an underlying theme about a vulnerable vigilante who is given the autonomy (and the responsibility) to balance his own needs with those of the community he wants to serve.

As a broadcast television show, *Arrow* faced different pressures than *Daredevil*. The push to broaden its audience, even within the parameters of The CW's narrow target audience and the requirements set by The CW brand, impacted the show's depictions of the American Dream. Although the wealthy, White, male superhero gives up his individual American Dream (though never quite the materialistic Dream) to focus on the moralistic Dream, *Arrow* consistently questions whether those being served are worthy of this sacrifice. *Daredevil*, on the other hand, mobilizes its relative freedom from commercial and regulatory interference by trying to uplift the superhero genre and recreate it, in line with the Netflix brand, as prestige television. While this encouraged the creation of a complex program that gave agency to the working class and questioned the alignment of the American Dream with upper-class ideals, it also replaced upper-class allegiance with a connection to a violent working-class stereotype. Both series, in their superficial embrace of diversity, problematically avoid considerations of systemic inequalities faced by marginalized groups, instead presenting the American Dream and problems achieving the dream as "colorblind." This approach mirrored the beliefs of many (White) Millennial viewers who, in contrast to those discussed in Chapter 3, wanted to celebrate diversity without acknowledging that race, ethnicity, gender, sexual orientation, class, and so on impact how people define the Dream and what it takes to achieve it. To take an optimistic view, these series, can be seen as a step toward future, more complex interrogations of the American Dream as later superhero series, such as *Watchmen* (HBO 2019) and *DMZ* (HBO Max, 2022) and, even, to some extent, The CW's own *Black Lightning* (2018–21), come closer to achieving Warner's call for a "'color consciousness' that acknowledges the culture carried by those with similar socio-historical contexts and skin colors and further seeks to understand how this racial-cultural experience informs the unique personality of a given individual" (2015, 25). In doing so, these later shows complicate ideas about individual versus communal responsibility and the autonomy available to diverse Americans in determining their own Dreams.

The series discussed here illustrate how the shifting industrial ecosystem in which television was created in the 2010s impacted televisual representations. They offer distinct renegotiations of the American Dream, both of which dealt with primary questions faced by Millennials, asked and answered in ways that engendered ideas about how to integrate individual goals and social responsibility in the American Dream. This chapter also demonstrated the significance of platform brands in shaping televisual representations. Throughout the 1990s and into the 2000s, branding became essential for developing viewer loyalty. The next chapter will examine how two television platforms attempted to remain relevant in the wake of the Great Recession by creating brands that also spoke to and about the American Dream.

Notes

1 Significantly, narratives predominantly focus on White, male superheroes, positioning them at the center of the exceptionalism that stokes the American Dream.

2 Though, superheroes, who could undoubtedly fix many of world problems involving inequality, hunger, and homelessness by thinking outside of neoliberal capitalism, rarely do so; while they protect people's basic freedoms, they still do so within the bounds of the existing structure of society.

3 James Truslow Adams, in fact, disliked the New Deal for, in its attempt to increase the economic prospects of all citizens, limiting individual autonomy (Cullen 2006, 4).

4 In *Spider-Man 2* (2004), for example, which overtly grapples with the balance of Peter Parker's personal desires and his responsibility to fight crime, Parker figures out how to live both as Spider-Man while still establishing a romantic relationship with the woman he loves. In *Captain America: The First Avenger* (2011), however,

Steve Rogers ultimately gives up his entire world (including his body, his love interest, and his time period) to save America from Hydra.

5   Initially, a tentpole referred to a star or character in the theater who was considered essential to a play. The term transferred to television as a reference to a character, primarily within soap operas, who was fundamental and irreplaceable (Zimmer 2015). In the late 1980s, the idea of the "tentpole" migrated to film. Frank Mancuso, as head of Paramount Pictures, explained in 1987 that tentpole films were those that "because of content, star value or storyline have immediate want-to-see and are strong enough to support your entire schedule" (Harmetz 1987, C21). Within the film world, then, tentpoles didn't just bolster one program, they supported an entire year's worth of films.

6   In 1979, CBS President Fred Silverman referred to *Diff'rent Strokes* (NBC, 1978–85; ABC, 1985–6), *Quincy* (NBC, 1976–83), and *The Rockford Files* (NBC, 1974–80) as tentpoles (McGee 1979, 28).

7   A point that is glossed over but significant is that Malcolm was really buying sections of The Glades so that, when it came time to rebuild, he would own the property. While the show focuses on Malcolm's delusional vision of "saving" the city by destroying the crime, in many ways this is also a business undertaking designed for profit.

8   In 2017, Kreisberg was suspended as executive producer from *Arrow* and other DC/CW shows for sexual harassment and inappropriate physical contact.

9   There is also a DC animated movie universe that is separate from both the films and the live-action television shows. That DC Entertainment could—and did—nimbly create television shows based on its superhero characters without regard for the film storylines may help account for the aggressiveness with which DC Entertainment approached television production. Before Marvel entered television with its Defenders franchise on Netflix, it had produced only two live-action programs, *Agents of S.H.I.E.L.D.* (ABC, 2013–20) and *Agent Carter* (ABC, 2015–16), both of which tied closely into the Avengers storylines. In that time DC Entertainment produced *Arrow, The Flash,* and *iZombie* (2015–19) for The CW, *Constantine* (2014–15) for NBC, *Gotham* (2014–15) for Fox, and other shows, such as *DMZ* (HBO Max, 2022), *Titans* (DC Universe/HBO Max, 2018–23), and *Scalped* (undeveloped) were planned. Certainly, not all of DC's shows exist within the Arrowverse, but The CW shows were arguably the most well-known of the DC Entertainment television fare.

10 The potential conflicts that arose between Warner Bros./DC Entertainment's interests and those of The CW demonstrate the difficult position faced by a television platform expected to both function as a successful distributor and meet the needs of its corporate parents. Divisions within media conglomerates walk

something of a tightrope as they navigate "the potential contradictions that emerge from the continued desire to reap the benefits of, and meet its responsibilities as, part of a corporate family" (Selznick, "Freeform: Shaking Off the Family Brand within a Conglomerate Family" 2018, 226). The CW had, perhaps, an even more difficult balancing act to perform as it was co-owned by two media conglomerates, Warner Bros. and CBS, until Nexstar Media Group bought a 75 percent stake in the network in 2022.

11 The episode "Legacies" centers on a series of bank robberies being perpetrated by a nuclear family whose patriarch lost his job and pension when the work was outsourced to China. This betrayal by capitalism in general and the Queen family in particular, sent him over the edge; he took his family "off the grid" and they began robbing banks to get "set for life." The final robbery results in the father jumping in front of a bullet meant for his son (similar to the way Robert shot himself to save Oliver). Before dying, he tells Oliver "It wasn't his fault. I turned my son into this."

12 Some of the show's parent-child relationships highlight the connection between fathers and daughters including Laurel and Quentin Lance and Helena and Frank Bertinelli. Moira Queen's relationships with both Oliver and her daughter Thea also factor into the show. These relationships can be read differently—and not necessarily with a consistent message—about the perception of the American Dream for women.

13 It's later revealed that Malcolm actually travelled to a hidden city in Asia (very much depicted as the mystical "Orient" in the series) where he trained to become the "Dark Archer." Like many characters on the show, over the course of the seasons, Malcolm is revealed to have a much more complex backstory.

14 See Rodney Thomas (2017) for a fascinating discussion of the way that Asian characters are depicted within *Arrow*.

15 The show does acknowledge some larger social issues such as gentrification, racial stereotyping, and income inequality, but these concepts are quickly dismissed.

16 The industrial pressures on the DC/CW Arrowverse, in fact, impacted the way the entire franchise shaped its representations. The tent that *Arrow* held up ended up including shows with diverse representations of the American Dream. Although they could exist in the same universe (or multiverse) with crossover episodes, *Arrow, The Flash, Legends of Tomorrow, Supergirl, Black Lightening*, and *Batwoman* often had different tones and themes that allowed The CW to reach for slightly differentiated audiences through varied depictions of success and happiness.

17 Marvel's turn to live-action television began in the 1970s when it sold Universal the rights to create content based on twelve Marvel characters for $12,500 (Blumberg 2016, 119). The 1989 movie was not considered a failure, but the Daredevil series died in development after moving from NBC to ABC (Blumberg 2016, 125).

18 These series emulated the Netflix shows, if not in tone and content, then in their focus on diverse characters and complex, real-world issues, demonstrating Marvel's televisual strategy. This approach most likely ended when Marvel and Netflix parted ways in 2018 and Disney pulled Marvel content from all other platforms.

19 Referring to an even more morally ambiguous superhero, *Daredevil's* showrunner Steven DeKnight observed that Matt Murdock is "literally one bad day away from becoming The Punisher" (Alloway 2014).

2

Believing the Dream: Network Rebranding

As the previous chapter demonstrated, the promise of the American Dream is built on a foundation of optimism and hope. For the Dream to hold, people must believe that, if they follow the rules by working hard and cultivating meritorious qualities, their lives will improve, and they will be happy. Optimism allows for faith in the future—a faith in both personal improvement and social progress. Being "confident in expecting positive outcomes," as Richard Cervantes et al define optimism (2021, 136), undergirds the belief in the potential of individual freedom and upward mobility. Confidence in a better future also stokes the conviction that the United States is, or at least can one day be, a truly equitable meritocracy.

As a personal trait, optimism is seen as a positive quality, tied to many mental, physical, and social benefits. Research has shown that people who are considered optimistic are physically healthier and more motivated; they achieve a higher socioeconomic status, are more successful in school, and optimistic people have more positive relationships (Cervantes et al. 2021, 136–7). Carol Graham links a positive mindset to the ability "to invest in the future rather than simply living in the present" (2017, 126–7). Thoughts about the future were transformed by the Great Recession. Americans' tendency toward optimism was shaken by fear and uncertainty as aspirations for upward mobility faltered. To appeal to viewers, television was caught between the call to upbeat escapism that held out hope in the American Dream and a darker cynicism that acknowledged the Dream's precarity. This chapter will examine how traditional cable networks losing their audience base redesigned their brands to connect with viewers more effectively. Focusing specifically on the Hallmark Channel and the USA Network will reveal how the platforms changed their underlying messaging about the American Dream as they rebranded to meet the emotional needs of target audiences and the business objectives of advertisers.

The Optimism of the American Dream

You're optimistic because you know it is a possibility, but you are skeptical because you know what it is going to take in order to achieve it.

De Groote 2013

Optimism is woven into the American Dream in myriad ways. John White and Sandra Hanson write, "At its core, the American Dream represents a state of mind—that is, an enduring optimism" (2011, 3). The Dream's embrace of individualism, expectations of social mobility, and belief in self-reinvention all rely on a trust in future possibilities. Analyses demonstrate that the conviction that better things are possible is "an essential feature not just of the abstract 'American Dream,' but also of the social and economic institutions of American civil society" (Keller 2015). The functioning of social structures intertwined with the Dream, such as family, the housing market, and much of the retail economy, depends on an assumption that the future will improve on the present. Early Puritan values and virtues that shaped the American Dream drew on expectations of a better future. In coming to America, the Puritans left England in search of a place where they would be free to practice their religion without discrimination; they believed that such a place was possible and that their lives could be better. Moreover, religious doctrine required that Puritans, without certainty of God's divine plan for them, "live their lives hoping for signs that things would turn out for the best" (Cullen 2006, 18). Although they believed that their fate had already been sealed by God for either salvation or damnation, Puritans moved through the world acting as if they had been chosen for deliverance, convinced their future would be exalted. This way of life was rife with a hope requiring that one live in expectation of "positive outcomes."

Puritan values also focused on the primary role of the individual, with each person having responsibility for the trajectory of one's life, a trait that, as seen in the previous chapter, is essential to the American Dream. According to Dr. Edward C. Chang, a clinical psychologist who runs the Perfectionism and Optimism-Pessimism Lab at the University of Michigan, individualism correlates with optimism (Keller 2015). People who believe that they have control over their lives tend to be more optimistic about their potential. If they, and only they, determine their potential for success, then surely "one could realize the fruits of one's aspirations through applied intelligence and effort" (Cullen

2006, 159–60). As optimists, Americans imagine that unrestricted and equally available opportunity to move up in the world is only constrained by their own hard work and abilities (the structural inequities elided by this optimism will be interrogated in the next chapter). As a result, optimism in their own abilities and merits allows people to cultivate the certainty that "tomorrow can and will be better than today" (Samuel 2012, 6). Or, as Janny Scott and David Leonhardt write, "Americans, constitutionally optimistic, are disinclined to see themselves as stuck" (2005).

As discussed in the previous chapter, the importance of the individual for the American Dream is counterbalanced by a focus on the community. Not surprisingly, then, Americans also draw on innate positivity to extend the Dream to others, primarily family members. Again, Puritans, came to the New World, in part to create better lives for their children (Cullen 2006, 16). Often, even when the Dream seems to fail individuals, Americans maintain hope that their children will still see the benefits of their hard work. Bob Williams writes:

> The reality of general improvement from one generation to the next has sustained the American Dream to the present. The U.S. economy has served as a powerful engine for improving the material conditions of most Americans and affirming the prospect of upward mobility. Even among those who experienced little gain in their own lifetime, they watched their children grasp increased opportunities and claim greater rewards. Most of us can see material improvements in subsequent generations as we trace back our ancestry. Even among those excluded from this history, the Dream's pervasive appeal offers hope they can change their family's fortunes. (2017, 2)

So, although the idealized future may not emerge in one's own lifetime, optimism can be preserved for future generations.

Considering the Great Recession, John Archer wonders, then, "what happens when a myth fails? Or, more precisely in this case, what happens when US citizens find that the American dream-myth doesn't work for them the way that it is supposed to? What happens when those playing by its rules discover that success eludes them, that they haven't made it—indeed, that they can't make it?" (2014, 8). According to Leslie McCall, the inclination toward optimism potentially helps Americans weather periods like the Great Recession and its aftermath. McCall explains that Americans tend to see US society as just, with people getting what they deserve, engendering "an optimistic view of how effort is rewarded and a skeptical view of the need for a social safety net . . . Optimism is thus adaptive in its potential to motivate effort in an insecure economic environment" (2013, 32). Even as times got tough, people could be expected to hold on to their belief in a just world, which was only possible if people had faith not only in themselves but in society. As Robert Perrucci and Carolyn Perrucci observe, "A feeling of hope might have little to do with one's personal situation or the situation of others, but may be based on a generalized optimism about one's country" (2009, 9). Optimism linked the individual and the nation, as discourses surrounding the promise and potential of the United States influenced people trying to maintain faith in the American Dream even as it became more difficult to obtain.

Concerns for the prospects of the American Dream certainly began before the Great Recession, which exacerbated existing socioeconomic troubles. In their book *America at Risk: The Crisis of Hope, Trust, and Caring*, Perrucci and Perrucci write that socioeconomic changes dating back at least to the 1970s resulted in a "deficiency in hope, trust and caring" and restricted social mobility in the United States (2009, 3). They chart the rise of a neoliberal mindset that shifted responsibility for job losses from political and corporate institutions onto individuals (Perrucci and Perrucci 2009, 6). As a result, failures of the American Dream "were understood to be individual exceptions, tales of glitches and misfits, not yet the wholesale disillusion that spread during the massive economic crisis that would come early in the new millennium" (Archer 2014, 11). Even while job insecurity expanded from blue-collar to white-collar workers in the 1990s (Schafer 2015, 1D), belief in the American Dream remained "stalwartly intact" as economic stagnation was framed as a consequence of individual shortcomings rather than problems with social institutions (Archer 2014, 12).

In the early 2000s, as the United States was beset by a horrific terrorist attack, ensuing wars, and deepening economic recessions, questions about the American Dream percolated. A Pew Study in 2006 reported that "there is declining contentment with the present and growing pessimism about the future" (Pew Research Center 2006, 5). The lead-up to the Great Recession, however, was, according to Archer, marked by excessive optimism in part fueled by the very thing that would eventually devastate the economy: homeownership (2014, 12). As will be discussed in Chapter 3, owning a home is considered a significant marker of achieving the American Dream. Predatory mortgage loans, along with magnified credit card debt, allowed many people to live a middle-class lifestyle with illusory, materialistic markers of social mobility. In fact, however, many people were victims of a system preying on their economic precarity even as financial stability moved further out of reach. In 2007, a report by Lake Research Partners titled "Economic Anxiety and the American Dream" found, perhaps unsurprisingly, that there was a growing sense of anxiety as "the middle class feels that the rules for economic success have changed and they are on their own to figure them out" (Report Details Anxiety 2007). Nevertheless, the report found that this anxiety was still tempered by an element of optimism that things would get better (Report Details Anxiety 2007). As the economy collapsed, presidential candidate Barack Obama capitalized on Americans' ambivalence about the future, as he "expressed an unfailing, steadfast sense of optimism and hope" (Atwater 2007, 128). Obama's rhetoric gave voice to a confidence in the future despite the difficulties of the present, allowing voters to fall back on the country's natural inclination toward positivity. He said in a 2007 campaign speech in Iowa, "There has been a lot of talk in this campaign about the politics of hope. But the politics of hope doesn't mean hoping that things come easy. It's a politics of believing in things unseen; of believing in what this country might be; and of standing up for that belief and fighting for it when it's hard" (Speech on the 'American Dream' 2007). In a call to see the American Dream as a communal dream, Obama, in his campaign and during the early years of his presidency, conveyed the optimistic expectation that America could be set right if its citizens played by the rules, worked hard, and aspired toward a just society.

But, as the United States moved through the economic meltdown and into the "recovery" phase of the Great Recession, Americans demonstrated a contradictory attitude toward the American Dream and faith in its potential. Polls found that people were hopeful about their personal potential to achieve the Dream yet apprehensive that it would be more difficult for their children and others in society. Moreover, people were concerned that the meaning of the Dream had changed to mean financial security rather than social mobility. These poll results illustrate a struggle to maintain hope in the face of harsh realities. As one interviewee said in a 2013 Northwestern Mutual Survey, "You're optimistic because you know it is a possibility, but you are skeptical because you know what it is going to take in order to achieve it" (De Groote 2013).

The slow and uneven recovery from the financial crisis compounded the frustration. During the financial free fall, people may have been hopeful that things would, eventually, even out. However, the realization that the recovery was not going to restore people's homes, retirement funds, or other pre-Recession semblances of success, sapped the belief in opportunity. The Black Lives Matter movement contributed to the disillusionment by foregrounding issues of equality and fairness, challenging the notion of the "just world" that nurtured the American Dream as well as the colorblind idealism of Millennials discussed in the previous chapter. As the recovery period dragged on, the American Dream shifted from the aspiration for upward mobility to the desire to simply avoid sliding further backward. In an interview in 2012, Michael Dimock of the Pew Research Center explains, "There are people struggling, and what you're seeing, especially right now, are people who feel like they played the game the right way, like they did what they were supposed to do, that the rules they thought they could play by and be OK have changed on them somehow" (A. Shapiro 2012). Directly questioning the relevance of the American Dream, a writer for *The Atlantic* observes, "Dreams imply things are getting better, growing, but many people are just focused on hanging on to what they have. They want to keep their families intact and safe" (Arnade 2015).

Article after article and study after study indicated that the optimism that undergirded the American Dream—the belief in upward mobility, that the future could be better than the past, that the next generation would live better than the current generation—was not as steadfast as it once was.[1] Markers of the American Dream, such as homeownership and family growth, declined in importance as people demonstrated a fearfulness of the future rather than an excitement about its potential. According to a survey done by *The Atlantic* with the Aspen Institute, in describing the American Dream, respondents focused less on home and children but instead emphasized "flexibility and economic security" (Baer and Penn 2015). While research showed that many younger Americans wanted to own homes and start families, their reluctance to do so signaled not only a preference for urban living as discussed in Chapter 1, but also a shift in their willingness to take a chance on the future (Xu et al. 2015, 208–9).

Meanwhile, politicians and social activists mobilized the concept of the American Dream for various purposes. For some, opportunities arose to highlight institutional imbalances, suggesting that individual effort might not be all that stood between people and achieving the Dream. The blatant transparency of some (not all) inequalities created the potential to "limit perceptions of opportunity and dispose Americans toward a more structural interpretation of unequal outcomes as opposed to one rooted in individual responsibility and just desserts" (McCall 2013, 39). Ben Mangan, a lecturer at the University of California-Berkeley's Haas School of Business and the CEO and co-founder of a non-profit that helped low-income Americans achieve their financial goals, observes, "Put aside high unemployment and underwater mortgages, and even gainfully employed folks are souring on their prospects. With real wages falling, people feel their own economic status eroding even as they work harder than ever" (2011). Mangan notes, the lack of fairness and equity within the system was draining American optimism which he described as "Americans' secret sauce" (2011). The focus on structural concerns that limited access to the American Dream resulted in several actions. In 2011, the Congressional Progressive Caucus put forward the "Restore the American Dream for the 99% Act," a failed measure that called for reduced funding for defense and industry in favor of bolstering support systems for the working and middle class (Archer 2014, 15). That same year, the Occupy Wall Street movement gained recognition. Occupy Wall Street used public protests and the occupation of public spaces to draw attention to the socioeconomic institutions, such as banks, oil companies, and mass media, that fostered "political disenfranchisement and social injustice" (Bolton et al. 2013, 6). Although the momentum of the movement waned in 2012, Occupy Wall Street drew attention to wealth inequality, with the rallying cry of "We are the 99%," referring to the fact that 1 percent of the population holds most of the world's wealth. According to James Anderson, writing in *Time*, Occupy Wall Street also, "cemented notions of economic inequality squarely in DC policy debates. Ideas that were thought to be too socialist since the demise of the Eastern Bloc—class struggle, wealth distribution across social strata, or even flaws in the capitalist system—were suddenly aired loudly and frequently for the first time since the Great Depression" (2021). By drawing attention to injustices within the US socioeconomic system, Occupy Wall Street contributed to the discourse that questioned the foundation of and equity of access to the American Dream, particularly for younger, Millennial Americans, even as the movement "struggled with how to include people from many different racial and ethnic background, people of a range of gender identities (men, women, transgender persons, and people of nonconforming gender identities), and people of diverse sexualities, nationalities, abilities, and disabilities" (Hurwitz 2020, 8).

The 2012 election also contributed to a rhetoric of concern about the American Dream, as candidates for the Republican nomination promised to "revive" and "restore" the Dream (Boesveld 2012, A22). Senator Mike Lee, for example, separated himself from President Obama's sustained message of hope. In a statement about his own "Saving the American Dream" plan, Lee said, "While optimism is an important part of the American dream, hope simply is not a strategy for the kind of course correction our country needs" (2012). At the Republican National Convention, speakers touted US exceptionalism as, according to Florida Senator Marco Rubio, "dreams that are impossible anywhere else come true here" (Boesveld 2012, A22). But Virginia Governor Bob McDonnell noted the waning of optimism, warning that Americans' "lost hope is why we need a big change this November. This election is about restoring the American Dream" (Boesveld 2012, A22). The way to restore the American Dream was, of course, up for debate. President Obama campaigned for reelection by promoting social programs that Republicans reviled. After the election, in a 2013 speech to the Center for American Progress, Obama said that his goal was to make sure that "every striving, hardworking, optimistic kid in America has the same incredible chance that this country gave me" (Remarks by the President on Economic Mobility 2013). Through most of the speech, he acknowledges the difficulties facing working- and middle-class Americans, outlining the plans and policies he hopes to enact to ameliorate them.

In addition to politicians' angst about the American Dream, research done by academics, think tanks, and market research groups, demonstrated the public's wavering optimism. As noted above, for the most part, this research uncovered inconsistencies as people wrestled with contradictions between what they experienced in their own lives, what they expected for their children, and what they saw as possible for the nation as a whole (ideas discussed in greater detail in Chapter 4). Jared Keller observes, that

> optimism has certainly dimmed with the Great Recession. . . . But Americans continue to see life on the up and up despite the burdens of economic downturn, social and racial unrest and the specter of terrorism. . . . On Main street, the average American *thinks* the country will improve in 2015, despite years spent caught in a cycle of frustration about the political and economic state of the union. (2015)

Meanwhile, a 2014 Pew survey "showed that American optimism about the US economy has sunk to its lowest level since the recession kicked in" (Davidson 2014). Despite the waning optimism, there was still a yearning for hope, as people chose to "redefine the dream without abandoning it" (Archer 2014, 14). Research indicated that while people held on to their optimism, they did so by recasting the Dream. A survey by Aaron's Inc. in 2014 reported that people lowered their expectations for the American Dream, focusing on security rather than opportunities (Aaron's, Inc. 2014). And the 2016 Northwestern

Mutual Planning and Progress Study concluded that, while 66 percent of those surveyed thought they could achieve the American Dream, according to a Northwestern Mutual executive, "the goal today seems to be more about outcomes-happiness, security and peace of mind rather than material wealth or the opportunity to advance. . . . The white picket fence is still important, but today, Americans seem to care more about what's going on inside the house" (Barney 2016). The Great Recession "shows that despite crisis and despair, the power of the American dream-myth remains durable. Instead of blaming the myth—which would effectively entail rejecting deeply held beliefs—the crisis has thus afforded opportunities to look inside and behind the myth, to question whose interest it favors and whose precipitated its breakdown." (Archer 2014, 8). Even while asking questions about the economic failure of the United States and worrying about the possibilities of upward mobility, many Americans held onto an optimism for the future that, at times, required reconfiguring, but not abandoning, the hopeful expectation of achieving the American Dream.

Finding Audiences for the Television (Re)Brand

It is not the brand itself that counts, but what you can do with it, what you can be with it.

Arvidsson 2005, 248

As this book argues, in their interactions with audiences, media institutions contributed to rhetoric about the American Dream. This chapter looks not at how individual programs participated in the conversations, but how television platforms mobilized Americans' hopes about the Dream to target audiences. Legacy television networks searched for ways to hold on to audiences within a quickly changing industrial ecosystem. In this process, networks modified their brands to tap into different conceptualizations of optimism to speak to their target audiences about their American Dream and the possibilities that it held.

Growing competition since the 1980s shifted the relationship between television networks and their viewers. As scholars have shown, the marketing strategy of branding took hold within television as platforms tried to foster loyalty among audience members by shaping the ways viewers thought about networks and programming (see, for example, Jaramillo 2002, S. Murray 2005, and Selznick 2009).[2] Most viewers, research has shown, select from only a few stations, cultivating a repertoire of 8–14 channels that they regularly watch (McDowell and Batten 2005, 5). In the 1990s through the early 2000s, the goal of cable networks was to become part of that repertoire for as many viewers as possible. As one Superstation WGN executive explained in 2004, "People in general aren't loyal to networks anymore. They are loyal to TV shows, but in a fragmented universe of 500 channels, there's a need to be top of mind as a place where I can go" (Haley 2004, 12a). To do so, networks position themselves—their brands—as different and better than other networks that are vying for viewers. Gary Edgerton and Kyle Nicholas argue that "brand recognition . . . has emerged as the most valuable form of currency as programming content is now widely adapted to other print, audio, video, and Web-based technologies to be marketed to network consumers" (2005, 248).

The connection between brands and viewers is designed to encourage audiences to make brands part of their lives; to do more than simply watch a movie or a television program, and to pay extra for DVDs, downloadable content, ancillary products, licensed goods, and extension products. The push to connect with viewers on an emotional level reflects the widely held marketing belief that "'emotionally attached' consumers . . . are the brand's most profitable customers" (Rossiter and Bellman 2012, 295). Craig Thompson et al explain the importance of trying to form affective links between the product/service and the consumer to make the brand part of the user's social network. They write, "From an emotional-branding standpoint, brand strategists should focus on telling stories that inspire and captivate consumers. These stories must demonstrate a genuine understanding of consumers' lifestyle, dreams, and goals and compellingly represent how the brand can enrich their lives" (2006, 51). As one E! executive explains, "The most powerful brands are the ones that focus on the customers. We stand for what you want. We put emotion behind it, like Nike's 'Just Do It'" (Whitney 2002, 23). Deborah Jaramillo demonstrates, for example, that HBO developed a connection with a "quality," niche audience by separating its brand from "regular" television. With the slogan "It's not TV, it's HBO," "HBO brands itself an outsider in the televisual terrain a channel more akin to a grandiose cinematic heritage than a broadcast one" (Jaramillo 2002, 73). By appealing to viewers' desire to think of themselves as cultured cinephiles, HBO established an emotional connection with an untapped audience that felt like there was finally a television platform for them.

Platform branding took on an even greater importance as competition increased in the 2000s. Not only did the number of digital cable networks grow in the early 2000s (Sung and Park 2011, 87),[3] but by 2011, subscription video on demand (SVOD) platforms like Netflix were also drawing users away from traditional television with second-cycle shows that could be seen on cable but without the schedule (Wayne 2017, 734). Additionally, DVDs, DVRs, and streaming services disassociated programming from the network on which it originally aired. A strong brand identity would hopefully encourage viewers to tune into a network regardless of what particular program is currently on air, so that the brand "acquires a phantasmatic life of its own, floating free of the products it subsumes" (Frow 2002, 64–5).

Douglas Holt and Douglas Cameron's Cultural Innovation Theory of branding can help to understand the ways that some cable networks adjusted their brands in the face of intense competition and socioeconomic change. The desired emotional connection discussed above can be created between a brand and a user by fostering a brand identity that taps into beliefs held by viewers, helping them develop their own sense of self. Adam Arvidsson writes, "It is not the brand itself that counts, but what you can do with it, what you can *be* with it" (2005, 248). Holt and Cameron's Cultural Innovation Theory examines brand construction in relation to identity formation. They propose that some brands deliver an "innovative cultural expression" that "serve as compass points, organizing how we understand the world and our place in it, what is meaningful, what is moral, what is human, what is inhuman, what we should strive for, and what we should despise. And cultural expressions serve as linchpins of identity: they are the foundational material for belonging, recognition and status" (2010, 173). Powerful cultural expressions use cultural codes to depict a particular story (a myth) that expresses a point of view on a cultural construct (an ideology) (Holt and Cameron 2010, 174). Holt and Cameron explain that "cultural innovations break through when they bear the right ideology, which is dramatized through the right myth, expressed with the right cultural codes" (2010, 176). In other words, consumers develop emotional attachments with brands that use carefully implemented slogans, logos, promotions, websites, and so on to construct brand stories that help them make sense of themselves and their world. Holt and Cameron further note that the "right" cultural values and cultural codes are prone to change: "at some point, as history unfolds and social structures shift, one or more of these shifts will be disruptive, challenging the taken-for-granted cultural expressions offered by category incumbents, and creating emergent demand for new cultural expressions" (2010, 185).

The Great Recession instigated such shifts, leading some television networks to rethink the brands that worked for them through the 1990s and early 2000s but were, perhaps, cultural expressions for a time that no longer existed. Rebranding, research has shown, is generally initiated by a trigger (Miller and Merrilees 2011, 282), instigated by internal or external causes (Roy and Sarkar 2015, 342). Changes within the media ecosystem along with the financial crisis and the ensuing recovery can certainly be seen as the "social disruption" that created "ideological opportunities" that would "unmoor consumers from the goods that they have relied on to produce the symbolism they demand and drive them to seek out new alternatives" (Holt and Cameron 2010, 185–6).

Rebranding can be a risky endeavor, threatening to damage existing brand value. For a platform that has positive connections with audiences, changing the cultural expressions of a brand can "affect these associations and the underlying network leading to a dilution of its existing brand equity" (Roy and Sarkar 2015, 343). Nevertheless, several television networks at this time chose to rebrand, changing their logos, slogans, and in some cases even their target audiences to establish stronger emotional connections with viewers. For example, as more television platforms mimicked HBO-style quality programming, HBO rebranded in 2009, moving away from the "It's not TV. It's HBO" brand of distinction, to a focus on "passionate engagement" that, using the tagline "It's More Than You Imagined," encouraged enthusiastic fan interaction, whether online or in the real world (Parmett 2016, 9). And, in 2013, AMC rebranded by changing its slogan from "Story Matters Here" to "Something More," introducing a new logo that featured a gold box that according to the network indicated "premium quality" and "popular appeal" (Goldberg 2013). AMC's vice president of marketing said that the rebrand "refines our focus on- and off-air and speaks to our promise to viewers to provide an experience that is unexpected, unconventional and uncompromising. . . . However we express the brand, we want to give our audience something deeper, something richer, *something more*" (Goldberg 2013).

The remainder of this chapter will explore two cable networks that participated in this wave of post-Recession rebranding, examining how their marketing strategies shifted the stories they told about the American Dream. The Hallmark Channel's rebranding in 2012 and USA Network's similar efforts in 2016 demonstrate that these networks used cultural codes to speak to specific post-Recession audiences and construct brands that reflected optimism about the Dream. Rather than focusing on specific television series, this chapter will look at the network brands writ large, drawing on all the elements that go into creating a platform brand, such as logos, slogans, promotional videos, print ads, and, of course, programming. Examining the cultural codes employed by these networks will demonstrate how the industrial entities of television navigated and reflected their audiences' shifting ideas about the American Dream in the post-Recession world.

Accentuating the Positive: Hallmark Channel

We have a 24/7 news cycle—it's a constant need to be fed—and we have a lot of dark, edgy programming out in the world that's fantastic, but as in the human experience, it's a huge spectrum, and where we live is with positivity and celebration and emotional connection, and that's unique to what we do. . . . If you choose to spend two hours of your time with us, you're going to feel a little better about the world and yourself and your community.

Turchiano 2019
Hallmark: "The Heart of TV"

The Hallmark Channel has, for the most part, been overlooked (and at times, scorned) by the popular press and media scholars. As Kayti Lausch notes, "Television studies has largely focused its attention on the channels that pushed the boundaries of television content (HBO, Showtime), rather than those channels that sought to reclaim the television of the past" (2021, 621). Hallmark, without a doubt, revels in the past by relying on the archaic TV movie format and recycling wholesome stories about love and family in (primarily) rural America. These televisual practices are undeniably part of Hallmark's business strategy and shape its brand identity. In staking out a position grounded in upbeat stories of love and expressing its brand through specific strategies, as the Cultural Innovation Theory explains, Hallmark Channel tells a story that reinforces certain ideas about the hopes and possibilities circumscribed by the American Dream for an audience outside of the sought-after Millennial generation.

The Hallmark Channel is unusual in today's media ecosystem as it not owned by a media conglomerate. Rather, the network is part of Hallmark Media (formerly Crown Media Family Networks), which is a subsidiary of the well-known greeting card company Hallmark Cards Inc. Hallmark first became involved in US television in 1998 as a co-owner of the Odyssey Channel, along with the Jim Henson Company and the National Interfaith Cable Coalition.[4] In 2001, after the Jim Henson Company sold its stake in Odyssey to Crown Media Holdings, the network was rebranded as Hallmark Channel, dropping all explicitly religious programming (Beckelhimer 2020, 51). Hallmark announced plans to target viewers aged 18–54 with a skew toward women, using family-friendly programming with the stated goal of becoming part of viewers' regular repertoire of channels (Hogan 2001, 48).

Over time, Hallmark solidified its brand, becoming well-known for its Christmas movies. In 2004, Hallmark was the fastest-growing cable network in the United States (Dempsey 2004, 2) and in 2005, it was "on track to harvest more than $110 million from advertisers in the upfront sales season" (Dempsey, "Hallmark Valentine" 2005, 4). By 2006, Hallmark was one of the "top 10 ad-supported cable nets among total viewers" (Dempsey, "Hallmark in 'Golden' Age" 2008, 5). The network, however, continued to stumble, remaining unable to reach the younger, Millennial demographic sought by advertisers. Hallmark Inc. unsuccessfully tried to sell Hallmark Channel starting in 2006 but took it off the market after figuring out ways to turn what had seemed like the network's shortcomings into its strengths.

As discussed in the previous chapter, the early 2000s saw the rise of complex television and its morally ambiguous antiheroes in series like *The Sopranos* (HBO, 1999–2007), *Breaking Bad* (AMC, 2008–13), and *Mad Men* (AMC, 2007–15). These series broke with several existing cultural orthodoxies of television including the assumptions that major characters should be likable, and that profanity should be limited to subscription services. By the 2010s, these shows had created their own cultural orthodoxies, establishing the expectation that for a television platform to succeed, it must appeal to Millennials and their gloomier preferences. This was not Hallmark's audience, which in 2008, had a median age of sixty-one, higher than any other general entertainment cable network (Dempsey, "Hallmark in 'Golden' Age" 2008, 5). Its programming, both original movies and syndicated series, appealed to the "nostalgia of an older audience less coveted by other networks" (Tyler 2020, 25). Rather than trying to change the brand to attract a younger audience, Hallmark talked up the value of older viewers. In 2008, Hallmark commissioned "The Consumer Television and Technology Study" from research agency Millward Brown. The study included several findings that reinforced the value of Hallmark's older audience. According to the study, adults aged 35–64 watch more television than younger generations, have more money and buying power than younger viewers, are more likely to sit through commercials even if they've recorded a show on a DVR, are less likely to change channels in the middle of a show, and are growing in number (particularly in the over fifty age group) (Hallmark Channel 2008, C52; Ground Breaking Study Reveals 2008). Jesse Aguirre, Hallmark's vice president of research, remarked, "With these findings in mind, it's no surprise that the media buying bull's eye—which not long ago shunned adults 25–54—is now widening to embrace the increased value of boomer adults 35–64" (Groundbreaking Study Reveals 2008). Hallmark, then, chose to embrace its older audience and, in the midst of an economic crisis that was particularly impacting younger workers, paint these viewers as financially appealing for advertisers.

In addition to the age of its viewers, Hallmark was also seen as a source of predictable and simplistic family-friendly content. In the wake of the financial crisis, Hallmark leaned into the idea that it could offer predictable programming that made people feel better. At Hallmark's 2009 upfront presentation to advertisers, Henry Schleiff, toward the end of his tenure as CEO of Crown Media Holdings, affirmed Hallmark's competitive advantage: "These are unpredictable times, said Mr. Schleiff. Will you lose your job? Will your family collapse into poverty? Will you end up destitute and heartbroken? In 2009, who really knows. During unpredictable times, he continued, people want predictable entertainment. With Hallmark, he said, you know exactly what you're getting" (Gillette 2009). Schleiff then announced a partnership with NYU's film school in which students would compete to create Hallmark-style content that "celebrates or uplifts the human spirit" (Gillette 2009). That same year, Hallmark also began its renowned "Countdown to Christmas" slate of Christmas movies and brought on Bill Abbott as the new CEO.

Under Abbott, the network settled into its brand identity promising light and wholesome family-friendly distraction. Not only did Hallmark offer an escape from the trauma of the financial crisis and the subsequent slow recovery, but it also provided a reprieve from the dark television content gaining popularity on many television platforms. Embracing an older audience with reassuring and heartwarming programming worked for Hallmark in the post-Recession period. While in 2005, Hallmark had access to substantially fewer cable viewers than any other networks (it reached sixty-seven million viewers while other general entertainment cable networks reached eighty-eight million), by 2012 it had been picked up by more cable systems to reach eighty-seven million subscribers (Hallmark Channel Captures 2012).

In 2012, Hallmark unveiled a rebranding that can be seen as more of an evolution of this existing brand position. The platform mobilized anxieties about the recession and the shake-up within the television industry to construct an inspirational brand myth that would connect with viewers around a social identity that was optimistic and comforting. Borrowing a page from The Family Channel circa the 1990s (where Abbott worked at the time), Hallmark would "accentuate the positive" (Lausch 2021, 624). In 2012, Hallmark developed a rebranding campaign that solidified the emotional connection it wanted to make with its viewers by promising them a "safe space," where bad things didn't happen and there were always happy endings. As Jeb Lund later wrote for *WashingtonPost.com* about Hallmark Channel, "The real world is horrible, and this one is not, even if it is sometimes unwittingly absurd and its pacing, plotting and characterization often need work. Nobody gets hurt in Hallmark movies. There are never bad guys, only the wrong ones" (2019).

Hallmark commissioned brand strategist Lee Hunt who worked on network rebrands such as USA Network's Characters Welcome and FX's Fearless to create something that the channel could "stand for" (L. Hunt 2023). According to Hunt, Hallmark was in search of a strong brand identity that they could "own." He recalled that creating a brand around emotions was similar to USA constructing a brand around characters in that all shows have emotions and characters "But it's about putting a flag in the ground. So, I said, you guys can own emotions, particularly positive emotions. And that ties you back into Hallmark cards, too, which makes that familiar connection really work" (L. Hunt 2023). The tagline for Hallmark was changed from "Where Great Stories Come to Life" to "The Heart of TV," foregrounding the emotional qualities of the Hallmark Channel. Hunt noted that this tagline "kind of works two ways in that it [Hallmark] is the emotional center of television. It is the heart of television. But also it sort of says, here's our place in the television universe. It is taking a stand" (2023). The new tagline, according to Susanne McAvoy, executive vice president of marketing and creative services for Crown Media Family Networks, "captured the essence of what Hallmark Channel stands for and what it does best—heartfelt, aspirational programming that evokes a wide range of emotions and responses" (Hallmark Channel Captures 2012). The network connected to a nostalgic impulse that "celebrates Hallmark Channel's core values and reinforces the network's position as a leading destination for life-affirming, celebratory, and quality programming that families come together to watch again and again" (Hallmark Channel Captures 2012).

Simplicity of tagline and design, became a touchstone for the campaign. As the brand strategy presentation deck states, "Emotions are complex. They need simple solutions" (Hallmark Channel Rebrand). To this end, Hallmark generated short 10- to 15-second promos that offered an "emotional spark" to complete the phrase "We feel" with words like impulsive, adventurous, and merry. These emotional spark promos feature a Hallmark daytime personality standing in front of a solid, vibrant background, relaying a simple story that reinforces the joy of family and home. In the "Impulsive" promo, for example, Marie Osmond, who premiered a daytime show on Hallmark in late 2012, stands in a simple black dress before a vibrant lime-green background telling the story about a spontaneous driving lesson that led to a memorable mother/ daughter conversation. She explains that "you can't miss those moments, even if it's a school night." The spot cuts to the word "Impulsive" in Hallmark Card's signature purple color against the lime-green background, which then cuts to Hallmark Channel written in its signature script with the Hallmark crown and the tagline "The Heart of TV" (Hallmark Channel Rebrand). The cultural codes in these spots—vibrant colors, a breezy font, energetic personalities, a direct and simple direct address to the audience—reinforces a positive and upbeat story about the happiness found through family, home, and love (Figure 3).

The network also produced several "Mood Bites," 10-second promos that similarly focus on a single feeling (eager, proud, irresistible, sweet) connected to

Figure 3   The conclusion to Hallmark Channel's "Impulsive" Emotional Spark promo © Hallmark Channel 2012.

specific holidays. These promos don't use network personalities but very short, single-shot vignettes that evoke an emotion. The "Eager" mood bite starts on a close-up of two pair of children's socked feet running down a staircase. As the camera follows the feet down the stairs we see their pajamaed legs as they move away from the camera and out of focus toward a Christmas tree in the background. The audio is serene yet upbeat piano music under which we hear muffled but excited children's voices. As the children sit by the Christmas tree out of focus in the background, the stair banister wrapped in silver tinsel frames the word "Eager" written in red which then cuts to the Hallmark logo and tagline (this time in red). These 10 seconds simply (and nostalgically) invoke the excitement of children on Christmas Day. The "Proud" mood bite opens on a shot of what appears to be an adolescent boy's midsection as he waves sparklers surrounded by a group of friends at night. There are other young teens in the background also waving sparkler who are more fully framed but out of focus. Simple non-diegetic guitar music plays but the primary sound is from the kids' whooping and cheering. As the boy dances with the sparklers, the word "Proud" appears on screen in a rich blue, which is then replaced again by the Hallmark logo and tagline (Figure 4). Here again, this short interstitial arouses feelings of carefree, summer-time fun with friends, intertwined with national pride, during the celebration of the US' Independence Day. As Hallmark's brand material explains, these mood bites are "distilling different aspects of said holidays into simple, emotional takeaways" (Hallmark Channel Rebrand).

Figure 4 Hallmark Channel's "Proud" Mood Bite for Independence Day © Hallmark Channel 2012.

The minimalistic yet vivid cultural codes used in this rebranding—the tagline, the promotions, the selections of colors—kept the campaign simple and emotional. As the network's rebrand strategy plan outlined, these materials were designed to spark "a feeling, a passion, a memory. Our voice is alive, vibrant, inviting, immersive" (Hallmark Channel Rebrand). Importantly, all the emotions being called on are positive and personal, tapping into a myth that ignored sociocultural, political, and economic troubles to highlight the promise of individual happiness. The optimism and hopefulness that Americans retained for their individual potential was reflected and mobilized to establish Hallmark Channel as a place where the promise of the American Dream was unthreatened, rooted in personal connection, family, and home.

Of course, like with any successful network brand, Hallmark Channel's content reinforced its identity. Hunt explains that one of the essential elements in establishing a network brand is its "assets," including the network's programming. Hallmark's content certainly dovetailed with a brand identity centered on positive emotions. By 2012, Hallmark was known for its romantic Christmas movies that celebrated love, family, community, and a work/life balance that always favored "life." Abbott said of the 2013 Countdown to Christmas lineup, "So much of the [television] universe features younger, sexier, more violent programming and around the holidays viewers are really looking for that destination of warm-and-fuzzy programming" (Umstead 2013, 16). Scholarship as well as trade and popular press articles have analyzed and critiqued this portrayal of American life. Walter Metz, for example, observes that the films are "deeply conservative" in their depictions of family and gender (2018). In 2020, Emily Newman and Emily Witsell write that Hallmark's films are "almost entirely white, Christian, middle class and heteronormative" (2020, 5). In 2024, Hallmark is still struggling to create more inclusive content as it attempts to make movies featuring non-Christians, gay couples, and people of color, all people that have found more opportunities for Hallmark-style romance on more Millennial and now, Gen Z-focused platforms such as Netflix and Hulu. Furthermore, Hallmark's content, grounded in nostalgia, can be safely (if reluctantly) watched by children, while also resurrecting adult viewers' childhood notions of adult-life. Lisa Tyler notes, Hallmark movies rarely depict women doing the everyday, boring activities that often take up time like grocery shopping and cleaning (2020, 20). Instead, women in Hallmark movies work outside the home often in creative jobs that they fully enjoy—unless they end up quitting to be close to a love interest and work within a rural community

(Tyler 2020, 20). Neither men nor women ever struggle logistically to balance family and work, the decision is always a personal choice with a clear message that focusing on work over family is a personality flaw that either makes someone an unsuitable romantic interest or is "fixed" by falling in love. The focus on positive emotions, then, comes at a cost in that these movies preserve individual optimism about the American Dream for a circumscribed set of people who demonstrate predetermined meritorious characteristics.

The power given to love and family to fulfill the American Dream in Hallmark content creates a complex depiction of work. This focus on family over occupation demonstrates a level of discomfort with neoliberal capitalism, which champions the subordination of the personal to labor. Additionally, as Tyler observes, Hallmark movies value community and local activities in ways that often result in the rejection of "big city" capitalists and consumerism. At the same time, Hallmark movies create a fictional world in which individual grit and a strong community are all that is needed to successfully navigate the post-Recession world. Economic precarity is only vaguely mentioned and usually overshadowed by concerns about the decimation of an important community event/institution. As Lund writes:

> Hallmark's movies are stridently anti-metropolitan, almost always beginning with a heroine fleeing the city on some pretext or another. The geography of her personal rescue takes the form of small towns and pastoral settings, where everyone has a nice house and a car and is probably a small-business owner or about to improve themselves by becoming one. Blue-collar jobs exist, but they pay at artisanal rates. And cratered school budgets and bankrupt shelters are rescued by private donors; in a world that cannot mention taxes, the commons only ever existed via the goodness of unnamed hearts. (2019)

The American Dream is thriving in small towns where community and love are the most important factors for building a fulfilling and happy life, primarily because the focus on nostalgic escapism leaves no room for real socioeconomic concerns. Hallmark evacuates all references to systemic failures, social anxieties, and economic traumas—particularly those that cannot be solved by simply choosing family/community over work or by a supportive community banding together.

Not surprisingly, the content created to coincide with the Hallmark's Channel's 2012 rebrand reinforced many of these ideas and focused on a particular variety of positive emotions. While Hallmark movies already supported the brand, the network bolstered its position with original series. According to Hunt, Abbott recognized that Hallmark was a small, general entertainment cable network that didn't have the budget to compete in prime time, but he saw an opportunity in daytime television,

> And so he was very much focused on that. And cause he also said, this is where I can get advertisers in who are looking for the particular demo that we know watches morning television which tended to be stay-at-home moms and women who were home during the day. And that became fairly successful. I don't think it ever really took off, but what I understand is that it helped raise the revenue. So, he was able to invest more in the original movies. (2023)

Daytime content was a way to bolster the brand while also bringing in money through advertising and product placement to help fund the movies. Hallmark originally entered daytime television in 2010 when it made a deal with Martha Stewart Living Omnimedia Inc to air *The Martha Stewart Show* (Hallmark, 2010–12) and an additional ninety minutes of daytime programming.[5] The content was produced and owned by Martha Stewart Living Omnimedia, not the Hallmark Channel, and did not do well in the ratings. Along with the rebrand, Hallmark announced two new daytime series that it would produce and own: *Marie!* (Hallmark, 2012–13), a one-hour talk show starring Marie Osmond, and *Home & Family* (Hallmark, 2012–21), a two-hour DIY show hosted by Paige Davis and Mark Steines.[6] Both of these series were promoted for their ability to speak to their demographics of women aged 25–54 (Umstead 2012, 14). Marie Osmond's promotional interviews emphasized her relatability, being asked, for example, if she thought that "being open about your weight struggles, divorce and postpartum depression increased your popularity particularly with women of a certain age?" (Sheridan 2012, C1). Osmond's answer to this question included her saying, "Some of the best advice I ever got was from my friends. Women are so strong and knowledgeable" (Sheridan 2012, C1). Osmond contributed to the network's brand identity as she spun each topic to emphasize the positives that comes from her love of family and community. Nevertheless, *Marie!* was cancelled after only one season, as Abbott explained in a shareholder meeting,

> on closer examination our daytime slate and analysis of costs versus benefits, we determined that the best direction for the day part is to develop more service-oriented lifestyle shows, similar to "Home and Family," which not only entertain and inform our viewers but provide us with ownership of content, which can

> potentially monetize multiple platforms and offer as unique content to our
> distribution partners. (Q2 2013 Crown Media 2013)

The success of *Home & Family* was likely related to how well it accommodated
product integrations. For this series, Hallmark built an entire house on the
Universal lot, creating opportunities for integrations related to appliances in
the kitchen, cars in the garage, technology in the office, and so on (Lafayette
2012, 4). At the same time, Abbott notes that the series dovetailed nicely with the
larger Hallmark Cards focus on "celebrating life's special occasions and turning
the everyday into something special. . . . We'll cover topics such as decorating,
travel tips, technology developments, and celebrity interviews. We think this
type of show will really resonate with the Hallmark enthusiast" (Kiefer 2012).

Hallmark Channel also announced its move into scripted series in 2012,
starting with *Cedar Cove* (Hallmark, 2013–15). The series, starring Andie
MacDowell, was based on a series of books by best-selling romance writer Debbie
Macomber that explores the familial, work, and romantic relationships of a judge
in a small, lakeside town. The series, which premiered with a two-hour movie
on July 20, 2013, was expected to "mirror the family-friendly dramatic format
that has proven to be successful for [Hallmark's] original movies" (Umstead
2012, 9). *Cedar Cove* demonstrates many of the same themes as the Hallmark
Channel movies, featuring a White, female character with a fulfilling job (judge)
who, in the pilot movie, must choose between a federal judgeship in the "city"
or life in her small Pacific-Northwest community surrounded by family and a
new love interest. Not surprisingly, Olivia Lockhart stays in Cedar Cove, and,
throughout the series, we follow the development of her relationships as well as
those of her family and friends. Reviews of the series repeatedly noted how well
it fit with the Hallmark-style of content, calling it "comfortable, uncomplicated,
unchallenging entertainment, which makes it ideal for Hallmark's brand" (Owen
2013, TV1). *The New York Times* review observes, "Viewers accustomed to the
intricate, fast paced, high-anxiety dramas that now dominate television will be
jarred by the relative slowness and simplicity of 'Cedar Cove,' but the Hallmark
Channel is built on the realization that not all viewers want their television time
to be nonstop trauma and adrenaline" (Genzlinger 2013, C3). Neil Genzlinger
notes the slow pacing of the "quiet" personal dramas that play out on the show
(2013, C3). Like in Hallmark's movies, the series' stories of love, family, and
community take place within a small town that is a serene and beautiful haven,
that marks "home" as a safe place, where, as Billy Stevenson notes, the idea of

locking one's door is scoffed at and the mention of local crime is passed off as a joke (2020, 182). If, on *Cedar Cove*, there are more "real life issues" (such as alcoholism, war, divorce, death) than seen in other Hallmark movies, the series itself is positioned as, according to co-star Bruce Boxleitner, a "safe harbor in the evening . . . a refuge where people can have an engrossing storyline and get away from their lives for an hour or two" (Cutler 2013). The peaceful, serene, and safe qualities associated with *Cedar Cove* contribute to audience expectations that, in the end, everyone will be okay; the positive emotions with which people face their problems allow for a steady optimism and expectations for a better future.

In their 2012 rebrand, Hallmark used cultural codes that picked up on and "planted a flag" for its brand position as the "Heart of TV" providing shelter from the storm of complex television and a precarious reality. The myth that Hallmark created for its viewers was that the world, specifically small-town United States, is a safe and hopeful place. Concentrating on home and family, focusing on the personal rather than the political, fosters a middle-class life that is full of love, family, community, and fulfilling employment. The reassuring feeling that Hallmark Channel chose to reinforce in 2012 is summed up nicely in 2019, by the executive vice president of programming and network publicity for Crown Media Family Network, who said

> We have a 24/7 news cycle—it's a constant need to be fed—and we have a lot of dark, edgy programming out in the world that's fantastic, but as in the human experience, it's a huge spectrum, and where we live is with positivity and celebration and emotional connection, and that's unique to what we do. . . . If you choose to spend two hours of your time with us, you're going to feel a little better about the world and yourself and your community. (Turchiano 2019)

This story of "positivity and celebration," in line with the Cultural Innovation Theory, confirms the benefits of personal optimism in the face of a precarious American Dream and reinforces the expectations of the many Americans at the time who still believed that they themselves would find the American Dream but were anxious about the state of the nation. The Hallmark brand, however, in its embrace of post-feminism and post-racial cultural codes, reserves this encouragement for a circumscribed set of viewers. For some, by excising larger political and social anxieties, Hallmark Channel reinforced personal optimism and provided a safe haven from the complicated economic recovery and social turmoil of the time. The American Dream was (and still is) alive and well on the Hallmark Channel, encouraging its viewers' faith in the future and in themselves.

From Blue Skies to Silver Lining: USA Network

*The USA team was surprised to find how deeply the trauma of the economic
meltdown has lingered in the culture. There's also a deep-seated distrust of
governmental institutions and big business.*

Littleton, USA Network Revamps 2016, 13

USA: "We the Bold"

While the Hallmark Channel, after the recession, embraced its optimistic brand
myth grounded in positive emotions, the USA Network began to walk back
its own upbeat branding that had been in place since the early 2000s. As the
network's existing series ended, USA programmed what it described as "bold"
content that would better reflect the post-Recession atmosphere. USA turned to
a darker, grittier brand that walked a fine line between hopefulness and cynicism
designed to reach the growing Millennial audience.

In 2005, USA, then recently folded into GE-owned NBCUniversal, garnered
attention using a successful branding campaign that positioned the general
entertainment cable network as a place to find upbeat, lighthearted, procedural
dramas featuring quirky characters.[7] The network adopted a new logo, replacing
its American flag icon with a stylized graphic of the letters USA, and a new
slogan, "Characters Welcome." By highlighting its characters, USA connected its
original series, which at the time included *Monk* (2002–9), *Dead Zone* (2002–7),
and *The 4400* (2004–7), its syndicated shows such as *Law & Order SVU* (NBC,
1990–) and *Nash Bridges* (CBS, 1996–2001), and the network's very successful
run of *WWE Raw* (USA, 1993–2000, 2005–present; Spike TV, 2000–5). Despite
its lack of focus on a specific demographic (women, men, children, Latinos)
or genre (drama, comedy, science fiction), Characters Welcome defined a
brand for USA. This success was not because of the idea of characters; as brand
strategist Hunt noted, "every piece of content has characters" (2023). Rather, the
USA brand identity was shaped by shows that featured quirky characters who
inhabited series with what the network characterized as "blue skies" and that
"had a kind of positive spin" (L. Hunt 2023). Andy Bryant and Charlie Mawer
note that "At a time when rival networks were going darker and edgier, USA
Network took the view that blue skies—both figuratively and literally—would
give their characters broad appeal" (2016, 37). USA's gamble paid off, and it soon
became, and remained for many years, the number one general entertainment
cable network in the US (Bryant and Mawer 2016, 39). Like the Hallmark

Channel, the USA Network offered viewers "fun escapism" (A. Smith 2018, 448) that Josef Adalian described as "popcorn procedurals, the video equivalent of beach reading" (2015).

Starting in the 2010s, viewership of linear television declined due to the rise of streaming platforms as both distributors of existing content and producers of new programming. Traditional television viewers aged 18–34 fell by 4 percent every year starting in 2012 (Frankel 2015). These shifts impacted USA, and its viewership began to slip in 2012 (Adalian 2015). In 2014, USA "shed 20% of its primetime audience, falling behind ESPN for the total viewer crown among cablers, ending its eight-year winning streak" (Baysinger, USA Leaves 2015, 22). At the same time, the median age for linear television inched up to fifty, slipping out of the desired demographic of 18-49-years old sought by advertisers (Frankel 2015, 1). At fifty-four years, the median age of USA viewers in 2015 was higher than that of FX (41) and AMC (42) (A. Smith 2018, 446). Chris McCumber, then president of NBCUniversal Cable Entertainment, observed that younger viewers had diverse interests and were attracted to a different kind of content than they had been in the past (Adalian 2015). Unlike Hallmark, USA did not embrace its older viewers; rather, the network shifted its brand to appeal to the younger, Millennial audience discussed previously. Many of USA's original series, including *Psych* (2006–14), *Burn Notice* (2007–13), *White Collar* (2009–14), and *Covert Affairs* (2010–14), ended their runs, and the network moved to slightly darker, morally ambivalent shows with more serialized storylines. *Suits* (2011–19), for example, featured characters who didn't always do the right thing, unabashedly smoked pot, and participated in power plays that stretched across seasons; *Suits* was also, in 2015, the USA scripted series most watched by Millennials (Katz 2015, 14).[8]

Networks executives at USA were vocal about their interest in the Millennial audience (Bryant and Mawer 2016, 40), who comprised two-thirds of the 18-49-year-old audience in 2015 (Baysinger, USA Leaves 2015, 22). Advertisers were particularly attracted to the size of the Millennial audience as they overtook Baby Boomers in number (England 2016, 35) and their $200 billion in annual spending power (Serazio 2013, 600). The research that regularly painted this generation as marked by contradictions influenced USA's conceptualization of how to best reach this audience. According to Louisa Stein, and as demonstrated in *Arrow* and *Daredevil*, incongruities found within Millennials resulted in televisual depictions of and for Millennials that illustrated both "millennial hope" and a "millennial noir." Millennial hope picked up on the tendencies toward hope and optimism, caring for others, and trying to make the world better (Stein 2015, 29). Millennial noir texts "depict millennials as morally ambiguous, as adult before their time, and as digital pirates with no respect for institutions—unless they themselves own those institutions" (Stein 2015, 78). This unease connects to Millennials' tension about the digital universe in which they were raised that both creates community but also ensconces them within a branded, commercialized world. Recognizing that Millennials are hyperaware of their global and corporate ecosystem, marketers identified the need for authenticity when trying to appeal to these consumers. As explained in the Nielsen "Breaking the Myths" Report, Millennials have

> been hit particularly hard by poor economic conditions and have a higher Misery Index than the older population, further confirming the difficult situation in which they have come of age. And this misery cannot be ignored in communicating with Millennials—especially in late holiday season. Honesty (in a direct and forward fashion) and authenticity are the best policies when communicating with this group. (Nielsen 2014, 8)

According to Michael Serazio, advertisers try to create branding that doesn't seem like branding, content that is empowering and that can be shared without appearing too commercial and that may come across as empowering (2013, 610–11). Authenticity became a buzz word when trying to reach Millennials (A. Smith 2018, 453), and in television, this meant crafting brands that connected to social issues and experiences with which Millennials identified.[9]

In preparation for its rebrand, USA's research on the 18–49-year-old audience found that viewership interests had changed in ways that dovetailed with existing information about Millennials. After 9/11, according to Alexandra Shapiro, NBCUniversal Cable Entertainment's marketing and digital executive vice president, the mood was "weirdly optimistic," thus allowing for the success of the upbeat Characters Welcome brand (Marian 2016). Years later, as Millennials took over this age group, "the USA team was surprised to find how deeply the trauma of the economic meltdown has lingered in the culture. There's also a deep-seated distrust of governmental institutions and big business" (Littleton, USA Network Revamps 2016, 13). Similarly, a 2015 report found that "millennials in particular are drawn to post-apocalyptic shows, as well as series that feature conflicted and flawed leaders and heroes" (Katz 2015, 12). McCumber also notes, "they've all become very sophisticated about the kinds of dramas they want to see: more serialized, more characters that come from the real world and face real problems" (Adalian 2015). USA's focus on escapist, blue sky entertainment, "the easy, breezy, self-contained stories for which USA had become known" (Adalian 2015), no longer worked to reach the network's desired audience. To stay current with the 18–49-year-old audience that was increasingly made up of Millennials, USA had to reconfigure its brand, shifting its lighthearted approach toward its characters and their place in the world to raise questions about equity and responsibility within society.

USA tested the waters for a possible rebrand in the summer of 2015 with *Mr. Robot* (USA, 2015–19), a series that departed from the blue skies brand and fully embraced an appeal to a more socially conscious and cynical Millennial audience. *Mr. Robot* focuses on Elliot, an introverted hacker experiencing mental illness, who gets involved with a secret society (the fsociety), out to destroy the global capitalist system embodied by the fictional company that Elliot dubs Evil Corp. The series was embraced by critics who appreciated its attitude as demonstrated by Emily Nussbaum's summary: "A dystopian thriller with Occupy-inflected politics, the series was refreshing, both for its melancholy beauty and for its unusually direct attack on corporate manipulation" (2015). In addition to favorable critical reviews, *Mr. Robot* won the audience award at South by Southwest, was an official selection at the Tribeca Film Festival, received several Golden Globe Awards, and was nominated for numerous Emmy Awards (with star Rami Malek winning in 2016 for Best Actor in a Drama Series). Perhaps most importantly, it was the top-rated new drama with viewers under fifty in the summer of its release, at least until *Fear the Walking Dead* premiered two months later (Adalian 2015).

Although the series didn't have ratings as high as some of USA's earlier series, it did attract younger viewers and, therefore, advertisers (Adalian 2015). *Mr. Robot* successfully connected with Millennials, presumably by moving away from the unwaveringly upbeat, brightly lit series associated with the Characters Welcome brand. This show, with its dark shadows and muted colors, features an antihero who not only hasn't achieved the American Dream but wants to destroy the system on which the Dream rests. James Murphy writes that "*Mr. Robot* gives us a hero who wants none of the traditional markers of success, and a failure who already has them, which amounts to a rejection of not just capitalism's but Hollywood's ultimate fantasy, namely, the idea that he who wants success most will and should get it" (2015). *Mr. Robot* repudiates the idea that the American Dream is equally available to all within a fair and meritocratic system.[10] Yet, embedded within *Mr. Robot*'s revolutionary vision remains an optimism for the future. The goal in destroying Evil Corp. is to make life better for the 99 percent, the regular people; the idea is that by wiping out all debt, the fsociety will create a more just society.[11] Underneath the show's cynicism and anger is a layer of hope that change is possible. The world can be made better, particularly by young, technologically savvy, anxiety-ridden, introverted Millennials.

The success of *Mr. Robot* and *Suits*, which throughout its run embraced greater degrees of moral ambiguity, demonstrated a path for USA. In April 2016, just under a year after the success of *Mr. Robot*, USA officially rebranded with the tagline "We the Bold." This campaign weaved a brand story that acknowledged Millennial anxieties about the state of the world and the future but also depicted Millennials as resilient, knowledgeable, good people who will solve the existing problems. The concepts of Millennial hope and Millennial noir permeated the branding campaign, from the show's promotions to its color palette. Loyalkaspar, the design firm that worked on the campaign, describes the intention of the rebranding in its brand strategy deck: "USA sharpened their lens to better reflect the people populating their increasingly daring programming: Unlikely heroes who defy the status quo, push boundaries and are willing to risk everything for what they believe in. Characters who are BOLD" (loyalkaspar). According to the firm, the boldness of design used "space and simplicity" that expressed confidence, "it's bold to be simple" (loyalkaspar). Additionally, the focus was on promoting the shows not the network, a move that also contributed to a more authentic vibe as viewers didn't necessarily feel overwhelmed by branding, particularly as the new promos created for the series "organically feature the tagline within the context of each franchisee's world" (Marian 2016).

The initial promos created around the platform focused on bold characters from three USA series: *Mr. Robot*, *WWE*, and *Colony* (USA, 2016–18). According to Joshua Hertz, who was an editorial director, creative at USA in 2016, these were a "series of character-narrated, show-specific spots, each interpreting 'boldness' through the lens of that show's world—demonstrating how the tagline worked for our various programming" (Hertz). One of the first We the Bold promos highlighted *Colony*, a series set in Los Angeles about a dystopian future in which the Earth is controlled by extraterrestrials who rule through a human-run military organization. The 40-second video is narrated by main character Katie Bowman, a wife and mother who is secretly part of a resistance cell. We see images from the series that focus on Katie and her husband Will, who is reluctantly working to track down resistance fighters. The music underlying the narration begins with a slow and sad piano theme which gradually adds in drums; the percussion picks up in frequency until the piano is no longer heard. The driving beat is accompanied by an increase in edits as the shot lengths gets shorter and shorter, matching the frenetic pace of the music. Over this, Katie narrates:

> When the time comes we all have to make a choice. Do we keep our heads down and follow orders, even if those orders go against everything we believe in? Or do we take a stand? Do we challenge the authority of those who demand obedience? Do we defy them even when they seem all powerful? Do we risk our lives and our loved ones to fight for a cause that is bigger than any of us? There is no choice. If we risk nothing, we risk everything.

The promo ends with the phrase "We the Bold" scrawled in graffiti-like font in dark red paint on a distressed off-white wall, supposedly in occupied LA. After a cut to black, the USA logo appears, against the same wall with the U and A in the same dark red color and a transparent S through which the wall is visible (Figure 5).

This promo demonstrates the rebrand's appeal to Millennials. It generates a nervous energy as the tempo of the video picks up. Additionally, the branding for the promo attempts to be subtle, incorporating the We the Bold tagline into the world of the series, and only referencing the USA Network at the very end. This is not a hard-sell of USA, which would potentially turn off Millennial viewers, but, rather, it offers a character study that could serve as an interesting paratext that enhances the

Figure 5   USA Network's *Colony* promo featuring the new tagline © USA Network 2016.

meaning of the series. Most importantly, the narration underscores the optimism of the We the Bold campaign. Millennial noir and Millennial hope merge as the narration drives home the dystopian anxiety seen in the images by emphasizing the danger of fighting for freedom, but the character clearly indicates that standing up for what is right is the only real option. Katie positions herself as a person who will oppose tyranny, despite the peril, because it's the only option. She provides hope for a better future. She is bold. The promo raises ethical questions, but it offers a hopeful resolution. Because individuals can be brave, there is room for optimism.

After the initial three show promos, USA released additional videos in this style for *Suits*, *Queen of the South* (2016–21), and reality show, *Chrisley Knows Best* (2014–23).[12] The campaign also included a sizzle reel for all of USA's content that focused on the network's current original series. With the song "Home" by indie-pop musician Morgxn pulsating in the background, clips from the different series are interspersed and occasionally the dialogue is heard (e.g., during a clip *Mr. Robot* we hear: "Why did you do it?" "I wanted to save the world"). Intercut between the show clips every few seconds are two images of text in bold white lettering centered on a black background. The first image repeats each time with the words "We the" and the second image, different each time, finishes the thought with a different "bold" quality: Risktakers, Unafraid, Heroic, Defiant, and Unstoppable. The promo then runs through each of USA's current series using an image of the show's title using the font/logo associated with the individual series followed by a short clip from the series. The tempo of the music and the editing pick up significantly and the promo ends with a return to the text image of "We the" followed by "Bold" and then an image of the USA logo in black and white. The use of stark black and white helps to keep the messaging simple, and an indie musician reinforces the shows' outsider status. Like in the *Colony* promo, we see a focus on character traits that embody bravery and strength; these are qualities that will allow the characters to not only persevere but succeed. These characters are connected to attributes that Millennials may want to associate with themselves as they try to navigate an uncertain world.

Finally, USA created short 3-second bumpers, seemingly intended for social media posting and sharing, to highlight its shows. Each bumper features a single shot from the series in the background with large white capitalized text overlaying (and obstructing) the image, with a single word or a small group of words flashing on screen at a time. The WWE bumper shows a man in a wrestling costume in a ring punching the floor in slow motion. The white lettering reads

WHEN SOMEONE DOUBTS YOU PROVE THEM WRONG. *Suits* had multiple bumpers highlighting different characters. For main character, Harvey, the medium shot of him, dressed in a suit, walking in slow motion through an office, tells us IT'S NOT BRAGGING IF IT'S TRUE. Another main character, Mike, is seen in a dress shirt and jacket walking, again in slow motion, toward the camera. The words tell us I DID WHAT I HAD TO DO. The *Queen of the South* bumper, promoting the series about a woman who becomes head of a major drug cartel, shows a woman in a chic white dress in front of a group of men all in black as they walk away from a helicopter. The group of people move in slow motion toward the camera as the large text flashing across the screen reads I'M HERE TO CLAIM MY THRONE. Each bumper ends with a single image reading WE THE BOLD in white letter on a black background and then a second shot of the black and white USA logo. These short bumpers were ideal for social media sharing, and kept the USA branding to a minimum, with the network only being promoted at the very end. Even the show names didn't appear on these bumpers. Instead, they focus on what makes the characters bold and strong, designed to appeal to people who were probably already fans of the show and hopefully intrigue those who were not (Figure 6).

These video promos use a simple font and stark colors (primarily black and white) to support the idea of "bold." Viewers were invited to identify with the characters' strong qualities that positioned them as Millennial stand-ins who would navigate a difficult world and come out on top. As a slogan, "We the

Figure 6 USA Network's *Queen of the South* bumper © USA Network 2016.

Bold" situated USA as an inclusive space for its viewers. It wasn't just Bold, like FX was Fearless, but through its use of the word "we," USA created a sense of belonging and identification to create a community of Millennials. Watching USA would encourage viewers to self-identify as bold and see not only the prospect of optimism but also the possibility that they themselves could be part of the solution to the problems plaguing the world.

This tinge of hopefulness not only speaks to Millennial optimism for the future but also to USA's goal in rebranding. Bryant and Mawer observe that USA's attempt to move to darker content "has not been a race towards copycat edgy and challenging dramas" (2016, 40). Rather, Jason Holzman, the senior vice president, brand creative, for the USA Network told them,

> We think our white space is what we call "silver linings." Very much not blue skies, because that feels completely out of step with the reality that people are experiencing now, not dark skies because: a) that's not true to who we are; and b) we don't want to be the last person to join the parade of dark, nihilistic programming. (Bryant and Mawer 2016, 40)

The original series created to extend this brand from *Mr. Robot*, such as *Colony* and *Queen of the South*, moved away from the brightly lit, blue skies optimism of the Characters Welcome era and instead, USA "developed a brand around images of troubled and/or sullen drama protagonists with whom it anticipates millennials might identify" (A. Smith 2018, 452). *Queen of the South*, for example, is based on *La Reina del Sur*, a best-selling Spanish language novel which was adapted into a Mexican telenovela about a woman who becomes the head of a major drug cartel. The US series highlights the drama and violence within the world of the cartel and the main character's struggle to maintain power. At the same time, through narrative, casting, and language choices, the series offers "an inept attempt to claim diversity" (Albarran-Torres 2021, 79) while appealing to "edgy" White, Millennial viewers. The angst and pessimism conveyed through USAshows' "muted color palette and downcast aesthetic of the series" (A. Smith 2018, 451), however, are balanced by the series' traces of optimism and hope. According to McCumber, USA was "going for this idea of unexpected heroes who are bravely emerging against all odds. That is something that the country right now, especially the millennial audience is going to really connect with" (Baysinger, USA Leaves 2015, 22). McCumber also noted that, while USA was moving toward flawed characters, they still needed to be seen as heroes: "What it comes down to is: Is that unlikely hero trying to do something for good. . . . We call it a silver lining. At the heart, is the character trying to do good, even though they might make some questionable decisions, or make some decisions that are a little grayer than blue sky" (Adalian 2015).

The USA rebrand continued to draw on the idea of characters but positioned them not as quirky and upbeat but as daring and audacious. These are characters who are not afraid of the world even as they are faced with precarious situations. Instead, they embrace challenges and make difficult choices in order to help themselves and most importantly others. In this way, the promos paint a brand story that contributes to the Millennial merger of hope and noir. The world is a dangerous place, but there is hope and optimism that it will be better—that they can make it better. A better life, the American Dream, may seem distant or fleeting, but it is attainable by those who are bold.

Conclusion

Unlike Hallmark, USA didn't just evolve its brand but changed it substantially. To attract a younger audience, USA shifted away from the upbeat positivity that Hallmark embraced. Each of these brands reinforced different elements of the cultural zeitgeist, casting different stories about the American Dream. As the Heart of TV, Hallmark promised viewers depictions of a Dream achieved through and with love, family, and community. The Dream thrived in small-town America where needs were simple and larger socioeconomic issues didn't exist. The network's brand story, which continues to this day, opens up space for optimism about the Dream even if viewers undoubtedly recognize it as fantasy. Hallmark faces increasing competition. Former Hallmark CEO Bill Abbott started the new platform Great American Family (GAF) in 2021 to directly compete with Hallmark.[13] GAF, which has drawn away stars such as Candace Cameron Bure from Hallmark's regular stable of actors, is expected to depict "traditional" (read, heterosexual) relationships. Other platforms, such as Lifetime, Hulu, and Netflix also began producing Hallmark-style romance movies, particularly around the winter holiday season. Unlike GAF, these other platforms, have approached the genre from a more inclusive perspective, centering same-sex couples and people of color. The creation of direct competitors—one that would be expected to attract even fewer young viewers than Hallmark and others that reach out to more inclusive Millennial and Gen Z viewers—suggests the ongoing demand for Hallmark's optimistic and escapist programming.

USA, on the other hand, has, in the years since its rebrand, markedly reduced its number of original series. NBCUniversal's focus moved to its streaming platform Peacock, and as USA's programming failed, it was not replaced. As of this writing, the only original scripted series on USA is *Chucky* (2021–present), a series based on the horror film that USA shares with both the Syfy network and Peacock. USA, instead, increasingly airs reality programming and sports, particularly since the demise of NBCUniversal's sports network. Although it's impossible to know if USA's earlier blue skies programming would have survived, the network's darker vision did not. Interestingly, a couple of the blue skies shows have been revived as stand-alone movies (*Monk* [Peacock, 2023] and *Psych* [Peacock, 2017, 2020, 2021]), and *Suits* found success with new, younger viewers on Netflix. Perhaps USA staked out a position that was too similar to what was available on other platforms, while still trying to maintain a sense of optimism through its silver-lining strategy. To appeal to Millennial hope, USA rested its brand story on characters who wanted to make a difference to achieve the American Dream not only for themselves but for others. This American Dream relied on resilience and determination shored by faith that a better tomorrow was available to all, even while refusing to acknowledge the significant barriers that obstructed this goal for many Americans. It was exactly this optimism that, as will be examined in the next chapter, was being questioned by television's signature comedies.

Notes

1 As one interviewee told Chris Arnade in 2015, "The American Dream is long gone. Long, long gone. Politicians have ruined it, broke our values, sold out to folks with money who only care about themselves. Nobody cares about anyone who works with their hands anymore. We got to get this country straight again, before it all keeps sliding down into hell" (Arnade 2015).

2 Portions of this discussion were included in Selznick (2009, 177–203), used with the permission of Liverpool University Press.

3 According to Yongjun Sung and Namkee Park, "the number of basic and digital cable network increased from 308 in 2002 to 565 by the end of 2006" (2011, 87).

4 The Odyssey Channel had been created in 1996 as a re-envisioning of the Faith and Values Channel by moving from overt religious content to family-friendly programming.

5 These series included cooking shows *Emeril's Table* (Hallmark, 2011) and *Mad Hungry with Lucinda Scala Quinn* (Hallmark, 2010–11).

6 *Home and Family* is a revival of a DIY show that aired on The Family Channel from 1996–8.

7 USA's history leading up to this brand strategy is detailed in Amanda Lotz's book *We Now Disrupt this Broadcast* (2018).

8 Fascinatingly, *Suits* was also named the most streamed show of 2023 when it gained popularity with Gen Z on Netflix (S. Adams 2024).

9 Of course, and as will be discussed in the next chapter, what was considered "relatable" differed for many within the very large Millennial cohort. Most of these generalizations about the Millennial generation stemmed from research focused on wealthy, White Millennials (Serazio 2013, 601).

10 The series does, purposefully, avoid discussions of the impact that race and ethnicity may have on the characters and their goals. Showrunner Sam Esmail, an Egyptian-American, explained that in creating a diverse cast, "when I made those choices, some of them in the screenplay, some of them in casting, which then inspired certain character choices, it was never to talk about it. Elliot is obviously of mixed race, his mother and father are different ethnicities, but we do not talk about it" (Chaney, Emami and Seitz 2016).

11 That fsociety's success in wiping out the debt and taking down Evil Corp. only leads to greater levels of insecurity and inequality results in questions about the series' position about progressive reforms.

12 *Chrisley Knows Best* was the trickiest show to fit into the We the Bold campaign, yet it was also the longest running series, surviving USA's move away from We the Bold and back to a campaign strikingly similar to Characters Welcome ("Here for the Characters," adopted in 2021). Unlike USA's other series, *Chrisley* would probably still be in production if the main characters hadn't been convicted of tax evasion and sentenced to prison.

13 Abbott left Hallmark in the wake of a much-publicized controversy over Hallmark's decision to pull a commercial from a wedding planning website that featured a same-sex couple kissing.

3

Transgressing the Dream: Signature Comedies

The American Dream's foundation of optimism discussed in the previous chapter is intertwined with the central tenet that the Dream is available to all. Anyone who works hard and/or has natural abilities can attain the freedom, independence, security, and contentment promised by the Dream. In other words, the American Dream is fair; it is founded on a meritocracy with equal opportunity. Merit, however, didn't prove effective at protecting Americans from the Great Recession. The economic crisis didn't discriminate between those who worked hard and those who did not. Many people found themselves out of work; many lost their pensions and their homes. The Great Recession tattered the sense of security promised by the American Dream, ultimately exposing and expanding inequities within the system.

While many marginalized groups were accustomed to being let down by the promises of the Dream, the economic breakdown impacted others who had routinely been privileged within the United States. As previously discussed, the White middle class, particularly, found itself realigning its vision of the Dream, leading to greater identification with and empathy for those who were historically disenfranchised. Social movements like Occupy Wall Street nurtured tenuous connections across racial, ethnic, and class lines to connect people who felt "left out" of the Dream. At the same time, influenced by transformations within the television ecosystem, distribution outlets leaned into growing opportunities to innovate television programming. This chapter will argue that the shifting bonds of sociocultural identification along with the demands of the expanding television industry contributed to new television stories about family, home, and success at the center of US television, and especially prestige comedy.

Comedy, as Jonathan Rossing writes, "distinctively confronts contradictions and constructs possibilities for meaning and action because it gives voice to the unspoken and ignored, particularly in times of social and political repression" (2012, 46). As will be discussed, since the Great Recession, television comedy has been reconfigured in ways that open new possibilities of representation that "tell us a great deal about the reality that has been disrupted, as well as the dominant underlying concerns of society" (Sands 2018, 3). Yet, at the same time, comedy often softens the edges of potentially oppositional ideas by presenting them as humorous and easing tensions with laughter. Writing about the relationship between comedic films and the American Dream, Zach Sands explains that, in recent years, "At a time when the neoliberal world economy has failed so many of its practitioners by distancing them from their own humanity, comedic films have once again entered into the debate about a new American Dream" (2018, 157). Television comedies, like movies, offer an opportunity to examine the cultural reimaginings of the Dream. While Sands focuses on the continued primacy of the middle class, White man as the center of US comedic films, we can see an attempt within television, borne of sociocultural and industrial influences, to center the experiences of underrepresented groups as they celebrate and struggle with the ideas of equity and security within the new economic order. Central to these stories is the concept of the meritocracy, what makes one "deserving" of the American Dream, and the rewards that may or may not come to those seen as "other."

Two series that demonstrate the changes to television comedy in the post-Recession period are *Unbreakable Kimmy Schmidt* (Netflix, 2015–20) and *Atlanta* (FX, 2016–22). While these programs may seem dissimilar, there are connections. *Atlanta*'s co-creator, Donald Glover began his television career as a young writer on *30 Rock*, which was co-created by Tina Fey and Robert Carlock, the team behind *Unbreakable Kimmy Schmidt*. Additionally, and as will be discussed below, both comedies were used as signature shows to shore up the emerging brands of their platforms, Netflix and FX. And these series received both rave critical reviews and subsequent criticism for their representations. However, the differences between these series in tone, style, content, and comedic approach provoke questions about how diverse television comedies reflect concerns about opportunity in the mid-2000s. The ways that these programs differ, and are more surprisingly similar, underscore the impact that the economic collapse had on US television comedy's mobilization of the genre's focus on family, home, and success to allow for an alternative view of the meritocratic American Dream.

Working through Trauma: The Meritocracy

Those at the apex of the American Dream were somehow at the center
of a massive instability. Their avenue to wealth had not been the mythic
application of thrift and discipline, for which society might profit as well.
Many had been speculating with others' money.

Kimmage 2011, 35

In the article "The Mirage of Meritocracy and the Morality of Grace," Victor Tan Chen calls attention to the failures of meritocracy, and, as a result, the American Dream. Chen proposes the morality of grace as "a direct and targeted antidote to meritocratic extremism," which allows those with the most resources to continue to shore up their merit (Chen 2021). Arguing against a meritocratic system predicated on people working to deserve what they get, Chen writes,

> grace abandons the idea of evaluation altogether. It rejects categories of right and wrong, just and unjust. It is not about retribution or restitution; it is about forgiveness. The simple commonsense idea here is that life is short, and in the final analysis, it is not worth spending that time fighting over who has what or who is on top. (2021, 67)

The rising call for "grace" (or compassion) after the Great Recession reflected the growing recognition of the failure of the meritocracy in the wake of an economic meltdown. If, as Chen writes, "the principle of competition is the basis for American meritocratic order" (2021, 59), the Recession uncovered significant problems with the meritocracy's ability to determine who is worthy of the American Dream.

As discussed in Chapter 1 in relation to *Arrow* and *Daredevil*, a meritocratic society, as Stephen McNamee and Robert Miller define it, is one in which "individuals get ahead and earn rewards in direct proportion to their individual efforts and abilities" (2018, 2). They suggest four factors that determine merit: talent, the right attitude, hard work, and moral character (McNamee and Miller 2018, 23). Furthermore, as Wilfred McClay explains, some types of merit are innate in that people are born with these qualities (essential merit) while other types of merit can be acquired or learned (institutional merit) (2016, 39). In all cases, the assumption is that those who work hard can make use of their essential merit and develop institutional merit. Portraying the United States as a meritocracy in which all people have equal access to the tools through which to achieve, allows for the justification of inequality as "those in a position of wealth and power were presumed to be in their social positions due to their inherent superiority and worthiness" (Bush and Bush 2015, 95). Additionally, those who don't succeed are those who don't try hard enough (Kozan, Gutowski, and Blustein 2020, 195).

This conception of equality is essential to maintaining the idea of the meritocracy that undergirds the Dream, limits resentment, and reinforces social stability (Bush and Bush 2015, 5). The belief in the meritocracy can only be upheld alongside a trust that there is equality of access to the tools to develop merit and equality of outcomes for all those who demonstrate merit. Often, emphasis is placed on ensuring equality of opportunity so that all Americans can attain education and employment. As several researchers have shown, however, opportunities within the American Dream are impacted by many forms of inequality in the United States including resources (such as bank loans, wealth, cultural experiences, etc.) and conditions or circumstances (such as safe housing, education, or good health) (see, for example, Hochschild 1996, 28; Cullen 2006, 108; Roemer 2018, 21–2). Of all the values behind the American Dream, the idea of equality is the most illusory, requiring that we, as a nation, avoid acknowledging the ways that so many people have been denied equality in terms of opportunity, resources, conditions, circumstances, and outcomes.

Unsurprisingly, a country built on racist slavery practices, patriarchal ideologies, and tenets of national exceptionalism, inevitably impedes access to the tools needed to thrive in a meritocracy. People historically relegated to exist "outside" of the American Dream, experience the meritocracy differently than those imagined to be on the "inside" (primarily White, upper/middle-class, heterosexual men). The meritocratic American Dream was used to create socioeconomic silos with promises of the Dream made accessible to poor, White men and held back from Black Americans, women, and immigrants (Bush and Bush 2015, 21). By offering the White lower classes the potential for opportunity, those in power encouraged their loyalty, effectively severing allegiances with other oppressed groups (Bush and Bush 2015, 21). Over time, the lower and middle classes continued to support the ideology of the meritocracy as they maintained the hope that, through their own hard work, they could increase their socioeconomic status "thereby distancing themselves from those whose political interests they may otherwise share" (Sands 2018, 151). Historical inequalities at the foundation of the meritocracy haunt those on the margins of the Dream. A 1962 study found that Black Americans "'experience a perverse sort of egalitarianism'—neither the disadvantages of poverty nor the advantage of wealth made much difference in what they could achieve or pass on to their children. Discrimination swamped everything else" (Hochschild 1996, 44). Writing in 1995, Jennifer Hochschild found that the American Dream continued to be elusive for Black Americans regardless of any measure of merit (1996, 40). And, Saliha Kozan et al found that the structural barriers that impact women's access to decent work "make it harder for them to achieve the American Dream" and impact their ideas about the meritocracy (2020, 196).

The intersecting ideals of meritocracy and equality only continue to complicate the feasibility of the American Dream. As Kozan et al explain, since the 2008 recession, "there is a growing disparity between meritocratic ideals and reality for many, causing this belief to play a complex role in the lives of Americans" (2020, 196). People who appeared to be meritorious—they worked hard, saved money, and cared for their families—experienced economic precarity, losing their homes, their savings, and their retirement funds. One report estimated that during this recession, approximately eight million homes were foreclosed on and about $7 trillion in home equity was lost (Goodman and Mayer 2018, 31). The housing crisis only increased the disparity between the classes. Laurie Goodman and Christopher Mayer argue that homeownership is a significant means of maintaining and accumulating wealth, particularly during economic downturns; however, minorities and those with lower incomes often face more difficulties holding on to their homes during times of financial adversity thus further increasing the wealth disparity (2018, 32). The systemic inequalities that persisted throughout the economic collapse highlight the failure of the American Dream.

Some Americans, particularly those who did not face extreme financial instability, continued to support the meritocracy, validated by the idea that those who were flailing simply weren't working hard enough. Chen observes that meritocratic extremism was used to blame those who suffered during the Great Recession in the "form of screeds against unemployed workers, distressed homeowners, and other perceived parasites being helped by the government" (2021, 65). Even people strongly impacted by the Recession could be expected to support meritocracy as the basis for the American Dream, as a means of psychological reassurance that their position in society could improve (Jost and Hunyady 2003, 145–7). The idea of the meritocracy is also intertwined with the notion of a post-racial colorblind society that helps satisfy "liberal guilt" about systemic discrimination (Warner 2015, 4). On the other hand, as discussed previously, many in the middle and working classes recognized that, as Michael

Kimmage writes, "Those at the apex of the American Dream were somehow at the center of a massive instability. Their avenue to wealth had not been the mythic application of thrift and discipline, for which society might profit as well. Many had been speculating with others' money" (2011, 35). This realization worked as a "situational trigger" sparking resentment and weakening the allegiance between the middle and upper classes (see S. Shapiro 2016) as well as raising questions of equity around the meritocratic basis of the American Dream (Newman, Johnston and Lown 2015, 328). Benjamin Newman et al predicted that as economic inequality became more recognizable (particularly within local communities), it would "stimulate rejection of meritocracy by increasing the salience of their disadvantaged position within a conspicuous local economic hierarchy" (2015, 327). Some research suggests that the continued belief in meritocracy in the midst of economic failure could potentially harm a person's self-image. Kozan et al also found that "critically resisting the meritocratic ideology may help marginalized people by offering less individualistic explanations for their disadvantage or lack of success and by allowing them to preserve their esteem as well as plan and prepare for social injustices they might encounter" (2020, 197).

As we can see, in the face of economic crisis, Americans developed a complicated relationship with the concept of the meritocracy, potentially changing the way they thought about the Dream. This reconfiguring of the Dream can be seen starkly in thoughts about homeownership, a foundation of both the American Dream and the financial crisis. The idea of "home" is at the heart of the American Dream. The home emblemizes not only material success through property ownership but also the promise of safety and stability. A home offers Americans a retreat from work, a place to nurture one's family, and a sense of control over one's own corner of the world. And it was the failure of the housing market that rocked the foundation of the US economy. Before the recession, "the run-up in home prices created what economists call a 'wealth effect' that led to surges in consumer spending and borrowing that proved unsustainable" (Pew Research Center 2011). Despite the anxieties discussed in previous chapters, even after the recession, many people viewed homeownership as a good investment. Because homeowners had seen the value of their homes increase in the past, they remained optimistic that the value would again increase in the future (Pew Research Center 2011). Additionally, homeownership continued to be seen as meaningful beyond its financial benefits. The "Home Sweet Home. Still." Pew Research Study explains, "A home is more than a financial investment. It's a place to raise a family, an anchor of community life, a haven for retirement, an emblem of the American dream. When survey respondents say it's the best long-term investment a person can make, it's likely they are making evaluations that go beyond dollars and cents" (2011). A home provides a safe haven from the outside world, a refuge with one's family, and a source of wealth that can be passed on to one's children. Homeownership is not simply seen as a display of socioeconomic status but also an earned marker of freedom and safety that are inherent values within the American Dream. But, as we'll see, the desire for a safe place of belonging, a home, can also raise questions such as, "what is the price paid for belonging, and what does it mean to be safe?" (Haggins 1999, 24).

Authentically Funny: Signature Comedies

Comedy does have a unique power . . . in that laughter can be so seductive.
It allows us to think about and explore those forbidden and difficult little
topics that we might not otherwise, by taking the pressure off a bit.
Broadnax 2018, 33

Significantly, the concept of home links the American Dream and television. As Bambi Haggins writes, "Notions of home in the United States are inextricably tied to constructions of family, nation, and the myths of the American Dream. No medium is more responsible for reflecting and refracting these notions than the electronic hearth: television" (1999, 23). Television comedy in particular is historically intertwined with the domestic both through its familial target audience and in terms of setting. The home is the center of many sitcoms, often confirming the comfortable middle-class status of their characters (even if the homes were demonstrably more upscale than those lived in by "real" middle-class families); the home is also the place where characters live, learn their lessons, and find comfort and understanding. Comedies like *Unbreakable Kimmy Schmidt* and *Atlanta*, however, use the post-Recession insecurities imbued within the idea of home to comment on the "visible cracks in the national faith in the meritocracy" (Chen 2021, 63). The ability to speak to national (and subnational) traumas in complex and often transgressive ways was possible for these shows because of the opportunities and responsibilities afforded them as prestige, signature comedies.

As previously discussed, just as the recession hit the United States, the television industry was adjusting to the growth of streaming television. Platforms such as Netflix, Hulu, and Amazon Prime Video only further fragmented the audience, contributing to the availability of a large library of older content and reconceptualizing what it means to watch television. Getting the attention of viewers, who were newly overwhelmed with programming, became increasingly challenging, especially within the financial constraints set by an economic downturn.

The rise of cable television, home video, and gaming consoles already initiated narrative and aesthetic changes for television programs as platforms created identifiable brands, as discussed in Chapter 2. While the tentpole programming discussed in the first chapter offered one strategy for achieving this, signature shows offered another (Dunleavy 2018, 16). *TV Guide* critic Matt Roush observed in 2012 that cable networks, "don't program nearly as many shows as the broadcasters do, so each one has to make a mark. They're looking for signature shows" (Hahn 2012, 16). Unlike the tentpole series, these shows, such as *Monk* (USA, 2002–9), *The Shield* (FX, 2002–8), and *Battlestar Galactica* (Sci-Fi, 2004–10), often generated more buzz than ratings as their "conceptual, formal and stylistic distinctiveness" garnered attention for the platform and helped establish a brand image (Dunleavy 2018, 17). As John Dempsey wrote, these shows "beam a dazzling spotlight on the cable networks that carry them" (1998, 1). While broadcast networks relied on shows that attracted mass audiences, cable networks, because of their dual sources of income from both advertisers and cable operators, could afford to air low-rated yet high-profile shows that appealed to a smaller, niche audience and served as loss leaders for the platforms; they may not make money, but they would attract viewers to the network. Quickly, dozens of cable networks were creating original programs and the "signature features of the complex serials produced to date were all well-established by 2008" (Dunleavy 2018, 28). These shows, often described as "quality" or "complex," highlighted antiheroes, serialized storylines, and moral ambiguity as well as narrative and aesthetic complexity to mark their difference from broadcast programming (see Mittell 2015).

The development of streaming platforms increased competition, encouraging television programmers to approach the growing Millennial audiences in new ways. Streaming services created their own original content, like *Daredevil*, to keep audiences engaged, but also to own the rights to programming as the cost of licensing rights to older shows climbed (Slattery 2015, 8). Netflix quickly gained a reputation for its quality original series by adopting and adapting the stylistic features of cable's complex, signature dramas with programs like *House of Cards* (Netflix, 2013–18) and *Orange Is the New Black*. Hulu, on the other hand, remained wedded to a focus on providing catch-up viewing for programming from its corporate owners, NBCUniversal, Fox, Time Warner, and Disney. And Amazon Prime Video, whose video services were frequently seen as an afterthought for Prime members, initially started original programming with comedies, highlighting diversity with shows like *Transparent* (2014–19). Like the cable networks before them, streaming services initially catered to niche audiences by airing programs that could not be found on existing platforms. According to one Amazon Prime executive, the platform would ask, "Is there a good reason we shouldn't make this?" To find series that would stand out in the flood of programming, Amazon was only interested in programs that they "shouldn't" make because they were considered too risky by other platforms (Havas and Sulimma 2020, 82). Furthermore, streaming platforms were afforded more flexibility because they didn't have to try to build a schedule around a difficult/complex series (Weinstein 2015) or worry about cutting to commercial after a disturbing scene. The structure of the streaming business, especially in these early years, set a course for innovative and inclusive programming.

Some of the best-known signature shows created before and during the Great Recession, such as *The Sopranos* (HBO 1999–2007), *Mad Men* (AMC 2007–15), and *Breaking Bad* (AMC 2008–13), were, as discussed above, dramas that focused on White men negotiating their role in a changing world. As these complex series became more commonplace, the need to innovate inspired programming that pushed the boundaries of the "male perspectival centrality" seen in many quality dramas. Comedy programming was seen as a less threatening way to experiment with new themes and styles, but comedy also has a complicated position in the realm of quality TV (Lagerwey, Leyda and Negra 2016). When HBO first started original programming, it created comedies, such as *1ˢᵗ & Ten* (1984–91) and the more popular *The Larry Sanders Show* (1992–8). Only later did the network produce dramas such as *Oz* (1997–2003), *The Sopranos*, and *Six Feet Under* (2001–5). Nevertheless, by 2012, it was assumed that signature shows would be dramas in part because, according to one TV producer, "dramas sort of seem more important because the subject matter would suggest a kind of gravity, and comedies don't necessarily" (Hahn 2012, 16). According to then Starz CEO and president Chris Albrecht, it's also more "economical, effort-wise" to focus on one drama rather than try to find two comedies to fill an hour slot

(Hahn 2012, 26). Dana Walden, co-chair and CEO of Fox, said that "Comedy lacks, just inherent in its the storytelling form, the kind of urgency that the big dramas have, that create a tendency in the audience to watch in a quicker period of time, which is how we're being judged" (Lynch 2015). Writing in *AdWeek*, Jason Lynch explains that audiences still want to watch comedies, but there's less immediate demand to do so. Combining this with the fact that networks often cancel series if they don't find ratings quickly enough, means that comedies have a difficult time staying on legacy television platforms (broadcast and cable) long enough to find a loyal viewership (Lynch 2015).

FX president and general manager John Landgraf also observes that it's difficult to find comedies that will attract a large number of viewers for general audience broadcast networks: "Taste in comedy is even more fractured than taste in drama. . . . . What moves people, what scares them, what engages them, is more consistent than what makes them laugh" (Berkshire 2015). With smaller, targeted audiences cable platforms created comedies like *Key and Peele* (Comedy Central 2012–15), *Inside Amy Schumer* (Comedy Central 2013–), and *It's Always Sunny in Philadelphia* (FX 2005–13; FXX 2013–), which were critical successes but only appealed to niche audiences (Lynch 2015). In this way, comedies could act as signature series that helped to brand platforms, particularly, as TV critic Matt Roush notes, "if it's the right kind of comedy or if it is stretching the boundaries of the genre of comedy" (Hahn 2012, 26). According to Mindy Kaling, "You have to be relevant, because if you're not getting the numbers you hope you get, it at least has to be the kind of show people are always talking about" (Lynch 2015).

Comedy, then, had potential to work as signature shows, particularly for those platforms with narrowly targeted audiences of younger, Millennial viewers. In a *New York Times* article titled "Viewing Habits of the Complex Millennial," Sarah Lyall describes the bid for the Millennial audience as "the great challenge for media companies. How do you appeal to people with such splintered, diffuse tastes, who crave novelty and individual experience and who do not want to be part of the herd?" (2016, B6). Tom Ascheim, then president of Freeform, explained, "Nothing gets all of them, but there are themes that do seem to matter" (Lyall 2016, B6). Shared conviction for many Millennials was the value of diversity and inclusion. Between 2000 and 2013, the "racial minority" population of the United States increased from 30 percent to 37 percent, showing industry insiders that "one thing is clear: television is not being broadcast to a nation of white boys" (Halloway 2014). One marketing executive noted, "They're the most diverse generation of adults in U.S. history, so that's a big issue for the entertainment industry" (Lyall 2016, B6). The emphasis on inclusion, therefore, became essential "as the search for diverse programming has gone from being a nice do-good to an economically logical pursuit" (Albiniak 2007, 26). A CBS executive observed, "The first thing out of people's mouths now is can we make it diverse" (Siegemund-Broka 2014). Television executives recognized that the country's shifting demographics meant that the tendency to tell stories written by White men about White men would no longer draw in the desired audiences. To maintain and gain audiences, television content needed to appeal to both previously marginalized viewers as well as the "cultured Millennials" (Lyall 2016, B1) who value inclusivity, authenticity, and originality. As Wesley Morris and James Poniewozik write,

> Representing more people in more ways is the right thing to do, and it has made TV better. But it happened largely because there was money in it. . . . TV audiences for everything are smaller now, which means networks aren't programming each show for an imagined audience of tens of millions of white people. On top of that, there are younger viewers for whom diversity—racial, religious, sexual—is their world. That audience wants authenticity; advertisers want that audience. (2016)

For some viewers, questions of authenticity and inclusivity countered the colorblind approach discussed in Chapter 1. A 2014 poll by MTV (using a national sample of 12–24-year-olds) found that Millennials "wanted a colorblind society and believed that 'never considering race would improve society'—while at the same time they also said 'embracing diversity and celebrating differences would make society better'" (Demby 2014). Programming that directly addressed topics of equity and inclusion could stand out—and comedy offered a safe way to explore these potentially transgressive subjects.

As many theorists have demonstrated, and many viewers have experienced, comedy can be a "comfortable" way to deal with ruptures and changes within society. Questions are raised and problems revealed only to be closed off by a joke that makes light of the situation. Furthermore, while comedy can create connections between people "defining them as a group of like-minded individuals" (Sands 2018, 16), it also "has often been used to define inside and outside groups, reinforcing an 'us versus them' mentality" (Sands 2018, 14). Comedy, then, has a progressive potential to expose problems within society and create connections between people as well as conservative tendencies to separate people into silos and shut down social concerns by brushing them aside with a joke.

Television comedy is no different. Analyses often link the genre and the traditional situation comedy style to its ideological qualities, as will be discussed further in Chapter 4. Sitcoms tend to be thirty-minute episodes (twenty-one minutes of content without commercials) in which familiar characters reenact similar (and presumably humorous) plots in recurring settings week after week. Sitcoms have also conventionally been seen to appeal to a broad, family audience. Traditional sitcom episodes are shot using multiple cameras on a set reminiscent of a theatrical stage. Often live audiences are used for the filming, and their laughter (combined with a recorded laugh track) is included in the soundtrack. Commenting on the familiar sitcom style, Brett Mills notes, "This stability has been seen as running parallel to a constancy in sitcom content, with the genre criticized for its simplistic use of stereotypes, outmoded representations and an apparent failure to engage with social or political developments" (2009, 63). As a result of these conventions, sitcoms often reinforce dominant ideas about family, gender, sexuality, class, and so on (Mills 2009, 64).

Even before the stylistic elements of the sitcom were fully formed, television comedy, George Lipsitz writes, was used by advertisers as "a vehicle for ideological legitimation of a fundamental revolution in economic, social and cultural life" (1990, 42). From the 1940s and into, at least, the 1970s, television family comedies essentially promoted consumerism as a means of solving problems within postwar nuclear families (Lipsitz 1990, 50). Yet, Lipsitz also explains that "while they unfailingly offered only individual solutions to problems, the mere act of exposing the contradictions of the nuclear family created the structural potential for oppositional reading by viewers" (1990, 57) and that "the same communications apparatus that presented consumerism as the heir to the moral legacy of the working class past also legitimized aspirations for happiness and community too grand to be satisfied by the lame realities of the commodity-centered world" (Lipsitz 1990, 73). Lipsitz's analysis recognizes that while the television comedy ultimately resolved problems by grounding the American family in traditionally conservative values—the primacy of the nuclear family, individual achievement, happiness through materialism, the equity of the American Dream—it first posited situations that threatened these values and opened them up for scrutiny.

Some classical sitcoms acknowledged sociocultural concerns and shifts, whether by mocking the military in *M*A*S*H* (CBS, 1972–83), examining the role of women in society in *The Mary Tyler Moore Show* (CBS, 1970–7), highlighting the intersection of race and poverty in *Good Times* (CBS 1974–9), or generating empathy with gay people in *Will & Grace* (NBC, 1998–2006). But the exploration of contemporary social issues truly proliferated as television faced growing competition from cable leading to the development of comedies that at different times were labeled "quality TV," "dramedy," and "narratively complex." For industrial reasons that will be discussed in greater detail below, comedies have increasingly taken on serious issues, allowing for programming that "hits the sweet spot by getting real, and rarely sacrificing a raw emotionally impactful moment for an easy laugh" (Landau 2018, 6).

The focus on personal trauma in TV comedies in the 2010s coincided with national traumas that included the murder of Trayvon Martin and the rise of the Black Lives Matter movement, the fallout of the Great Recession, and the Occupy Wall Street movement. Television comedy, as it did in the past, offered "a unique site for society to work through its most serious moments in unserious ways" (Scepanski 2021, 14). As Philip Scepanski writes,

> Because the genre follows a different set of rules than others, television comedy acts as a key component to the way mass media makes sense of American nationhood in relation to national traumas. It does so by acting as a forum for testing and defining the limits of expressible ideas, negotiating popular memory and history, and policing the boundaries of group identity. (2021, 3)

Concurrently, television continued to innovate, embracing more transgressive comedy that expanded the limits of acceptability.

Transgressive comedy has many definitions, but essentially it pushes the boundaries "around who or what audiences are invited to laugh at, what it is acceptable to joke about" (Bore 2017, 121). Moreover, transgressive humor can encourage a reassessment of social norms and assumptions. When it moves beyond the idea of "gross-out" jokes and body humor, transgressive comedy can probe ideological norms and conventional beliefs. Anshuman Mondal explains that "offensive" humor is rooted in power relationships and "satire, in particular, is a discourse of power and arguably the most politically performative of all aesthetic forms, whether it is wielded against dominant forces, groups and individuals, or on their behalf" (2018, 35). Comedy is an ideal framework through which to expose that which is often unspoken, acknowledging problems in a way that allows them to be recognized but also mitigated through humor. Kenneth Ladenburg, for example, examines how comedy can effectively uncover the racial power structure in that it "spotlights the contradictions and absurdities inherent in the framework of whiteness and exaggerates them to comedic effect" (2015, 862). Transgressive comedy, then, is not simply about crass wordplay or body humor, but it also carries the potential to question the ideological, social, and economic status quo.

In the wake of the Great Recession, growing social unrest, and a changing industrial ecosystem, some television comedies embraced the idea of the transgressive, using it to flesh out the repercussions of US trauma. As discussed above, traditional television comedy provided "a narrative and generic space in which subversive material can be introduced, yet safely contained through such techniques as offloading disruptive politics onto controversial and/or flawed characters or through the narrative structure of the situation comedy itself, which revolved around the restoration of (patriarchal) order and the status quo at the end of each episode" (Patrick 2017, 238). Contemporary television comedy demonstrated less concern with this hegemonic containment. Michael Tueth writes in 2016, that "while transgressive comedy has amused audiences in so many public places and occasions, it has finally entered the relative privacy of the home environment where it shows no signs of leaving" (2016, 258). For television, there may be no bigger taboo than the capitalist system on which it relies and which it shamelessly promulgates. Through storylines that don't, immediately or ultimately, reaffirm the contemporary ideals of the American Dream, some comedies raise questions and uncover ruptures and don't suture the social fabric back together with a joke or a reaffirming message. In contrast to the colorblindness demonstrated in tentpole dramas like *Arrow*, these series acknowledge the hierarchies that exist within the US system and question the equity of the meritocratic ideas behind the American Dream. The transgression within these comedies is a rejection of the Obama-era post-racist and post-feminist ideologies that try to paint social divisions as a thing of the past; a calling of attention to the very real bifurcations within society and the ways that they create an unequal playing field in the attempt to achieve the Dream.

Television comedies of the 2010s, particularly those that we'll discuss below as "signature shows," embraced alternatives to the traditional sitcom style and content that transformed the representation of the Dream. Transgressions of sitcom style accompanied transgressive ideas in what Billy Stevenson termed "postcomplex television." Complex television, as explained by Jason Mittell, blends episodic and serialized narrative structure to create an operational aesthetic that encourages viewers to "simultaneously care about the story and marvel at its telling" (2015, 46). Dramas such as *The Sopranos* and *Breaking Bad* and comedies like *Arrested Development* (Fox, 2003–6; Netflix, 2013–19) use clever narrative techniques (breaking of the fourth wall, nonlinear time, unclear framing, genre hybridity, etc.) to inspire awe within viewers. Postcomplex television, according to Stevenson, continues to use the narrative techniques that make complex television distinct, but now they are "folded into more conventional effects and used to disrupt the relation between serial and episodic experiences, rather than converging these elements into a narratively spectacular seamless whole" (2021, 80). In other words, postcomplex television modifies the mainstream US style by destabilizing the primacy of narrative clarity as well as the clarity of television formats. Stevenson highlights the work of Steven Shaviro who introduced the idea of post-continuity. Shaviro explains that (some) films have abandoned their reliance on continuity, which instead has been "fractured, devalued, fragmented, and reduced to incoherence" (2012).

While Shaviro's work focuses on how recent films, primarily action films, have weakened the priority of narrative continuity, Stevenson connects these ideas to television comedy in the post-Recession period. Post-continuity, the fragmentation of time and space, in the service of comedy offers a means of transgression that disrupts traditional expectations of the genre. At the same time, however, "the violation of continuity rules isn't foregrounded, and isn't in itself significant" (Shaviro 2012). Unlike the operational aesthetic employed by complex television series, post-continuity and postcomplex television don't engender, or ask for, aesthetic acknowledgment. Television comedies that embrace post-continuity simply ask viewers to accept the chaos. Transgressive narrative techniques, in these series, are not mobilized to elevate the genius of the showrunner or the cleverness of the viewer, but are presented as ordinary, thus foregrounding and generating a more fluid understanding of identity and identification in the series.

Lili Loofbourow argues that postcomplex television also eschews complex television's focus on antiheroes (2015, 20). Instead, these series demonstrate "a wild, roving narrative sympathy" in which "subjects that prestige shows have usually treated fatalistically—disintegrating social structures, the loss of family, broken bonds—are shown as occasions for resilience rather than resignation" (Loofbourow 2015, 20). Shows such as *Transparent* (Amazon, 2014–19), *Getting On* (HBO, 2013–15), and *Orange Is the New Black* (Netflix, 2013–19), comedies primarily helmed by women about women and/or other underrepresented groups, depict characters who demonstrate strength and compassion (Loofbourow 2015, 20). Differentiating these characters from the antiheroes that inhabited many of the complex dramas of the earlier 2000s, Loofbourow writes:

> The characters in these new shows are no less prone to self-pity than Tony or Walt, but the camera's roving inattention undercuts rather than dramatizes moments that in the older style would invite us to be moved or to selectively analyze (and exculpate) the protagonist at the expense of everyone else. That egalitarian affect is promiscuous protagonism's angle on the story of American decline. Everyone, regardless of race, class, gender or sexual orientation, is on the sinking ship together. We're just sinking at different rates. (2015, 21)

These series and their depictions of "stoicism, resourcefulness and even hope" convey sympathy and empathy for a range of characters in the face of shared national trauma (Loofbourow 2015, 21). Thematic and stylistic transgressions of television comedy norms contribute to these series' potential to reshape the conversation about merit and its rewards, particularly for groups traditionally excluded from the American Dream creating (story)worlds tentatively calling out for Chen's morality of grace.

Loofbourow's emphasis on the showrunner (creator/writer) as the source of the distinctiveness of these series aligns with the industry's ideas about how to generate diverse content. Platforms searched for writers from marginalized communities to give voice to the pain experienced on the outskirts of US society and, most often, to do so through comedy.[1] And the increasing acceptance that a television comedy doesn't have to be funny all the time creates opportunities. Jason Zinoman writes in *The New York Times*, "More often than at any time in the past, television comedy, particularly the non-network kind, is willing to sacrifice laughs in pursuit of more varied pleasures. It's part of what makes it such an unpredictable and exciting time for this genre" (2015, 1). This allowance also facilitates a more authentic and complex examination of trauma. According to Justin Simien, the executive producer of *Dear White People* (Netflix 2017–21), "Comedy does have a unique power . . . in that laughter can be so seductive. It allows us to think about and explore those forbidden and difficult little topics that we might not otherwise, by taking the pressure off a bit" (Broadnax 2018, 33). In these post-Recession signature comedies, shows designed to appeal to niche audiences and create more buzz than ratings, we see the potential for questions about the US meritocracy and its ability to bolster an American Dream traditionally venerated in television comedies. *Unbreakable Kimmy Schmidt* and *Atlanta* use the narrative and aesthetic possibilities afforded transgressive signature comedies targeted at more inclusive and empathetic audiences to reconsider the accessibility of the Dream for those whose historic marginalization in US society was only exacerbated by the economic breakdown of the Great Recession.

The Merit of Cute: *Unbreakable Kimmy Schmidt*

Unbreakable Kimmy Schmidt . . . has attracted a lot of attention for its treatment of post-apocalyptic cults. But that's not actually the most radical or unusual thing about it. Instead, it's that this weird, lively little show that has the audacity to tell a story about surviving sexual trauma, is a comedy, rather than a competitive exercise in how far and how fast television can descend into the gritty darkness.

Rosenberg, "A Sardonic Comedy with Bite" 2015

You get to live your life the way you want. That's the whole point of not being in a bunker. No one gets to tell you what to do.

"Kimmy Kisses a Boy!"

Unbreakable Kimmy Schmidt (UKS) was created by Tina Fey and Robert Carlock as a follow-up to their NBC hit *30 Rock*. In the opening scene of the series, twenty-nine-year-old Kimmy Schmidt is rescued from an underground bunker, along with three other women, where she was held for fifteen years after being kidnapped from her front yard by Reverend Richard Wayne Gary Wayne, the absurdly named leader of a religious doomsday cult. A comedy about child abduction, sexual assault, cults, and PTSD seems unlikely fare for a broadcast network, yet the show was ordered without a pilot and planned as a midseason replacement for NBC in 2015 (Streaming Service Bent 2014, 44). Early that year, however, the series moved to Netflix. According to Fey and then NBC Entertainment chairman Robert Greenblatt, the shift from NBC to Netflix was not due to the show's content but to improve the series' chances for success. As *UKS* prepared for broadcast in 2015, NBC, like all the broadcast networks at this time, was "flailing when it comes to comedy" (Worth Watching, Driven by Demand 2015, 1). In February 2015, Greenblatt acknowledged, "We are really challenged by the comedy brand that we're trying to build on this network," adding, "I didn't want to put Tina's show on and have it fail because we couldn't launch it with the right lead-in" (Lynch 2015). That the series was produced by NBC's sister studio Universal Television incentivized all involved to find it a good home (O'Connell 2015).

While NBC struggled with its comedy brand, Netflix was strengthening its market image with original series. Netflix announced high-profile, signature shows such as *Grace and Frankie, Bloodline,* and *Daredevil.* Central to Netflix's plan was that these programs offer viewers innovative content that would not work on legacy television. *UKS* was seen as meeting this requirement. Ted Sarandos, at the time Netflix's chief content officer, noted that it would be difficult to create a schedule around a show like *UKS,* but this was not an issue for a streaming service like Netflix (Weinstein 2015). He also remarked, "There are jokes in the show that would make a network executive squirm, and we embrace it" (Levin 2015).

Cindy Holland, Netflix's vice president of original content, who praised Fey and Carlock's "unique comic voice and sensibility," said that *UKS*' "offbeat premise, hilarious and rich characters and serialized storytelling' made it 'a perfect Netflix comedy series'" (Itzkoff 2014). More cynically, Julia Havas and Tanya Horeck observe that *UKS* "taps into current discourses about female toughness and believing women, which also help Netflix establish its 'woke' brand" (2022, 267). This feminist (or post-feminist) view of the show was supported by Tina Fey's existing brand image (Streaming Service Bent 2014, 44). Fey's previous hit, *30 Rock,* was considered quality TV, and, even if it was debated among some viewers, Fey held an esteemed position as a successful female showrunner who provided a strong creative voice for (White, upper-middle-class) women. The series also paired well with the viewing patterns taking shape around Netflix: repeat and binge viewing. One reviewer noted that "This is the sort of show that could benefit from multiple viewings because the jokes are so packed in you're sure to miss something while laughing" and "I can think of nothing better than sitting through all 13 episodes in a row on a rainy afternoon when you need something to live for" (Moylan, Unbreakable Kimmy Schmidt 2015). For all these reasons, Netflix saw potential for *UKS* to generate critical acclaim and audience buzz as a signature series. The platform immediately ordered two thirteen-episode seasons (Streaming Service Bent 2014, 44).

The transgressive nature of *UKS* is apparent from its first episode, setting up the plot centered around Kimmy Schmidt's quest for freedom and independence as she pursues the American Dream that was denied her when she was taken from her front yard in Indiana when she was fifteen. The series steadfastly doesn't focus on Kimmy's time in the bunker. Within the first minute of the series, the women are rescued and emerge into a lush, green field, surprised to realize that the world had not been, as they had been told by the reverend, destroyed in an apocalypse brought about by the stupidity of women. Very quickly, news coverage of the rescue morphs into an energetic autotuned theme song that praises women for being "strong as hell." Within the first two minutes of the episode, the "mole women," as they are dubbed by the media, are in New York City being interviewed by Matt Lauer on *The Today Show*, a cameo that does not hold up well in the aftermath of Lauer's own sexual assault scandal.[2] Following the interview, Kimmy decides to distance herself from her past and a future in which she is perpetually seen as a victim by moving to New York City. In the tradition of the American Dream, Kimmy chooses to reinvent herself. She quickly finds a job as a nanny for the young son of the wealthy Jacqueline Voorhees and a place to live with her soon-to-be-friend Titus Andromedon, a jaded and cynical gay, Black man who moved to New York to become an actor.

Much has been written about the series' problematic representations of race, particularly the decision to cast White actress Jane Krakowski as Jacqueline, a character revealed to be a white-passing Native American woman who uses hair dye and contact lenses to pass as a blond, blue-eyed, blue-blooded trophy wife. The series also mobilizes stereotypes, and in some cases comments on them, in its depiction of Titus as well as Kimmy's Vietnamese friend/boyfriend, Dong.[3] While this discussion, which focuses on the first season of *UKS*, considers the series' representations of "otherness," here I emphasize the ways that this post-Recession signature show imagines the American Dream for its victimized White, female main character through the lens of trauma and transgression. Like the program's depictions of gender and race, which have been both celebrated as progressive and critiqued as ignorant, the series' conceptualizations of opportunity, equity, and fairness in the purportedly meritocratic US society embodies the conflict between progressive and conservative tendencies discussed above in relation to television comedies, as it gestures toward oppositional commentary, yet still retreats to more traditional ideas.

This duality can be seen in the show's stylistic qualities. While *UKS* is similar in some ways to more "complex" comedies like *Arrested Development* and *The Office* in that it is shot in single-camera style and doesn't include a laugh track, *UKS* also adheres to some of the traditional generic conventions of television comedy. Each episode is riddled with jokes centering around a particular "situation" or two (the well-known A plot and B plot structure of a sitcom), which is, somehow, resolved by the end of the episode. And, while some of the episodes in the first season that were edited after the move to Netflix run a bit longer than a traditional broadcast length, all fall close to the thirty-minute time frame established for comedies (Bauder 2015). As one reviewer observes, "beyond its dark premise, 'Kimmy' fits the familiar aspirational mold of comedies like 'The Mary Tyler Moore Show' or, reaching way back, 'That Girl'" (Pennington 2015, G23). Like these older shows, *UKS* centers on a main character who is incredibly (almost pathologically) likable. Most reviewers agreed with the sentiment that "we like and root for the character and soon find ourselves believing that the world will be a better place as long as Kimmy Schmidt remains unbreakable" (Wiegand 2015, A9). Through her ebullient support of those around her, as Jack Seale writes, Kimmy

> becomes a magic friend we should all strive to be a bit more like, starting with her perky spring wardrobe full of happy lemon cardigans, hilarious fuchsia trousers and cute floral minis. More profoundly, her efforts not to be recognized as "one of the mole women" caricature the fear everyone has of Being Found Out, and the struggle not to be weighed down by bad stuff in your past. (2015)

In their initial reviews of the series, critics focused on the buoyant tenor of the show, writing, for example, that "[lead actress] Kemper's midwestern enthusiasm and naturally upbeat attitude keep Kimmy from being a sad character, even when the worst things happen to her" (Pennington 2015); "Kimmy is a grinning optimist, self-assured to the point that she turns others' insults into compliments and whose cluelessness is balanced by an iron core, an absolute unwillingness to let any perceived flaw stop her" (Berry 2015, B1) and, ranking *UKS* as one of the 2015's "most culturally relevant shows," Emily Morris writes that Kimmy's "refusal to settle into the role of the traumatized victim . . . reflects emergent survivor culture. This shift aligns with the strain of feminism taking hold in pop culture, which emphasizes personal narratives of female empowerment and refusal of defeat at the hand of the patriarchy" (2016, 31). Throughout the season, for example, Kimmy, shares the tricks she created—such as persistent smiling; jumping up and down while yelling, "I'm not really here"; or repeatedly counting to ten because a "person can survive anything for ten seconds"—that allowed her to endure what some may consider an unendurable trauma. Presenting these tactics as ridiculous and comical lightens the reality of what Kimmy suffered and presents Kimmy as an empowered survivor. Charity Fox writes, "*UKS* encourages audiences to see survivors as the centers of their own stories rather than as traumatized players in the abuser's story. Because, ultimately, *UKS* argues and demonstrates that 'females are strong as hell'" (2019).

While *UKS* may mobilize some sitcom conventions, including Kimmy's depiction as an upbeat, character, the series also relies on transgressive, cringe comedy that centers around the trauma at the center of the show, Kimmy's abduction, and various characters' attempts to chase their dreams in what is often a cruel and difficult world. Alyssa Rosenberg observes that what's most radical about *UKS* is "that this weird, lively little show that has the audacity to tell a story about surviving sexual trauma, is a comedy, rather than a competitive exercise in how far and how fast television can descend into the gritty darkness" ("A Sardonic Comedy with Bite" 2015). According to Havas and Horeck, the series' prestige emerges from the dichotomy between its content (the aftermath of abduction and sexual trauma) and how it is represented (as an upbeat, often campy comedy) (2022, 255). Fox writes that the series uses "the lightness of camp to place viewers in an unexpected relationship with the dark subject of captivity" (2019). For example, the third episode opens with Kimmy returning to her apartment wearing a pink Disney-princess dress, accompanied by a Disney-style prince. They are laughing about the fun they had at the "king's ball." In this dream, Kimmy is clearly playing out some adolescent Disney-movie-based fantasy date. She excuses herself to slip into something more "comfy-womfy," and once in her room, the camera closes in on Kimmy's face as she begins to panic. We see that she is back in the bunker. As she pulls on the door struggling to get back to her dream date, we cut to Kimmy straddling a sleeping Titus, choking him. After pushing Kimmy off him, Titus quips, "this isn't the Chinatown bus—you can't just choke someone who's sleeping" ("Kimmy Goes on a Date!"). The juxtaposition of the excess of Kimmy's dream with the cynical joke about New York lightens the grounding of the entire incident in Kimmy's PTSD, offering both a humorous moment and a deeper understanding of Kimmy's anxiety (Figure 7).

In *UKS*, trauma doesn't initiate a dramatic exploration of recovery and survival. While Kimmy is clearly plagued by fear and she acknowledges that she experienced "weird sex stuff" in the bunker, the show never describes or depicts scenes of sexual trauma and doesn't even use the word "rape" until season three. Rather, we are asked to focus on Kimmy's meritorious traits as the series only provides "memories of resilience in the bunker that Kimmy curates for herself, which ultimately challenges viewers' expectations of the captivity narrative genre" (Fox 2019). Flashbacks to the bunker include scenes of Kimmy challenging the reverend or helping the other women by, for example, adjudicating disputes or boosting their spirits with her boundless cheerfulness. The choice not to focus on Kimmy's trauma—the abduction that took her independence, safety, freedom,

Figure 7 Kimmy dreams of a perfect date that ends with her back in the bunker in "Kimmy Goes on a Date!" *Unbreakable Kimmy Schmidt* © Universal Television 2015–19.

equality—but to center on the innate merit that allowed her to survive during and after her captivity shapes our understanding of Kimmy. We are discouraged from seeing her as a victim, but, as she was described in the show's numerous rave reviews, resilient, optimistic, hopeful, and caring.

Kimmy's goodness is a shining light in a world that is often painted with a dark cynicism. While the New York City in *UKS* may be brightly lit and decorated with vibrant colors, it is not always a kind place. People frequently behave in selfish and corrupt ways. Kimmy's wealthy boyfriend Logan, depicted as narcissistic and spoiled, reports her friend Dong to immigration because he sees Dong as a rival for Kimmy's affections. The teacher assigned to Kimmy's GED class sabotages his students' learning so that he will be suspended (with pay). In an oft-cited episode, Titus discovers that he is treated better while costumed as a werewolf than when he navigates the world as a Black man. Kimmy may see the world through rose-colored glasses, but *UKS* does not. Not all people are meritorious. Nevertheless, except for the reverend and Logan, the two White men who victimize marginalized people, most characters are afforded grace as they try to cope in a complicated world that sometimes requires reinvention. Jacqueline's teenage stepdaughter, Xanthippe, takes an instant dislike to Kimmy, who refuses to be impressed by or afraid of the teen's privilege and power. Xan tries to discover why Kimmy, who has kept her identity as a mole woman secret, is so befuddled by the contemporary world. Jacqueline chastises Xan, "Her past doesn't matter. People come to New York and start new lives, and it gets complicated. And you, of all people, don't get to judge her. Your greatest accomplishment in life is pulling off that lipstick. Which you have to let me borrow; it looks awesome. Now, take your spoiled ass upstairs and go to your rooms" ("Kimmy Goes on a Date!"). The right to start over, central to the American Dream, is essential in *UKS*, as all the main characters attempt to define and redefine themselves. Moreover, *UKS* suggests that individuals have the right to this self-determination without judgment. Kimmy, a "kind and thoughtful friend who understands the seclusion of being 'different'" (Setiaki and Destari 2019, 108), believes everyone deserves a second chance and the opportunity to live their lives as they see fit. While the series finds humor in Dong's decision to marry a much older woman to stay in the US, Kimmy doesn't judge him for it and supports his pursuit of the life he wants. Kimmy also comes to accept her friend and fellow-assault victim Cyndee's choice to use her fame as a mole woman to create the life that she wants. Kimmy is initially critical of Cyndee's willingness to accept goods, services, friendship/love, given out of pity. But she eventually concludes, "You get to live your life the way you want. That's the whole point of not being in a bunker. No one gets to tell you what to do" ("Kimmy Kisses a Boy!").

Kimmy, as we see, affords her friends wisdom and grace as they navigate their lives and determine what's important to them, encouraging them to pursue their dreams. At the same time, she herself only survives her trauma and is allowed the opportunity of reinvention by becoming a paragon of optimism, strength, kindness, and resilience; qualities intertwined with conventional feminine stereotypes. Although Stephanie Patrick writes, "the show uses comedy—more specifically, the ironic rendering of Kimmy as an otherwise happy, strong and 'unbreakable' survivor—to criticize contemporary gender relations in America" (2021, 31), Kimmy still takes on the traditionally gendered role of caregiver. She literally works as a carer for Jacqueline's young son, picking him up from school and planning his birthday party. And she also nurtures her new friends, as she did in the bunker, offering them life advice and serving as their cheerleader. Kimmy repeatedly encourages Titus as he pursues his failing acting career. At the end of the first episode, standing in the middle of Time Square, she tells him,

> Life beats you up, Titus. It doesn't matter if you get tooken by a cult or you've been rejected over and over again at auditions. . . . You can either curl up in a

ball and die, like we thought Cyndee did that time, or you can stand up and say, "We're different. We're the strong ones, and you can't break us." ("Kimmy Goes Outside!")

She also pushes Jacqueline to divorce her cold and absent husband, accompanying her to the meeting with her attorney, telling her, "You're stronger than you think" ("Kimmy Is Bad at Math!"). Kimmy encourages Jacqueline to redefine her American Dream to emphasize self-determination and self-respect over material goods. Despite her own troubles and traumas, Kimmy seemingly enjoys supporting and helping others, illustrating the vast extent of merit, and possibly her acceptance of a traditional female role, that makes her deserving of her American Dream.

The show's emphasis on worthiness and resilience reinscribes the myth of the meritocracy by portraying a world in which traumas are overcome by and success achieved by those who have the strength and determination to work hard and persevere. Jorie Lagerwey, Julia Leyda, and Diane Negra argue that, because of the economic precarity resulting from the Great Recession, a group of television shows emerged that reflected an understanding of the struggle faced by women within the neoliberal order and focused on female empowerment within this system. One result of the coexistence of feminism and financial insecurity is the reconfiguration of female empowerment as a "neoliberal, individualized female overcoming" (Lagerwey, Leyda and Negra 2016). They write, "We identify female resilience as a particular dynamic of the post-recession period and argue that its depiction becomes an animating principle across a range of newly celebrated female-centered texts" (Lagerwey, Leyda and Negra 2016). Television programs mobilized resilience to demonstrate "adaptability and competence in the face of precarity" as a means by which women navigate the world (Lagerwey, Leyda and Negra 2016). Lagerwey et al note that women in these series don't attempt to change the system but learn to work within it by controlling their emotions and focusing on their own success. In many ways, *UKS* fits in with these shows as it celebrates Kimmy's desire to work hard as a nanny, as a GED student, and as a friend to overcome her past.

Kimmy's steely determination is softened by her childish innocence, which sparks much of the show's humor and endears her to audiences. Brian Moylan writes in *The Guardian*, "Most of the comedy comes from the fact that Kimmy doesn't know anything about the modern world, and what she does know is incorrect, but she states with kind the pluck and sincerity [*sic*] that makes you wish she was right. This is a girl who wears light-up sneakers and doesn't say she was kidnapped but 'tooken'" (California Streaming 2015).[4] The show often depicts Kimmy's naivete as silly. David Hinckley writes, "Kimmy's cheerfulness can border on the irrational. It is, after all, a sitcom" (2015, 82). Writing in *The Toronto Star*, Heather Mallick takes this idea further, seeing Kimmy as a "reflection of national cluelessness" in a show that is "as devastating an attack on childishness as I have ever seen" (2015, A19). Cáit Neylon argues that Kimmy's childishness reframed as cuteness is actually "a weapon deployed in the name of resilience in precarious times," a reaction to her trauma being used to avoid being abducted again (2022, 14). Kimmy's cuteness, Neylon explains, generates compassion among the audience and other characters, and encourages people to want to help her (Neylon 2022, 10). Cuteness, in other words, is a strategy that Kimmy mobilizes to help her navigate this new, confusing, and dangerous world while remaining nonthreatening to the more powerful people around her. When Kimmy is catcalled by a construction worker, she turns to him with a smile and tells him how much she likes his yellow construction hat because it's her favorite color. The man takes Kimmy's open and friendly response as a maneuver meant to make him feel guilty and he turns from a threatening character to one who acknowledges his toxic masculinity and even questions the foundation of capitalism that has him working to build "another bank." Kimmy's bubbly innocence, her cuteness, disarms those around her, protecting her and reinforcing her independence, even if it requires that she play the part of the plucky caregiver who is not held back by the traumas of her past.

In its depiction of the American Dream for women, particularly a woman marked by trauma, *UKS* ultimately both reinscribes the meritocracy but also raises questions about equality of opportunity. Economic success does not seem possible for a woman if she does not want to marry into it (as did Jacqueline) or capitalize on her past (as we see with Cyndee) (Patrick 2017, 245). While Kimmy begins the series with a backpack full of cash donated by the public to help the mole women, she quickly loses that money due to her naiveté (she leaves the bag on the floor while dancing at a club). But Kimmy is not interested in money for its own sake; this is not central to her Dream. Kimmy's American Dream is simple (or as Titus would say, "basic"): she wants a place to live, a job, and a GED. In this way, *UKS* brings Kimmy "problematically back into alliance with postfeminist, neoliberal values of individualism" (Patrick 2017, 246).

The yearning for a home, for example, a central component of the American Dream, is scaled down for Kimmy as she searches for the safety and security afforded by a home. In the pilot episode, Kimmy observes that "the worst thing that ever happened to me happened in my own front yard," establishing her rural Indiana home as an unsafe place connected to her trauma. For the next fifteen years, Kimmy's home was the underground bunker, another unsafe place in which she was sexually assaulted. Part of Kimmy establishing her own life in New York involves her finding a place to live, and she is overjoyed when she moves into a shared basement apartment that Hinckley in the *NY Daily News* describes as "just slightly larger than a bed." He writes, "It could be used in a film about solitary confinement in a maximum-security prison, right down to the single tiny window somewhere above eye level . . . Yet Kimmy looks around and chirps, 'Oh, it's got a window!' with a level of enthusiasm only credible from someone who has been locked underground for the previous 15 years" (Hinckley 2015, 29). Kimmy is happy about this place because it's her own, but it's also indicative of her relentlessly hopeful and resilient personality, both of which are symptoms of her trauma. Kimmy accepts this apartment because it represents her freedom and reinvention. She earns her place by being a caring, hard-working, positive person who could not be broken by her tragic life experiences. Kimmy's innate merit allows her to find a home, but it's one that is much scaled down from the middle-class households that shelters traditional sitcom families pursuing the American Dream.

As a television comedy, *Unbreakable Kimmy Schmidt* embodies many of the contradictions of the genre, an inconsistency also seen in the conflicted scholarly work on the series—it empowers (White) women and it reinforces neoliberal post-feminist ideas; it offers complex characterizations of trauma victims and it trades on stereotypes of marginalized groups. As Patrick writes, the show "walked a fine line between feminist and post-feminist politics, often celebrating individualist discourses of 'doing the right thing' and perseverance, over solidarity and structural change" (2021, 32). The American meritocracy is alive and well in *Unbreakable Kimmy Schmidt*, in which women overcome their trauma and shake off their marginalization through resilience and perky optimism. Yet, the show also presents sexual assault victims as survivors and offers the potential for grace despite character flaws. In *UKS* (almost) all people deserve the opportunity to chase their Dream, particularly if they do not exploit those with fewer resources to get more and, most importantly, are willing to settle for less. In the end, *UKS* suggests that those searching for the American Dream would do well to scale back their hopes and accept that "the solution . . . is not dismantling or altering the system to ensure it better fits the needs of the marginalized, but the much less radical message of finding individual ways to 'make it work' for you" (Patrick 2017, 246). In its depiction of the American

Dream, *UKS*, like other television comedies before it, raises questions while shutting them down with jokes, reinforces hegemonic ideas while proposing oppositional positions, potentially leaving ideas lingering in the back of our minds about the opportunities available for today's young women and what they must do/who they must be to achieve their American Dream.

The Merit of Acceptance: *Atlanta*

Many viewers, of all races, are hungry for more shows that can weave outrage and narrative and everyday life together as effortlessly as this one does.

Steuver 2016, 12

I'm poor, Darius. And poor people don't have time for investments because poor people are too busy trying not to be poor, okay? I need to eat today not in September.

"The Streisand Effect"

Like *UKS*, *Atlanta*, Donald Glover's series about four Black people living in the titular city, speaks from a perspective that aligns with its creator. Yet, *Atlanta* was also celebrated for its ability to speak to a range of viewers. This discussion will home in on the first season of the series to consider how Glover's authentic voice, made available in FX's search for a signature show, linked television comedy, transgression, and trauma to offer its own take on the American Dream that can, like in *Unbreakable Kimmy Schmidt*, be seen as both innovative and conventional in its ideologies.

At the age of twenty-three, Glover was hired by NBC to write for Tina Fey and Robert Carlock's *30 Rock* during the show's first three seasons (2006–9). Glover later revealed he was hired as part of NBC's diversity initiative, which contributed to the imposter syndrome he felt as a writer for the series (Green 2023). Fey, nevertheless, served as a mentor to Glover, who said, "Tina Fey took me under her wing and really pushed me to find my own voice" (Blair 2009, A12). To do this, he left *30 Rock* and worked on the NBC series *Community* and found success as rapper Childish Gambino. Glover, like Fey, cultivated a brand image, appealing to a young fan base that appreciated quirky and innovative content. This brand also caught the attention of the FX Network as it was solidifying its own brand.

In the mid-2010s, FX Networks was looking to differentiate FX and FXX. John Landgraf, then president and general manager of FX Networks, was critical of the flood of television content, proposing that FX would make fewer shows in a "nonindustrial, extremely personal way" (Elber 2016, E8). In keeping with the issues of network branding discussed in the previous chapter, Landgraf explains in an interview,

> "For FX to be relevant to people as a brand—for there to be a reason for people to continue to pay attention to what we do and seek us out—we have to give them an experience they just can't get somewhere else," he says. "You have to continually replenish your brand equity." And that requires big swings like The People v. O.J. Simpson and Atlanta. "You can't just be different," he says. "You have to be different and good." (Lynch 2016)

Additionally, in 2015, a Directors Guild of America report found that in the 2014–15 season, only 12 percent of television directors were women or people of color, and FX had the worst record of all the networks (N. Smith 2016). Landgraf consciously wanted to shift the culture, scheduling *Atlanta* and the female-led *Better Things* (FX, 2016–22) for the 2016 season. Remarking on what many considered a failed programming decision, Landgraf said,

> I think back to making Damages instead of Breaking Bad. That was not the right decision from a programming standpoint; but it was the right decision in the sense that we aspired to be more than white-male antiheroes. . . . We were going to try to be a beacon of quality for everyone. That turned out to be where television was going, and we made the right sacrifices to be on that right trend. (Goldberg 2016)

FX, then, was invested in finding shows that could be seen as quality and also offer a range of voices, making Atlanta an ideal signature show for the network.

In October 2015, after seeing the pilot, FX ordered ten episodes of *Atlanta* (Littleton 2015). Although it became one of the most anticipated series of the season (Rhone 2016, 2D), like most signature shows, *Atlanta* was not expected to pull in a mass audience (T. Goodman 2016, 63). The program, however, did prove a resounding cable success. The show premiered on September 6, 2016, airing two episodes back-to-back. With three million viewers in Live+3 ratings, the first episode drew in the largest viewership for an FX premiere since *Wilfred* (FX, 2011–13; FXX 2014) in 2011 (Umstead 2016). Among the 18–49-year-old demographic, it was the best premiere of any basic cable prime-time scripted show in three years and the most watched new comedy with the 18–49-year-old audience since April 2014 (Redfearn 2016). The series also gained a lot of buzz on social media, with #AtlantaFX trending while the show aired on Tuesday nights (Jurgensen 2016, D5). As FX's highest rated comedy (Lynch 2016), *Atlanta* was renewed for another season after its first three episodes aired (Redfearn 2016). The series connected with FX's younger viewers and helped to reinforce the platform's quality brand when it was nominated for six Emmy Awards for its first season (with two wins, both for Glover for best director and best actor in a comedy). The program also won a Peabody Award "for its seamless blend of vibrant character study and rich sociopolitical commentary in a detailed and textured exploration of a Southern city" (Peabody Awards 2016). In May 2017, FX announced that Hulu would become the streaming home of *Atlanta*, with the first season becoming available before the second season premiere to allow new viewers to catch up (Otterson 2017).

Atlanta was positioned as a quality series in that it avoids common tropes of television comedy and upends expectations regarding the representations of Black Americans on television. The series revolves around Earnest (Earn), a poor, young Black man who is on a "one-year break" from Princeton that has extended into its third year. In the first episode, Earn learns that his cousin Alfred is gaining traction in the Atlanta rap scene as Paper Boi and decides that he wants to be his manager. The series focuses on Earn, Alfred, Alfred's friend Darius, and Vanessa (Van), the mother of Earn's three-year-old daughter with whom Earn has an uncommitted romantic relationship. While *Atlanta* can be, and has been, described as being about two men trying to "make it" in Atlanta's rap scene or about a young man trying to find himself or about four young Black people trying to survive poverty and violence in Atlanta, all these descriptions are both accurate and completely inadequate. The series' style and narrative eschew essentialist depictions of Black life, revealing "black subjectivity beyond how it is merely imagined from the outside to how it is complexly lived on the inside" (Guerrero 2020, 16). The nuanced picture of urban Black life, presented in stylistically innovative ways, distinguishes this comedy, which acknowledges, but isn't about, the structural racism and inequality that threaten the security, individual achievement, and freedom promised by the American Dream. At the same time, like *Unbreakable Kimmy Schmidt*, *Atlanta* also falls back on some conventional characterizations that reinforce the meritocracy and neoliberal notions that life after the Recession can be navigated through hard work and resilience.

As a signature series created by Donald Glover, *Atlanta* was expected to provide an authentic voice of Black America. So, this show was circumscribed not only by tropes of television comedy but also expectations regarding the representations of Black Americans on television, particularly in comedies. Much research has focused on the problematic depictions of Black Americans on mainstream US television. Herman Gray, for example, demonstrates how television offers two very different portrayals of poor and middle-class Black Americans. Looking at non-fiction programming from the 1980s, Gray notes that depictions of poor Black people as lacking "family values," violent, lazy, and drug addicts, "appeal to and contribute to the notion of the black poor as menacing and threatening, especially to members of the white middle class" (1989, 385). Meanwhile, television also offers representations of the "idealized middle class black Americans" who "confirm a middle class utopian imagination of racial pluralism" (Gray 1989, 378) as seen in sitcoms like *The Cosby Show* (NBC, 1984–92), *Family Matters* (NBC, 1982–9), *Sister, Sister* (ABC, 1994–5; The WB, 1995–9), and many other comedies of the 1980s and 1990s.[5] Haggins demonstrates that even series that depict "respectable," middle-class Black characters reflect the instability felt within marginalized communities. Comparing *The Cosby Show* to *Family Ties* (NBC, 1982–9) and *Living Single* (FOX, 1993–8) to *Friends* (NBC, 1994–2004), Haggins argues that despite their similarities, the series with Black casts depict a different underlying outlook in which success can be fleeting and hard work never ends (1999, 31–4). Importantly, as David Stamps writes, these series that tell us "that everyone can succeed if they work hard dismisses the truth that many lack access to education, wealth accumulation, and/or community support" (2017, 407). And, more recently, Racquel Gates questions the assumptions surrounding the discourse of positive and negative representations that has surrounded many analyses of Black representation on US television. Gates writes that "Conventional uses of 'positive' and 'negative' support politics of respectability and close off possibilities for multilayered conceptions of and performances of identity. At their worst, to invoke these categories uncritically reinforces racist ideologies that use discourses of black exceptionalism to further marginalize black behaviors and people that deviate from white, middle-class, heterosexual norms" (2018, 12).

More considered views of these systemic issues became fodder for television in the post-Recession industrial and socioeconomic context discussed above. The ideals of post-racism that undergirded calls for a colorblind society proved murky. The election of President Obama ushered in a general sigh of relief as many (primarily White) people imagined a world in which skin color no longer impacted society or individuals. A Black president, it was imagined, demonstrated that our society provided equal opportunities for all, and that the meritocracy was alive and well; clearly, anyone could succeed if they worked hard enough, regardless of race. However, the murder of Trayvon Martin in 2012 followed by the acquittal of his killer, the string of other deaths of Black men by police and "scared" (White) citizens, the arrest of Harvard professor Henry Louis Gates at his own home, the rise of the Black Lives Matter Movement, and the candidacy and election of Donald Trump along with the barrage of hate that he encouraged, exposed the deep divide that one Black president could not repair.

For Black Americans, the economic precarity of the Great Recession, which already disproportionately affected them, was exacerbated by continued systemic racism and life-threatening challenges to their safety. While mainstream television may have continued to provide superficial diversity, the long tradition of transgressive comedy, grew within the Black community and, thanks to the internet, became more visible. As Terrence Tucker explains, comic rage within Black culture gives voice to anger, a call for change, and humor; it expresses a "desire to tear normative values to tatters" (2018). Lisa Guerrero connects comic rage to trauma, observing that "contemporary black satire is more deliberate about focusing on the damaging toll to the black psyche inflicted by the unrelenting conditions of anger, sadness, and protest" (2020, 8). Guerrero writes that Black satire looks to upend the typical depictions in which Black people are seen as enduring a racialized world that is not of their own making, allowing a Black subjectivity in which Black Americans become the makers of the meaning not the "meaning that is made" (2020, 12). The potential is a more authentic depiction of Black American experiences that, as Tucker says of comic rage, although it may be "expressed in front of white audiences, it is not concerned with appealing to white audiences" (2018).

Making manifest the complexity of Black subjectivity, *Atlanta* established an audience for a series about Black trauma. Yet, *Atlanta*'s success with White and Black viewers speaks to the show's relevance in this sociocultural moment. Talking to the Television Critics Association, Glover said, "The thesis with the show was kind of to show people how it felt to be black. . . . You can't really write that down; you kind of have to feel it. So, the tonal aspect was really important to me" (Friedlander 2017, 21). *Atlanta* is a "love letter to black people and black culture" (Stephen 2018, 7), speaking to people who rarely see themselves represented on television in genuine ways. And the series also exposes White viewers to a more nuanced view of Black life. As Glover explains, "I wanted to show white people, you don't know everything about black culture" (Browne 2016). To appeal to both of these audiences, *Atlanta* disregarded many conventions of television and corresponding thematic ideologies.

From the start, *Atlanta* differed from traditional television in its production practices. To tell a new, authentic story, the series employed novice creators. As Stephen Glover, Donald Glover's brother and a writer on the show, explains, "This never happens. Five writers all black, all first time. First-time director, first-time showrunner" (Bakare 2016). Hiro Murai, for example, a Japanese man who directed most of the show's episodes, had previously been a music video director and, at the start of the show, didn't have experience with scripted television. Additionally, instead of working out of a conference room at a studio, the writers "gathered in a Hollywood Hills house they dubbed 'the factory.' Daylight hours were devoted to 'Atlanta' with long discussions transcribed on a laptop; at night the focus would shift to workshopping songs for Childish Gambino and other artists" (Jurgensen 2016, D5). This new group of television artists employed a range of stylistic strategies that corresponded to the postcomplex television style. Unlike most mainstream US series, *Atlanta* doesn't foreground narrative clarity for the viewer. Glover acknowledges, "Television shows are like novels now. You've just got to invest in them. So, like, I feel like the tone of this . . . it's going to take time for people to understand what's going on, which I think is a good thing" (Littleton, Donald Glover Celebrates 2016). Within the first season, there are episodes that begin in media res (including the pilot), flashbacks that aren't signaled, jokes that aren't explained, and a stand-alone parody episode (the much discussed "BAN" episode that spoofs a Black news roundtable show complete with embedded commercials). The pilot episode begins as the three male main characters get into an altercation with a man and a woman in a convenience store parking lot. Viewers don't know who any of the characters are or what causes the fight that escalates to Alfred holding a gun to another (armed) man's chest. The scene ends in a bird's-eye long shot in which we see the characters standing in the parking lot. There's a flash and the sound of a gunshot, but the camera is not close enough to show viewers who was shot by whom. After fading to black, the opening credits play. The next scene begins with a medium close-up of Earn, whom we recognize from the opening scene, lying in bed listening to music as a woman's arm flings out and hits him in the face. The previous fight scene isn't explained, and viewers don't know where it exists in the timeline until the end of the episode. There is also no exposition that explains Earn and Van's relationship. Rather, viewers must figure it out as the characters talk ("The Big Bang").

This refusal to center the audience's narrative comprehension is compounded by the show's somewhat episodic nature in which episodes often mobilize different styles ranging from satire to the absurd not just between but within individual episodes. Brian Tyree Henry, who plays Alfred/Paper Boi, says, "Perceptions really do define what our realities are. What we're hoping to do with *Atlanta* is to really shatter that. To shatter it completely wide open. To go from the furthest lane of absurdity to the furthest lane of reality and make them blend" (Grant 2016). Within a single episode, a naturalistic storyline can butt up against the surreal or absurd. Even within the opening scene, as Alfred amps up and Earn tries to de-escalate the situation, Darius talks about déjà vu and fixates on a nearby dog. The focus on Darius and the dog adds a sense of confusion and incongruity to the scene that reverberates throughout the series. Another example can be seen in the "The Club." Within the episode, references are made to, and jokes are made about, a rap artist who claims to have an invisible car. At the end of the episode, as Earn and Alfred talk outside of a club, we see them react to an off-screen situation that is followed by the sound of gunfire. As people run for cover, we hear a car and see people clearly being hit by what can only be an invisible car. In the midst of Earn and Alfred's ordinary conversation, *Atlanta* interjects both violence and the surreal to keep viewers off balance.

This dream-like tone of the series, in which anything could happen at any moment, fits with Glover's description of the series as "Twin Peaks with rappers" (Stanhope 2016). Bijan Stephen writes, "Hiro Murai, who's directed most of the episodes, does an excellent job of presenting the show's most surreal aspects straight. The effect is similar to the way the logic of dreams makes perfect sense while asleep; it only breaks down when you stop to think about the events and the order in which they occur" (2018, 10). In *Atlanta*, the streets can be populated by people dressed in various cow costumes, explained by one person telling Earn that "it's free chicken sandwich day" ("The Jacket"). Like in a dream, this motivation sort of explains why people are dressed up, but in a way that, under scrutiny, is totally inadequate. Like a student wearing white face at Van's school ("Value"), the cow costumes are narratively motivated but not in a way that offers clear resolution for the lingering confusion (Figure 8).

Placed within this uncertain and volatile world, the characters in *Atlanta* also grapple to maintain independence and self-determination (unlike Oliver

Figure 8 Earn walks past people in cow costumes celebrating "free chicken sandwich day" in "The Jacket." *Atlanta* © FX Productions 2016–22.

Queen in *Arrow* and even Matt Murdock in *Daredevil* discussed in Chapter 1). Throughout the first season, Alfred struggles with his persona as rapper Paper Boi. He explains that he's a rapper because "I have to. I scare people at ATMs, boy. So, I have to rap. I mean that's what rap is; making the best out of a bad situation" ("The Streisand Effect"). In a later episode, Alfred gets into a fight with a badly behaved Black Justin Bieber at a youth outreach basketball game (in *Atlanta's* universe, Justin Bieber is, inexplicably, a Black man, played by a Black actor). After the altercation, Alfred tells a (White) reporter that she has the wrong idea about him, and he'd like to do an interview so she can get to know the "real me." She responds, "Listen, I want to give you some advice. Play your part. People don't want Justin to be the asshole. They want you to be the asshole. You're a rapper, that's your job" ("Nobody Beat the Biebs"). Although Alfred is gaining some success, there's only so much that he can do to shape what he attains; the parameters of who he can be professionally are established by outside forces that he does not control.

Glover was adamant, though, that the series not focus on inequality and racial injustice as its subject matter, saying, "I never wanted this shit to be important. I never wanted this show to be about diversity; all that shit is wack to me" (Browne 2016). Glover may not have intended for *Atlanta* to talk explicitly about diversity, but it does depict life as lived in the margins of US society. As Henry says, "You can call it a black show, a hip-hop show, you can call it this or whatever you want, a hip-hop show, but I think it's going to surprise people at how human the show is—this is our lives" (Platon 2016). *Atlanta* approaches its characters and the traumatic realities of the world in which they live by playing with and adapting the tropes associated with Black Americans on US television. Although the show is ostensibly about a rising rap artist, the depictions of violence and drug use are upended. Stephen Glover says, "You are conditioned to see black people to get shot or hooked on something. It's really fun to write a show where you get to see black people living life every day. We all live life every day, and, knock on wood, I've never been shot" (Bakare 2016). According to Donald Glover, FX originally wanted Alfred to live in a run-down home, but he pushed back explaining that as a drug dealer, he would have enough money to live in a "regular apartment" (Browne 2016). And drug use doesn't turn the characters into violent offenders lacking family values; rather, when they smoke pot, they sit around, eat cookies, and talk (A. Hughes 2016). The "negative" image of the Black drug user/dealer gets turned on its head by instilling humanity into the characters. Still, brutality and the trauma that it yields are always behind the scenes waiting to take center stage. As seen in the examples from "The Club" and "The Big Bang," violence is always possible. In the second episode, while Earn is waiting to get bailed out of jail (after the first episode's shooting), he watches as the guards quickly switch from laughing at a mentally unstable man to beating him after the man spits urine on a guard ("Streets on Lock"). While many dramedies of this post-Recession period use comedy to end a dramatic scene and take the edge off the pain being depicted, *Atlanta* more often uses violence to end a comedic scene to remind us that, in this failure of the American Dream, safety can never be assumed and is always in jeopardy.

Atlanta also refuses to intertwine poverty and moral failures. Robert Bianco observes that "What sets the characters apart in *Atlanta* is poverty: This serio-comedy may be the first series in which poverty is a given, rather than some tragic jumping-off point for a story about drugs, gangs or crime" (2016, 1D). As a result, characters in the series are doing all that they can to get by regardless of legality, and we are not meant to judge them but to afford them grace. Regardless of their merit, we are asked to recognize that, as social media influencer Zan tells Alfred, "it's all a game. We're all just hustling" ("The Streisand Effect"). Alfred and Darius buy drugs from a Mexican cartel and sell it on the street; a club bouncer charges Earn $10 just to let him in to look for a lost jacket; a man who found a reflective vest and a light saber charges $10 to keep watch over illegally parked cars outside of a restaurant; after taking Van out on an expensive date,

Earn reports his debit card stolen to avoid paying the bill. All these characters are doing their best, they're "hustling," to survive. The closest the first season comes to explaining the pressures of poverty rather than showing the characters simply existing within it, is when Darius takes Earn to pawn his phone. In a series of bizarre stops, Darius encourages Earn to trade his phone for a sword and then the sword for a dog, finally explaining that Earn won't get any money for another few months, after the dog has sired puppies. Upset, Earn responds, "I'm poor, Darius. And poor people don't have time for investments because poor people are too busy trying not to be poor, okay? I need to eat today not in September" ("The Streisand Effect"). Darius hands Earn his own phone, telling him to pawn that instead, and the scene ends on an upbeat note as Darius happily tells Earn, "We're friends now" ("The Streisand Effect"). The scene doesn't end in anger but, instead of dwelling on the tragedy of Earn's poverty, concludes with an act of friendship and support. Ultimately, as Brandy Monk-Payton observes, "the program does not fetishize those who are marginalized by their economic status but rather treats such poor and working-class folks with care as valuable sources of racialized knowledge" (2024, 177).

In the world of *Atlanta*, people are poor and struggling, violence is always a possibility, drugs are regularly available, and success is never assured, but there is still hope. *Atlanta* demonstrates that "if the condition of precarity is simply accepted as a characteristic of black life instead of the black subject being in a state of fear of precarity, the threat of precarity ceases to hold power over determining the shape of black life" (Guerrero 2020, 140). The acceptance of poverty and insecurity moves the focus from these aspects of life and the fear they engender to allow a depiction of other hopes, aspirations, and anxieties. Wesley Morris writes in *The New York Times*,

> The lowly lumps of suffering that Mr. Trump imagines he's talking to when he presents himself as black America's white savior ("What the hell have you got to lose?") don't exist on this show. Anybody expecting a pathological monolith gets, instead, a kaleidoscope of personalities and class, of parents—married, single and somewhere in between. Violence and poverty are part of this world, but neither defines any of its characters. (2016)

The humanity within the series is noted in review after review as the show is described as "intimate and familiar" (Kostidakis 2016), "authentic" (Petrashko 2016), and "essential" (Varghese 2016). One review reads, "'Atlanta' immediately and effortlessly imbues its environs with a tender sense of home and community, where hardship is a backdrop rather than an agenda item" (Steuver 2016, 12). And Akilah Hughes writes, "It's not a 'black show,' but it very much is a black show. These characters are real, these situations are real, and yet somehow we never really get to see them on TV" (2016). *Atlanta*'s grounding in the everyday of life includes scenes of Earn cooking dinner for Van and their daughter, Van overcome with jealousy while having dinner with a rich friend, and Alfred troubled by his notoriety. *Atlanta* connects with audiences through its portrayal of lives lived in response to and despite scarcity and fear. These characters embody Kristen Warner's call for a "color consciousness" that rejects colorblindness but also doesn't define characters solely by their skin color (2015, 25). Rather, as Monk-Payton writes, "*Atlanta* goes beyond a superficial portrayal of black community on-screen through risky storytelling that infuses its characters as well as narrative environments and situations with subtle complexity" (2024, 170). In this post-Recession period, as Hank Steuver writes, "Many viewers, of all races, are hungry for more shows that can weave outrage and narrative and everyday life together as effortlessly as this one does" (2016, 12).

As we see, the postcomplex relaxation of the rules of narrative cohesion and pushback against existing stereotypes and expectations contribute to the ways *Atlanta* challenges assumptions about the American Dream. In its interrogation of success and the Dream, *Atlanta* reflects an already complicated relationship that Black Americans have with a myth that is based on ideals of equality that are absent from their lived experiences. *Atlanta* unequivocally depicts failures within the American Dream across many dimensions; promises of safety, equality, freedom, and self-determination for all who have merit and/or work hard come under scrutiny. Earn, Alfred, Van, and to some extent Darius are all "powerless to change their circumstances" no matter how hard they work (Clake 2021, 178–9). Yet, the characters (except for Darius, perhaps) still strive to find security and fulfillment. They push for some version of the American Dream. After Van loses her job as a teacher, she networks by attending a Juneteenth party hosted by a wealthy Black woman and her White husband, reminding Earn that their hosts "knows people" and that any benefit for Van would also be good for their daughter ("Juneteenth"). For Earn, particularly, the Dream means freedom to make his own choices and create a future of his own choosing.

As in *UKS*, we see Earn's relationship with the American Dream play out in his living situation, his home. Within this season, Earn identifies as homeless but not "real homeless" ("The Big Bang"). He moves between Van's home, where he lives the life of a loving father, and the homes of friends like Alfred, where he smokes dope, drinks, and plays video games. Significantly, despite seeming to have a good relationship with them, Earn is not welcome in his parents' home due to his tendency to ask for money ("The Big Bang"). In each of these places, Earn plays out a different part of his life, fractured by responsibilities and expectations. Like Kimmy, Earn demonstrates a desire for individual freedom and independence, even if it means his "home" is not what most would associate with the American Dream. Earn spends the last episode of the season trying to find a key that he misplaced while drunk. After a peaceful evening with Van and their daughter (during which the key is returned by a friend), Earn declines Van's invitation to spend the night with her. Instead, he leaves and uses the valued key to enter a storage locker in which he has been living and sleeping ("The Jacket"). This space that would seem to many a downgrade from Van's comfortable home is clearly important to Earn, who is struggling through the season to find what makes him happy. As Earn's father tells Alfred about his son, "Earn trying like the rest of us. But when he wants to do something, he does it. On his own terms" ("The Big Bang"). Earn also emphasizes this point, saying in a later episode, "I know I have a daughter and I know she deserves the best. But I don't think I have to compromise what I want out of life to do that. . . . I can do this I just gotta do it my way" ("Go For Broke").

Atlanta, in this way, demonstrates Guerrero's argument that "In so many situations in contemporary society, black subjects have to reimagine freedom in different ways, and these ways are frequently in conflict with normalized (read: white) practices of freedom" (2020, 140). Earn would likely agree with Guerrero that, "If you can't be safe, you might as well be free" (2020, 138). The series' portrayal of Black subjectivity contributes to its focus on how some Black Americans have reconfigured the American Dream to make sense for the America in which they live. In *Atlanta*, "The recognition of kaleidoscopic Blackness is an ethical move that leads to social justice in its revelation of the multiple ways of performing Blackness and being Black, where social justice is the freedom to be, freedom to articulate and perform one's own autonomous identity" (Morgan 2020). Yet, the series has been criticized for its apparent difficulty in representing a range of subjectivities for Black women (Ibrahim 2022). Over the course of the first season, Van often feels like a tangential character and throughout the series struggles with an identity that exists outside of her relationship with Earn. Nevertheless, even criticisms of Glover reference the quality of *Atlanta*, arguing for example, that "Glover's skill as a creator is more than evident, which is what makes his inability to provide fleshed-out characterization and narrative arcs with Black women characters so frustrating" (Ibrahim 2022). Van's depiction demonstrates, perhaps, the most extreme struggle with the autonomy that *Atlanta* imagines for its characters.

The capacity to take full advantage of freedom still requires that a willingness to work is paired with innate qualities of strength. Like Kimmy, the characters in *Atlanta* are resilient. While they certainly don't share Kimmy's caring optimism, their merit, what makes them deserving of the American Dream, is their willingness to work hard to take care of themselves and to make do with what they can get. The American Dream may be reimagined in *Atlanta*, but it still serves the neoliberal agenda that keeps people striving for more and working to achieve it. The series "admits that its characters are hopelessly stuck in a cycle of dreaming and being disappointed" (Clake 2021, 178).[6] In their acceptance of the instability of their lives, the characters don't try to change the world around them, they accept it and adapt. These adjustments involve sarcastic comments about injustice and acknowledgments of the absurdities that surround them, but they don't require social change. In this first season, the continued search for the American Dream serves neoliberalism well. As Jennifer Lee O'Donnell writes, "the good neoliberal moves on, changes place. Inertia is the death of personal growth and it is best to be rootless" (2021, 322). Earn, especially, is "rootless" as he moves from place to place trying to better his circumstances while also maintaining a sense of self-respect and fulfillment. Here, the American Dream may be redefined, but the elements that make it useful to the US capitalist system are not.

Conclusion

Unbreakable Kimmy Schmidt and *Atlanta* reveal a contradiction in that they expose the trauma sparked by the Great Recession and use it to create comedy. The signature series discussed in this chapter certainly mobilize very different kinds of postcomplex styles and humor. *UKS* is campy and transgressive; *Atlanta* uses cynical satire and absurdism. And while both series model grace, suggesting that people don't need to be perfect to deserve kindness, understanding, and even success, they both still reinforce the idea that the meritocracy will provide the most benefits to those with the innate strength to survive. Kimmy, a White woman who is a victim of sexual assault, is full of hope, and Earn, a young Black man who is a victim of systemic racism, is resigned, but they keep trying. They exhibit merit—the inability to be broken, a resilience—that leads them to chase their American Dream. Moreover, essential to this strength is the willingness to lower expectations. These shows demonstrate "making it work" through the characters' readiness, actual eagerness, to downgrade their ideas of home if it means they have their independence. So, again we see the television comedy cutting both ways. These series present transgressive and marginalized stories that acknowledge precarity and resulting trauma; at times, they encourage us to laugh, whether in surprise or in cynical understanding, at the new way of things. Yet, while they may not find solutions in consumerism, these series do support a neoliberal mindset. For all their progressive ideals, *Unbreakable Kimmy Schmidt* and *Atlanta* tell us that to achieve the freedom and independence promised by the American Dream, we may just have to work harder and lower our expectations. Meanwhile, as will be discussed in the next chapter, syndicated mainstream comedies available through an increasing number of second-cycle distribution windows continued to paint a rosy picture of the pre-Recession American Dream.

Notes

1   The search for inclusive and genuine stories on television centered on writers. Darnell Hunt explains that "when white writers write about people of color, the stories they tell are likely to be different from the ones people of color choose to tell. And this reality lies at the core of a prominent disconnect between the stories that routinely emerge from network television's production pipeline and the lived experiences of increasingly diverse audiences" (2015). For television platforms, the emphasis on authentic inclusion went hand in hand with comedy writing. In 2007, NBCUniversal's director of talent diversity initiatives explained that "it tends to be easier to find a fresh voice in comedy" (Albiniak, "Diversity for the Fun of It" 2007, 26). To this end, traditional media companies constructed diversity initiatives centered around comedy writing. CBS' Diversity Institute hosted a Diversity Sketch Comedy Showcase designed to find new comic talent. NBC created the Diverse Staff Writer Initiative, through which the network paid to add a "diverse" staff writer to its comedy series. This program, which put both Mindy Kaling and Donald Glover into writers' rooms, offered series' producers a free writer for three years with the expectation that these writers would leverage their experience into future deals. Many participants have noted serious problems with these initiatives as writers found themselves marginalized in the writers' room, typecast as only being able to

write racial/ethnic humor, or simply discarded once the network stopped paying their salaries (D. Hunt 2017).

2 Lauer's line, "I'm always amazed at what women will do because they're afraid of being rude" is particularly shocking ("Kimmy Goes Outside!").

3 For very interesting discussions of these issues, see, for example, Oh 2020 and Setiaki and Destari 2019.

4 The original title of the series, *Tooken*, was initially changed to be more broadcast friendly, and Netflix approved a return to this original title (Itzkoff, "Sprung from a Cult to Stream on TV" 2015). The decision to stick with *Unbreakable Kimmy Schmidt* demonstrates the importance of Kimmy's "unbreakable" strength as a defining element of the series.

5 The tendency to use comedy instead of drama to highlight stories of Black Americans has led to critiques that, within mainstream US television, "Black life and Black issues are not taken seriously" (Innis and Feagin 1995, 707).

6 Even in later seasons of the series as the characters achieve financial success, they still grapple with a dissatisfaction that keeps them working.

4

Rerunning the Dream: Television Syndication

In the wake of the Great Recession, many Americans felt abandoned by the assurances that hard work and merit would lead to the American Dream. The homes and jobs, often seen as a bedrock of the Dream, were in danger, and many of the institutions relied upon to support achievement appeared either impotent or culpable. While, as we have seen, many television shows in the 2010s offered viewers ways to come to terms with the new American Dream, others retreated into a nostalgia not just for an earlier version of the Dream but also for television of the past. As discussed in Chapter 2, the Hallmark Channel employed a nostalgic vision of the American Dream as a means by which to brand its network. Hallmark's programming relied on traditional versions of the Dream to engage contemporary audiences. This chapter will explore the mobilization of a different kind of nostalgia, one that tapped into viewers' own televisual histories to return them to the feelings of comfort shaken by the economic downturn. Through what Derek Kompare termed rerun culture (2006), the television industry navigated a changing economic ecosystem by offering viewers a sense of security through familiarity. In this process, pre-Recession television continued to influence how viewers understood the post-Recession American Dream.

Engrained within the American Dream is a sense of promise that the future will be not just stable but also better, in whatever way an individual may define this. Although the Great Recession may have been expected to erode this optimism, Chapter 2 demonstrated that polls found that many Americans maintained hope, expecting that their lives would improve and they would, in time, achieve the Dream. In 2009, while two-thirds of Americans reported that their family's income was falling behind the cost of living, "more than 1/3 of Americans (34%) say they have already achieved the American Dream and another 41% believe that they will achieve it in their lifetime" (Halpin and Agne 2009, 5). As the US recovery slowly unfolded, this confidence did not stem from a booming economy and robust job market. Many Millennials lived with their parents, struggled to find work, and faced a staggering amount of student loan debt. One report in *The New York Times* stated that, with the Millennial unemployment rate close to that found during the Great Depression, "for young adults, the prospects in the workplace, even for the college-educated, have rarely been so bleak" (Uchitelle 2010). Although the sense of optimism found within the polls may be somewhat confounding, examining the nostalgic bent within culture can help explain at least some of this positivity. On television, for example, rerun culture disseminated content that circulated images of an American Dream that was in flux—and in doubt. Popular syndicated series tapped into the longing for a bygone period, one that existed even before many of the viewers were alive, that offered depictions of a hopeful and fleeting American Dream. This chapter will explore how the fluctuating syndication market in the early 2000s overlapped with post-Recession anxieties to popularize particular sitcoms and keep their visions of the American Dream relevant for audiences. A focus on the two sitcoms that reportedly maintained the greatest popularity among Millennial audiences—*Friends* (NBC, 1994–2004) and *The Office* (NBC, 2005–13)—will highlight how shifting windows of television distribution overlapped with the angsts and fears of viewers to perpetuate a nostalgic relationship with the American Dream.

Safety in the Nostalgic American Dream

faced with a loss of faith in the grand narratives of the past, and lacking an alternative anchor for the understanding of the modern (or postmodern) world, we continue to operate as if the previous patterns were still operable. . . . Thus, the past becomes a central way to interpret the future.

Stephan 2019, 27

Nostalgic representations within films and TV series often depict a past that highlights the positive, or as David Lowenthal writes, "nostalgia is memory with the pain removed" (1985, 8). Nostalgia, as many researchers have noted, is not about revisiting history but "is more about a desire to remember not to re-experience; to recall not to recover" (Holdsworth 2011, 102). This form of uncritical nostalgia evacuates negative associations with the past. Michael Pickering and Emily Keightley use the term regressive nostalgia to identify "those forms of nostalgia which, through a limited set of idealized images of the past appeal only to the component of backwards longing in nostalgia, and conceal or deny the loss and painful sense of lack which elsewhere are its other two components" (2014, 84). As will be discussed, rerun culture is generally associated with this less analytical type of nostalgia, as it most frequently does not encourage a thoughtful reconsideration of a television series we once loved. We are also not meant to truly relive the time in which we watched the show, as that may include negative emotions and experiences, nor are we asked to analyze the series in the context of more contemporary ideologies. Rather, we are encouraged to engulf ourselves in the pleasant memories of another time.

Svetlana Boym differentiates what she calls restorative from reflective nostalgia, highlighting restorative nostalgia as a means to protect the past by reaffirming its superiority. Boym writes, "Restorative nostalgia does not think of itself as nostalgia, but rather as truth and tradition. Reflective nostalgia dwells on the ambivalences of human longing and belonging and does not shy away from the contradictions of modernity. Restorative nostalgia protects the absolute truth, while reflective nostalgia calls it into doubt" (2001, xviii). Restorative nostalgia, like regressive nostalgia, presents a past that is comforting, shrouded in a sense of security and safety. This arguably supports traditional, conservative ideologies, looking to the past rather than embracing potential progressive change. Nevertheless, this type of nostalgia can help people navigate difficult times like financial precarity. Although nostalgia was initially considered a psychological illness, it may also be used "to counter those symptoms" (Sedikides and Wildschut 2018, 48). Daniel Marcus argues that "recollections of the past take shape out of current needs and pressures. Nostalgia thrives when the stability of personal identity is challenged by rapid social change, discontinuity, and dislocation" (Marcus 2004, 67). The economic and social upheaval of the Great Recession created the exact "social complexity" that Barbara Klinger proposes, "drives nostalgia as people try to stave off the uncertainty" (2006, 178).

Constantine Sedikides and Tim Wildschut argue that nostalgia allows people to weather stress by providing a sense of meaning and purpose, instilling both confidence and a positive attitude (2018, 56). Furthermore, because we are the center of our own memories, they argue, nostalgia makes us feel important at times when we may be flailing (Sedikides and Wildschut 2018, 49). Looking specifically at nostalgic narratives that people construct about their own lives, Michael Maly et al note that "through storytelling . . . we construct communities and our notions of ourselves" by imagining a shared past with others (2012, 760). Nostalgic feelings have also been linked to generating the perception of a meaningful life trajectory (since we look at events of the past as integral to our present) and strengthening motivation to achieve life goals (Sedikides and Wildschut 2018, 51–2). Sedikides and Wildschut's research also indicates that nostalgic feelings prompt people to feel an important connectedness to others since our nostalgic remembrances often involve other people (2018, 51).

Nostalgia offered a means of navigating the unease generated by the Great Recession. According to Matthias Stephan, "faced with a loss of faith in the grand narratives of the past, and lacking an alternative anchor for the understanding of the modern (or postmodern) world, we continue to operate as if the previous patterns were still operable. . . . Thus, the past becomes a central way to interpret the future" (2019, 27). The weakening of the grand narrative of the American Dream was punctuated by a loss of optimism about its efficacy. The expectation that hard work and meritorious actions would result in upward mobility was increasingly eroded, replaced with a sense of uncertainty about the future. Michael Kimmage writes, "By the fall of 2008, the economic crisis had become visible and unavoidable. Those at the apex of the American Dream were somehow at the center of a massive instability" (2011, 35). The median family income, which had traditionally grown since 1950, albeit at varying rates, actually fell by 7.1 percent between 2000 and 2013 (Jillson 2016, 226). The resulting insecurities continued even as the economy began a slow recovery in 2009. The government pumped a great deal of money into failing industries, and, over time, unemployment rates declined, wages increased, household net worth began to rebuild, and home prices and sales increased. Despite signs of improvement, as late as 2013, a Pew Research Center study reported that "the views of most Americans about the economy can be summed up as 'meh'" (DeSilver 2013). As discussed in previous chapters, this tension around the economy and apprehension about the future impacted the ideologies that structure the American Dream. As David Kamp writes in 2009, "What needs to change is our expectation of what the dream promises and our understanding of what the vague and promiscuously used term, 'the American Dream,' is really supposed to mean" (2009).

Concerns about the American Dream outlined in previous chapters about autonomy, the meritocracy, security, upward mobility, and so on all exacerbated a sense of anxiety about the future. Kamp, writing for *Vanity Fair*, observes "These are tough times for the American Dream. As the safe routines of our lives have come undone, so has our characteristic optimism; not only our belief that the future is full of limitless possibility, but our faith that things will eventually return to normal, whatever 'normal' was before the recession hit" (2009). Ryan Lizardi explores how Millennial viewers, the most desirable of television audiences (as previously discussed), faced specific uncertainties centered around their coming-of-age during the Great Recession. These "emerging adults," Lizardi explains, are "perpetually stuck in an unstable environment in which they are expected to form and consolidate their identities without the guidance of ritualized and institutionalized practices that helped previous generations" (2015, 25). Nostalgia became a particular source of comfort for Millennials. In an article in *Forbes* focusing on the benefits of nostalgia when marketing to Millennials, Lauren Friedman notes, "Alongside hectic work schedules, unrelenting responsibilities, and more, fond memories make us smile—and that leaves us open to brand messaging. . . . Share a compelling blast from the past with a millennial, and you're likely to reach them on an emotional level" (2016).

As objects of totemic nostalgia that engender an "affective relationship with a fan-object, usually forged in childhood" (Proctor 2017, 1122), television series become important not necessarily because they include nostalgic content but because programs connect them to others who also remember the series. A TV program "ties fans' self-narrative to an object of fandom" (Stephan 2019, 26) and can contribute to the creation of a unified sense of self and confidence in the future. William Proctor writes, "a totemic text becomes profoundly enmeshed as a resource of meaning-making, of self-identity, self-narrative and self-continuity" (2017, 1122). Totemic television series work by engaging affective nostalgia, which Jason Sperb explains as a type of nostalgia that isn't embedded within the text but develops because it "triggers in the present a yearning for yesterday by virtue of its relationship to some distant audience memory" (2021, 19). Although the content of the media texts may not be overtly nostalgic, they spark affective nostalgia in their ability to return audience members to the (positive) emotions felt during the original viewing (Klinger 2006, 175).

The primary way that audiences engage with the nostalgia of television is through repeated viewings of older series, a practice that frequently offers comfort and security.[1] Although the repetitiveness of mass media is often critiqued for its ease and lack of critical edge, these qualities may be exactly why certain texts appeal to audiences during times of stress. As Klinger notes in her discussion of the repeat viewing of films, "Familiar material, then, brings enjoyment via a combination of both mastery and solace: mastery of the narrative and one's own world; solace in the sense of control that predictability brings and in the way the screening of the same narratives can transform a space into a secure environment" (2006, 155). By offering a "retreat from the additional responsibility that come[s] with age or the pressing concerns of everyday life" (Klinger 2006, 177), television series, like films, provide viewers with comfort during challenging times through the feelings of control and power that come from knowing what's going to happen next.

As will be discussed below, repeat viewings of television series and the associated nostalgia have become increasingly possible and encouraged within the contemporary US television marketplace. Lizardi explains that this explosion of nostalgia enabled by the digital media environment engenders a particular kind of narcissism among viewers who can create a personalized "archive out of their own media-soaked past, legitimizing and credentialing this way of viewing history as an individualized playlist compiled from nostalgic texts" (2015, 4). Furthermore, Lizardi argues that new forms of media distribution, especially streaming services, are economically incentivized to promote melancholia, a state of "perpetual nostalgia," in which we are steeped in our nostalgic past and discouraged from "moving on" from the totemic objects/television series that we loved. Lizardi writes, "Encouraging melancholic attachments to media properties is the perfect strategy for streaming companies built on archive-access and subscription fees, because consumers are made to feel they need to have continual access to texts that feed nostalgic longing" (2018, 383). Viewers, then, are motivated to feed their nostalgia and take solace in the past.

The affective nostalgia imbued in older TV series also potentially allows viewers to see the past as better than the present. Although the shows may not have been produced with nostalgic intentions, as they are rewatched ten or twenty years later, they generate nostalgia for not only the original feelings of watching that series but also for that time period—the hair, the clothes, the music, and, less obviously, the ideologies that they perpetuate. The comingling of these representations from/of the past with affective nostalgia for the programs lays the groundwork for regressive nostalgia that provides a "romanticized interpretation of the past" (Keightley and Pickering 2014, 87). In the post-Recession period, watching older shows on television gave viewers comfort and reminded them of the past, demonstrating that "the psychological dynamic of the rerun mentality is that when times become politically, economically, or culturally difficult, there is a tendency to rely on the comforts of a romanticized past to ease the anxiety through the consumption of the familiar regardless of era" (Lizardi 2015, 47).

A turn toward nostalgia within culture, including television, may help account for the curious optimism that continued to tether Millennials, as well as other anxious Americans, to the American Dream. Nostalgia allows people to develop a "sense of hope and fear, of dreams for the future rooted in the conditions of the past" (Cullen 2006, 40). Memories (with the pain removed) foster connections to traditional ideologies. Regressive nostalgia offers a means to calm insecurities without promoting critical thinking that may encourage a questioning of dominant ideologies. For example, as noted in Chapter 1, Sarah Banet-Weiser examines how post-Recession Levi ads turned to a nostalgic vision of American masculinity to "explicitly harness the fear and anxiety generated by global economic crisis in order to rescue viewers from the crisis—or perhaps more accurately, to encourage viewers, as consumer-citizens, to rescue themselves" (2014, 99). This example is only one that demonstrates US corporate culture finding ways to link and marshal anxiety and nostalgia as a means of enduring difficult times.

Television's Business of Nostalgia

The texts of the past are already produced, contain proven audiences, and focus viewers' attention away from a critical point of view.

Lizardi 2015, 63

The economic uncertainty felt throughout all industries in the wake of the Great Recession was compounded within the television industry. Emerging windows of distribution made possible by new technologies and made desirable by social and industrial shifts (reviewed in the introduction and previous chapters) destabilized sales of second-run television series. US broadcast television's reliance on deficit financing means that production companies depend on syndication sales to make up for the losses incurred when programs are sold to broadcast networks. When buying series, the major broadcast networks don't pay the entirety of production costs. Rather, production companies retain ownership of the series and count on second-cycle syndication sales to make up the difference between the network license fee and production costs as well as to generate any profits. As Kompare explains, this syndication market has been in flux since the 1950s, impacted by various changes within the industry, such as the rise of independent stations, cultural shifts within program formats, and, of course, the development of cable television.

The end of the Financial Interest and Syndication Rules in the 1990s, along with the growth of cable networks, impacted syndication sales in many ways, creating new markets for older shows while also devaluing local syndication. Local stations were no longer the only buyers for older series, generating demand for more shows but also expanding competition and introducing multiple ways to watch the same series. The increase in possible windows within the syndication market resulted in the breakdown of syndication exclusivity. While, in the past, local stations paid to be the only means by which to see older series for a set amount of time, as cable emerged, syndication distributors sought to sell series to both local broadcast stations and cable networks. This arrangement allowed local stations to have a certain number of years of exclusivity after which the series would begin its second cycle on a cable network as well. Additionally, through the early 2000s, series were released on DVD. Initially, DVD boxed sets were reserved for cult favorites and "quality" series. Matt Hills wrote in 2007, "At present, shows which are culturally and discursively positioned as being absolutely 'of their time' or as being a disposable part of 'that day's schedule' remain far more likely to permanently disappear from consumer availability" (2007, 50). Increasingly, however, many popular yet "ordinary" shows were released on DVD, creating, on top of cable, even more competition for local stations. Fragmentation of audiences across different viewing platforms meant that advertising rates could not justify the cost of the most popular off-network syndicated programs. Local stations weren't enthusiastic about paying higher prices for sole rights and, as a result, exclusivity was lost. One headline in *Broadcasting & Cable* proclaimed, "Off-Net Exclusivity May be Dead," as it reported in 2009 that *Two and a Half Men* "may be the last off-net program to be sold exclusively to TV stations" (Albiniak, "Off-Net Exclusivity May be Dead" 2009, 13).[2]

Transactional and subscription streaming television services—from iTunes to Netflix—only exacerbated the ubiquity of television and the control viewers had in choosing their content, frequently off-network programming. In 2005, iTunes began selling television episodes and AOL announced a television streaming service. Netflix started offering some streaming content in 2007 and initiated a stand-alone subscription streaming service in 2010. That same year, Hulu Plus launched, and iPads provided viewers with new ways to watch television. Despite the possibilities imagined for how the internet might create space for innovative media content, Amanda Lotz describes the important symbioses that developed between these new internet platforms and the distributors of legacy content, as the streaming services needed the content to attract viewers and the content distributors wanted new revenue sources (2018, 114). OTT platforms, internet options that didn't require a cable subscription or a television set, created content libraries that offered viewers free rein in their access to (some) older programs, resulting what appeared to be an "explosion of immediate and eternal syndication" (Robinson 2017, 19). As late as 2019, "nonoriginal 'library programming' made up 72% of the minutes people spent watching Netflix" (Flint and Sharma 2019). This cooperative relationship continued between the traditional media conglomerates and the new OTT platforms throughout the primary recovery from the Great Recession, meeting the economic needs of companies involved, providing viewers with access to both new/original programming and a great deal of older, second-cycle content.

Changes to the syndication system were particularly impactful on sitcoms. For a number of reasons, in the early 2000s, networks were creating fewer thirty-minute comedies (Dempsey, "Looking for Laffs" 2008, 18). Furthermore, the Writers Strike during the 2007–8 season limited the amount of new, fictional programs resulting in a decreased availability of sitcoms for future off-network sales. Yet sitcoms retained particular importance in the syndication market and audiences were, according to *Broadcasting and Cable*, "flocking to the off-net versions, even as sitcoms hit the DVD market" (Downey 2004, 29).

Sitcoms were traditionally seen as the ideal format for reruns. Their short run time (thirty minutes with commercials) made them flexible for scheduling and for viewing. They could also, for the most part, be screened out of order without confusion. The syndicated sitcom's importance was also due to it being a relatively inexpensive means to reach a desirable target demographic for advertisers, as sitcoms seem to appeal to younger viewers more so than hour-long dramas (Dempsey, "Looking for Laffs" 2008, 18). Additionally, the re-airing and licensing of existing television series is cheaper and less risky than the production of new content. According to Lizardi, "The texts of the past are already produced, contain proven audiences, and focus viewers' attention away from a critical point of view" (2015, 63). One television industry executive explained that some of the older sitcoms such as *Seinfeld* (NBC, 1989–98) and *Friends* continue to do well in second cycle because "the younger people are coming in, so the audience continues to refresh. The core audience, from a demographic perspective, kind of stays the same." (Downey 2004, 29). New distribution windows better allow "intergenerational viewers to consume nostalgic television content" (J. C. Murray

2019, 59). Some older shows are even treated as new shows by younger people who have never seen them (Flint and Sharma 2019), resulting in nostalgia-by-proxy, which develops as television shows "evoke nostalgia for an era before one's own life, a previous Golden Age available to those who have come after through media consumption and stylistic revival" (Marcus 2004, 94).

Although *Seinfeld* and *Friends* reported declining syndication ratings in 2007, right before the full force of the Great Recession hit, they increased by 20 percent in 2011, prompting the president of Warner Bros. Domestic Television Distribution to claim, "The overall picture is one that suggests a new golden age for syndicated comedies" (McLean 2012, 20). In 2013, another syndication executive observed that "we have found more demand for off-net sitcoms than there has been in a long time" as people don't seem to get tired of sitcoms (Albiniak, "Established Comedies Prove" 2013, 20). And, for audiences faced with anxiety—from the precarious sociocultural environment shaped by the Great Recession and perhaps also from the increasingly complicated television ecosystem—well-worn syndicated comedies offered nostalgic comfort, a reprieve from decision-making, and an opportunity to laugh. Past viewers and new audiences were presented with nostalgic objects that may never have been intended to be nostalgic but offered comfort during challenging times. Referring to the signature comedies discussed in Chapter 3, one television executive stated, "While more edgy comedies might attract a small, upscale audience, most viewers are looking for comfort food" (Dempsey, "Syndie's Sitcom Slump" 2007, 19). The reassurance associated with familiar characters and jokes met the needs of anxiety-ridden viewers, offering an escape from the unknown. These series and the nostalgia surrounding them also helped television companies facing a changing industrial environment allowing them to profit from already-existing content. These series served as totemic objects that became imbued with affective nostalgia, cultivating a melancholic retreat into a vision of the American Dream founded on the hope for opportunity and compassion that seemed so scarce in the post-Recession world.

Nostalgia for Opportunity: *Friends*

It's not dark, it's not twisted, it's not about corrupt people. It's comfort food.
Friends co-creator Martha Kauffman (Flint and Sharma 2019)

You're supposed to find your passion in life. You can be whatever you want to be now. It's exciting.

"The One Where Rachel Goes Back to Work"

A growing nostalgia for the 1990s aligned with an industrial ecosystem that allowed for *Friends'* continued success in the 2010s (Johnson 2015). The multi-camera sitcom about six young adults in their late twenties living in New York City initially aired on NBC as part of its "Must See TV" Thursday night schedule. By the time of the 2008 financial crisis, *Friends* had been off the air for four years and was in its highly successful second cycle of syndication sales. The first syndication cycle, negotiated in 1996 during the series' second season, brought in over $4 million in cash and barter sales for each of the show's first 100 episodes (Dempsey, "Buddy System" 2005, 2). Syndicated episodes began airing in 1998 on Tribune-owned as well as other broadcast stations around the country.[3] In a controversial move, Warner Bros. Domestic Television Distribution, the company responsible for distributing *Friends* outside of its NBC run, also required these stations to accept a limited exclusivity of three years, with the series going to TBS in 2001 (Dempsey, "Buddy System" 2005, 2).

Clearly, Warner Bros. had a profound economic incentive to encourage the continued popularity of the series whether with nostalgic audiences or new viewers. Some industry participants, however, questioned the residual potential of a series that seemed very much "of its time." One station group program director remarked on the target audience for the series observing, "Look, *Frasier* and *Grace Under Fire* attract the stable kind of 35-plus demos you also need for prime access. But right now *Friends'* real popularity is with the most fickle of demo groups. Any show that is so trendy that it spawns a hairstyle fad is probably too risky for airing in access syndication" (Freeman, "New Best 'Friends'" 1996, 4). Despite these concerns, in the 1998–9 season, *Friends* brought in the highest 30-second advertising rate of all the nationally syndicated shows—$140,000/30 seconds (Mandese 1999). For advertisers, syndication offered a way to reach the *Friends'* audience for a fraction of the prime-time network advertising cost; for broadcast stations, *Friends* reruns brought in new and young viewers and the advertisers that followed them; and, for Warner Bros. Television Domestic Distribution, the series' successful syndication run brought in cash, earned money from barter time advertising sales, and demonstrated the show's value to NBC and future platforms interested in the next syndication cycle.

The series' second syndication cycle was negotiated in 2001, with a starting point of 2006. Some television programmers balked at the fees requested by Warner Bros. in 2001, expecting the series' popularity to decline, particularly as the show was to begin airing on TBS (Frankel 2001, 12). The ratings for the series in syndication remained strong, however, and it was considered one of three off-network shows (along with *Seinfeld* and *Everybody Loves Raymond* [CBS, 1996–2005]) doing well in the syndication market even as DVDs were released (Downey 2004, 29). By the time the series ended on NBC in 2004, *Broadcasting & Cable* reported, "Warner Bros. has made a bundle on *Friends*. Sources estimate the show raked in $4.3 million as episode in license fees and barter advertising for its first off-network syndication cycle. . . . And the second cycle is already completely sold, at prices estimated to be in line with or a little better than cycle one" (Albiniak, "Quit Crying, Friends" 2004, 1). In 2005, *Friends'* reach expanded when it was sold to Nick at Nite for the years 2011–17. Nick at Nite would share the cable window with TBS (which extended the deal that started in 2001), with Nick at Nite airing episodes after 6:00 p.m. and TBS airing them earlier in the day (Dempsey, "Buddy System" 2005, 2). *Friends* served very specific industrial functions for both Nick at Nite and TBS. Nick at Nite was designed as a programming block on the children's Nickelodeon network using family-friendly programming from their own childhoods to appeal to parents after younger viewers went to bed (Kompare 2006, 181). By picking up *Friends* in 2005 for a 2011 premiere, Nick at Nite planned to draw in Gen X parents, just as it had done with Baby Boomer parents by showing *All in the Family* in the 1990s. Importantly, as Kompare explains, Nick at Nite not only counted on nostalgia to appeal to its audience but actually reinforced its programming as "television heritage"; therefore, through its promotions, Nick at Nite augmented the importance of *Friends* as a totemic object (2006, 183). For TBS, *Friends* was part of a branding strategy. As Josef Adalian explained in 2008, "TBS simply tagged itself as 'Very Funny' then went after brand-defining acquisitions, such as *Everybody Loves Raymond*, *Seinfeld*, and *Friends*" (Albiniak, "Does that Rerun Fit the Brand?" 2008, 20). By picking up "young-skewing offnet sitcoms," TBS cultivated one of the youngest audiences on cable (Dempsey, "Comedy Cavalcade" 2007, 17), demonstrating how, as competition increased, syndicated content became an essential asset for television platforms. In 2005, John Dempsey, writing in *Variety*, estimated that *Friends* earned well over a billion dollars in syndication alone (Dempsey, "Buddy System" 2005, 2).

Around 2007, the ratings for off-network airings of *Friends* began to decline. Despite still being considered "crucial to the health of tv stations" for its ability to work as "high-rated lead-ins to lesser comedies," the series' household ratings fell by 29 percent (Dempsey, "Syndie's Sitcom Slump" 2007, 17). And, in 2008, *Broadcasting & Cable* reported that ratings were down 59 percent (Albiniak, "The Sweet Sound of Laughter" 2008, 30). However, in the 2010s, during the recovery from the financial crises, syndicated sitcoms grew in popularity with *Friends'* ratings increasing by 20 percent in 2012 (McLean 2012, 20) and in 2015, it was the number one rated show on Nick at Nite (Ault 2015, 31). *Friends'* significance was cemented by its purchase by Netflix in 2014, ten years after it went off the air, for $500,000 per episode or approximately $118 million (Albiniak 2015, 15). Netflix purchased the streaming rights to *Friends* as part of what seemed to be a push for the platform to offer more mainstream offerings that appealed to international audiences. As Mareike Jenner explains, around this time, Netflix was expanding globally and sought content that would help offset its costs and bring in new subscribers around the world (2018, 148–9). As an international hit, *Friends* had name recognition that would attract a broader, more multigenerational subscriber base (Jenner 2018, 150). *Friends* went on to become one of Netflix's most watched shows (second only to *The Office*) (Low 2019, 126). As late as July 2021, *Friends* was reported to be the most "in-demand sitcom worldwide" (and the only sitcom in the top 10 of the most in-demand series) according to Parrot Analytics (Parrot Analytics 2021). This continued popularity, as Simone Knox and Kai Hanno Schwind explain, illustrates that the series successfully balances its globally familiar sitcom tropes with an openness that allows space for culturally specific readings about friendship, love, and the complexities of emerging adulthood (Knox and Schwind 2019, 245–50). The economic value of *Friends* as a series became evident when Netflix reportedly paid approximately $100 million just to maintain rights to the show in 2019, and Warner Media then reportedly paid $425 million to purchase the rights to this 25-year-old series for its new HBO Max streaming service (Low 2019, 126).

Friends' reemergence in the post-Recession period was undoubtedly related to its pervasiveness on television. The availability of the series on broadcast, cable, and streaming platforms provided viewers ample opportunities to watch the show (Cobb, Ewen and Hamad 2018, 684). Furthermore, the 2007 Writers Strike limited the amount of new content being made for television. And *Friends* benefited from the retreat into nostalgia advanced by the social and financial insecurities generated by the Great Recession that increased the desire for televisual "comfort food." One of the series' co-creators, Marta Kauffman, explains its continued appeal saying, "It's not dark, it's not twisted, it's not about corrupt people. It's comfort food" (Flint and Sharma 2019). Adam Sternbergh connects the series' popularity directly to the pressures of the post-Recession world, writing in *New York Magazine*, "the central pleasure of watching *Friends*— the feeling of being cosseted in a familiar place, free of worries, surrounded by friends—has never been quite so longed-for as it is now" (2019). The cultural value assigned to *Friends* was displayed in HBO Max's one hour and forty-five-minute *Friends: The Reunion* (2021), a special highlighting the series' global impact that viewers watched with nostalgic longing from the safety of their homes in the midst of a global pandemic.

Significantly, there were several shows airing in syndication at the time that didn't resonate with audiences with the same force as *Friends*. Even *Seinfeld*, hailed as one of the most innovative series ever created, did not become the touchstone for the post-Recession generation in the same way as *Friends*. Jillian Sandell notes that "by almost any measure of commercial and popular success, therefore, *Friends* is more than simply a television show but is also firmly situated within American popular imaginary as an icon of its time" (1998, 143). The show tapped into and eased some of the anxieties faced by Millennials and their parents through the mobilization of nostalgia. *Friends*, like many other television comedies of its time, touched on the fears exacerbated by the recession while offering a refuge from them. Neil Ewen uses the term "insulated precarity" to consider how the series "allowed anxieties about socio-cultural change, evident in the late 1990s, to be elaborated and played out in a 'safe space,' circumscribed by the conventions of the sitcom genre" (2018, 725). Apprehensions about the future, particularly surrounding the idea of achieving success and happiness, play out as these young adults design their American Dreams. The issues that are raised (and resolved) center on expectations of and opportunities for family, home, and career that spoke both to audiences in the 1990s and offered comfort to viewers in the 2010s.

Friends' ability to soothe post-Recession viewers can be linked to a broad nostalgic celebration of the 1990s, which was idealized as a time before 9/11, before the War on Terror, before the Great Recession, and before the inundation by social media. As Ewen writes, "Frequently lauded by liberal critics as a time of hope, during which the hard edges of Reaganism and Thatcherism were softened by the rise of the Third Way, the 1990s in this narrative is a decade that started in recession, but which grew hopefully toward the new century" (2020, 576).

Of course, this conceptualization of the 1990s ignores major socioeconomic problems in the United States, including increasing racial injustice and growing economic inequalities. *Friends'* "cultural afterlife and persistent ability to find new audiences reflects an anxious nostalgia for pre-Great Recession politics and economics" (Cobb, Ewen and Hamad 2018, 688) by offering the comfort of restorative nostalgia that mobilizes the desire for a return to less anxious times when young adults could move to the city and reinvent themselves, search out jobs that they found fulfilling, have plenty of time to sit in a coffee shop with their friends, and dream of buying homes in the suburbs with loving spouses. *Friends* also removed any liberal guilt about racism or inequity in its refusal to include people of color in any significant way. *Friends* reacted to anxieties surrounding race prevalent in the 1990s in the wake of the Rodney King trial and LA rebellion by ignoring them. That the series never diegetically acknowledges the lack of diversity within a group of friends living in New York City—and that, as Sandell notes, people of color are "explicitly coded as a form of disruption"— demonstrates the show's refusal to engage with White privilege (Sandell 1998, 152). This disavowal ultimately brought attention to the show's whiteness as it became a topic of conversation surrounding the show, with even Oprah Winfrey commenting on it at the time, but never a topic within the show. Without this discursive context, Millennial viewers in the 2000s could rely on restorative nostalgia, and their tendency toward colorblindness, to romanticize the lack of racial tension in the series and see the 1990s as a simpler, less divisive time in US history.

In addition to the general nostalgia associated with the 1990s, *Friends* provided a measure of affective nostalgia, as audiences could return to the emotions of earlier viewings when, perhaps, times were not so difficult. Repeat viewers also found comfort in what, as discussed above, Klinger referred to as "mastery and solace." Audience members who had already seen or knew about the last seasons of *Friends* (whether by watching the entire series, coming-of-age in time to watch the last few seasons, or reading about it in the endless press accounts) were doubly insulated from the problems raised by the series because of nostalgic access to the characters' fates. Part of the pleasure of rewatching series is the feeling of predictability and control we have because we know how things turn out. Any concern caused by Monica losing her job in the first season is not "serious" because we know that by the end of the series, she is head chef at an upscale restaurant. Unease about Chandler's empty work life is mitigated by our knowledge that he eventually quits this job to find one he loves. And, we don't have to worry about Ross and Rachel because we know that they are going to end up together. Viewers can watch each episode with an understanding that even the characters don't have, offering a sense of control that anxious post-Recession viewers certainly didn't have within their own lives. The simple process of rewatching, then, provided a refuge from the storm of insecurity felt at this time.

A further sense of security and proficiency comes from viewers' understanding of the sitcom as a genre. Even as the more thought-provoking, complex comedies discussed in the previous chapter gained popularity in the post-Recession period, audiences flocked to traditional sitcoms, most often available through syndication, to ease uncertainties. Of course, broadcast networks were still producing new sitcoms, but the familiarity and nostalgia of older sitcoms added to the sense of ease bestowed by these shows. Formal techniques associated with the genre, such as the use of multi-camera set-ups, the inclusion of a laugh track, and the proscenium staging that suggests a live audience, are all connected to expectations about what viewers will experience. As discussed in the previous chapter, sitcoms frequently address sociocultural shifts but then use humor to dispel tensions created by change and to (attempt to) reinforce dominant ideological positions. Traumatic moments—whether it's a character losing a job, a heartfelt breakup, or a discussion of suicide—are de-escalated with humor that minimizes the potential discomfort and highlights the resiliency of the characters caught in the endless loop of the sitcom. As with most sitcoms, problems on *Friends* rarely have serious consequences. Ewen notes that all the characters have a "safety net," usually in the form of another character, that keeps them from truly failing (2018, 731).

Interestingly, the show's use of irony, a prevalent form of humor for the initial Gen X audience, may have worked against the show's ability to assuage concerns. While the humor led to laughter, it did not erase apprehensions. To cut the caustic edge that may have resulted from too much ironic distanciation, *Friends* often "veers back and forth between ironic detachment and sentimentality—a reflection of the dilemma of the series as a whole which is: how seriously to take the lifestyle problems of these post-adolescent characters" (Skovmand 2008, 206). This duality mirrors the expectations laid out by series co-creator David Crane when he said there were two rules in the writer's room: "You had to care, and it had to be funny" (Sutton 2019, 22). The humor of the show, then, was consistently designed to navigate a balance between ironic humor and a gentleness that would allow viewers to care for the characters.

The balance that *Friends* found as it addressed young adult concerns of the 1990s within the mollifying form of the sitcom offered viewers of the 2010s a reassuring image of "success" within the American Dream. The series acknowledged growing problems within the Dream—particularly surrounding family and careers—but from the perspective of the 2010s, their depiction in the series seemed quaint and optimistic. After all, as has been noted by almost anyone who has written about *Friends*, all the problems facing the characters— from job loss, to failed relationships, to the inability to conceive a child—were soothed by good friends (and a sense of humor). Sandell notes, "The belief behind *Friends* is that the 'families we choose' can substitute for badly paid jobs and dysfunctional relationships" (1998, 148). Nevertheless, the series, through its relentless optimism, ultimately reinforces many dominant ideas about the American Dream, from the importance of the nuclear family (despite its problems) to the value of individual responsibility. The positivity, as well as perhaps some of the contradictions that underlie it, is evident in *Friends* from its opening credits. The lyrics to the upbeat pop song "I'll be There for You," made famous by the series, unleash a string of negativity—"my life's a joke, I'm broke, my love life's DOA"—while we see quick cuts of characters dressed in stark back and white (with flashes of colors from items such as umbrellas and toy ducks) dance, play, and laugh next to (and in) what is supposed to be a fountain in New York City's Central Park.[4] Things may be bad ("when it hasn't been your day, your week, your month or even your year"), but you can still hang out with your friends and laugh and have fun. The opening credits lay the foundation for the series in which problems/concerns/tensions are presented then eased not only by humor but the expectation/assumption that the American Dream is inevitable for these six (White, heterosexual, attractive) characters.

Friends offers a contradictory depiction of the nuclear family, a bedrock of the American Dream. As Sandell notes, the series acknowledges the increasing destabilization of the nuclear family, focusing instead on the characters' construction of a "family by choice." Their own nuclear families are all depicted as dysfunctional in some way. Parents, especially, are seen as ineffective and emotionally insecure, unable to effectively nurture their children, who instead find solace in their friends. The complications of family relationships are compounded by problems with romantic love as the series "focused obsessively on the failures, rather than the advantages of heterosexual coupling" (Sandell 1998, 142). Much has been written on the ways that *Friends* questions yet also reinforces the traditional heterosexual relationship even while it depicts (and ultimately marginalizes) one of television's first lesbian couples. Monica, with her hyper-domesticity and longing for marriage and children, particularly "embodies and articulates a discourse of neo-traditionalism that is centered on (white) heteronormative romantic love and the fetishization of the domestic sphere" (Hamad 2018, 695). *Friends* reflects the confusion generated by the desire for romantic relationships even as they repeatedly disappoint and potentially end in unsatisfying nuclear families. Ultimately, the series "works toward a . . . recuperation of the nuclear family, and the idealization of heterosexual coupledom" as Monica and Chandler marry, have children, and move to the suburbs (Cobb and Hamad 2018, 123). Phoebe marries Mike, though they continue to live in the city. And, the series finale reunites Rachel and Ross (and their child), presumably so that they can settle into the ideal nuclear family.[5] Only Joey remains single, a move undoubtedly connected to his impending relocation to California for his unsuccessful spin-off, *Joey* (NBC, 2004–6). Despite the difficulties seen throughout the series surrounding nuclear families, audiences are expected to set aside their ironic recognition that these characters may just be creating more dysfunctional families and cheer them on. These characters who spent ten years searching for the perfect relationship on which to build their American Dreams found love, had their children, and are expected to succeed in these relationships.

Similarly, anxieties about work and careers played into the ways *Friends* depicted ideas of success within the American Dream. In the 1990s, there were a number of series that portrayed the lives of young, White, singles in urban locations who were "generally attractive, well educated, and/or well respected in their professions" (Tueth 2000, 103), including shows such as *Seinfeld*, *Will and Grace* (NBC, 1998–2006), *Spin City* (ABC, 1996–2002), *News Radio* (NBC, 1995–9), *Ellen* (ABC, 1994–8), and *Caroline in the City* (NBC, 1995–9). The characters in *Friends* primarily meet these criteria; however, they are not, at least initially, at the apex of their careers, nor are they always seen as being "good" at their jobs. In early seasons, for example, Rachel is an incompetent server, Joey is a questionably talented and underemployed actor, and Monica, although depicted as an excellent chef, gets fired from a restaurant and takes a job at a kitschy diner that requires her to stand on the counter and dance. In other words, the young adults on *Friends* face failure, sometimes due to outside circumstances but often due to their own mistakes. Monica is fired when she takes steaks from a meat supplier that she interprets as a gift, but her boss considers a bribe (Figure 9). Joey is written off a soap opera when

Figure 9 Monica is comforted after getting fired from her job in "The One with Five Steaks and an Eggplant." *Friends* © Warner Bros. Entertainment 1994–2004.

he insults the writers in an interview, and Phoebe loses her job as a massage therapist when she is found kissing a client, which she knew was against the rules. Moreover, the disappointment that accompanies "setbacks" is often acknowledged. Trying to comfort Joey after he is fired from *Days of Our Lives*, Chandler tells Joey, "It's gunna be okay. You know that" to which Joey responds: "No, I don't. It's like, you know, you work your whole life for something and you think that when you get it, it's never gunna be as good as you thought it would be, but this so was. You know, it changed everything" ("The One Where Dr. Ramoray Dies").

While the show recognizes the disappointments that come with failure, it repeatedly reinforces traditional values of the American Dream to navigate obstacles. In a strong display of positivity and optimism, characters frequently demonstrate an unwavering (and unquestioned) belief that everything will be fine. As noted above, while Joey wallows in his sadness over losing his job for one episode, in true *Friends* (and sitcom) fashion, he then carries on. More importantly, the show's narrative continuously moves the characters toward their goals: a random stranger who overhears Rachel complaining about her job offers to set her up for an interview at Ralph Lauren ("The One with all the Jealousy"); Monica writes a bad review of a restaurant for a small newspaper and is offered a job as the head chef ("The One Where They're Going to Party"); Ross is asked to serve as a guest lecturer at New York University ("The One Where Joey Loses

His Insurance"), which somehow eventually leads to him getting tenure. It's easy to be optimistic when positive things continue to happen. Furthermore, the authentic problems that come with unemployment and underemployment are rarely anything but a set up for the next joke as seen in the episode in which Joey loses his SAG health insurance because he didn't work enough over the course of a year ("The One Where Joey Loses His Insurance") or when an unemployed Monica turns to day trading when she only has $127 in the bank ("The One with the Bullies").

In addition to optimism, *Friends* emphasizes the importance of individual responsibility. Certainly, community is important in the series, although the idea of community only extends to one's closest friends. However, the inciting incident of the series, Rachel's decision to leave her wedding and move to Manhattan and live with Monica firmly reinforces the values of self-reliance, as Monica celebrates Rachel "taking control of your life" ("The One Where Monica Gets a Roommate"). The show repeatedly depicts the characters rejecting help from one another in favor of self-sufficiency. In perhaps the only episode that deals with the economic disparity between the characters, the underemployed friends refuse to allow the others to pay for their concert tickets, saying "we don't want to feel like charity" ("The One with Five Steaks and an Eggplant"). Joey won't take money from Chandler to pay for a much-needed hernia operation, but instead gets an acting role as a dying man ("The One Where Joey Loses his Insurance"), and later Phoebe turns down Joey's offer of a loan but does accept a role he gets her as an extra on a soap opera ("The One Where Rachel Goes Back to Work"). The characters' eagerness to work to support themselves is perhaps the primary demonstration of merit in this series (other than the merit that comes from being White, attractive, heterosexuals). That the characters take jobs that they (and viewers) consider "beneath them" undoubtedly resonated in the post-Recession period, depicting this qualified self-sufficiency as meritorious. Nevertheless, the driving optimism of the show assures viewers, particularly repeat viewers who know the characters' fates, that these unwanted jobs are only pit stops toward more fulfilling careers.

The question of meaningful work is central within *Friends*, as the series incorporates some of the tensions being driven by the changing job market. Chandler, as Ewen notes, has perhaps the most complicated relationship with work, as he has a steady job but one that he hates and that none of his friends understands (2018). While many of the other characters face the (insulated) precarity of work, Chandler's career demonstrates the growing neoliberal expectations that workers faced in the 2010s, to the point that he is transferred to the company's Oklahoma branch with a moment's notice ("The One Where Emma Cries"). Chandler's work comes to stand in for two growing problems within realm of US work: the frustration of a meaningless job and the lack of work/life balance. In early seasons, Chandler's job is mocked because no one quite knows what he does, and he doesn't seem to care about it at all. The show privileges the idea that one should find a fulfilling career. This is best demonstrated by Rachel who initially takes a job at the friends' favorite coffee shop although she really wants to work in the fashion industry. Throughout the first two and a half seasons Rachel is depicted as a terrible employee who is unable to get a simple coffee order correct, spends much of her time at work sitting with her friends, and is only retained because the manager has a crush on her. In season three, when asked to go through retraining she complains, "I'm training to be better at a job that I hate. My life officially sucks" ("The One Where Rachel Quits"). Repeat viewers recognize that the problem isn't that Rachel is incompetent but that she's in the wrong field. After Rachel quits (telling Gunther, "I just don't care. This is not what I want to do so I don't think I should do it anymore"), she quickly gets a job at Ralph Lauren and proves to be a stellar employee who moves up the corporate ladder. When Chandler leaves his job, he also seeks out something more fulfilling. Monica tells him, "You're supposed to find your passion in life. You can be whatever you want to be now. It's exciting" ("The One Where Rachel Goes Back to Work"). By the end of the series, each character is engaged in a career that they enjoy and appears to have some measure of success within it (except, again, for Joey, who goes to California to chase success in his spin-off).

Chandler's effort to reinvent himself comes toward the end of the series, after he and Monica are married and are trying to have children. The tension of balancing work and personal life is briefly acknowledged when Chandler suggests that he should go back to his old (meaningless) job so that he can earn enough money to help support a child. Monica disagrees, telling him, "I want you to have a job you love" ("The One Where Rachel Goes Back to Work"). Not only does this reinforce the possibility of fulfilling work (which Chandler finds in, of all things, advertising), but it also imagines a world in which, like in the Hallmark Channel content discussed in Chapter 2, personal and work lives can easily coexist without compromise. The partitioning of personal and work time, a major problem in the neoliberal era, is unquestionably reconciled on *Friends*.

When he is forced to work over Christmas in Oklahoma, Chandler quits his job so that he can fly back to New York and be with Monica. Chandler makes a choice that privileges his family over work. Throughout the series, and in true 1990s sitcom style, the characters spend an inordinate amount of time at the coffee shop hanging out together, with Rachel joining them on the couch even when she's supposedly working. Characters demonstrate "typical successes and failures, without anxiety about their jobs becoming their defining characteristic" (Ewen 2018, 729).

Significantly, when the characters are sitting together at the coffee shop, they are talking (or sometimes reading), and always primarily present for each other. Discussing the increased ways that media have been integrated into our daily lives, Manuel Menke explains that "many people who do adapt to alterations are stressed by expectations of constant and instant communication, by managing their digital identities, and keeping pace with new media technologies" (2017, 632). This stress, Menke says, leads to nostalgia for a time before this new technology was prevalent—even if for some people that time may only be their childhoods (2017, 633). *Friends* returns (or introduces) viewers to a time of personal connection and free time. As Ewen writes, "from the perspective of the present—an era defined by anxiety—it [*Friends*] also invites the viewer to be nostalgic about an earlier culture whereby work was less stressful, competitive, and all encompassing—where there was time to be reflective, or even to just do nothing" (2018, 728).

While there were several syndicated sitcoms that could have provided viewers comfort and escape, *Friends*, spoke to particular economic and sociocultural anxieties that connected with both Gen X and Millennial viewers during the recovery from the Great Recession. And it did so in a way that offered audiences faith in future opportunities for individual reinvention and gratifying success; in other words, it depicted hope in the American Dream. For viewers navigating the fallout of the financial crisis by attempting to pay off student loan debt in a precarious job market and trying to be independent while moving back in with their parents, *Friends* portrayed an American Dream that rests upon authentic relationships that exist outside of social media, the potential of succeeding at meaningful and fulfilling work, and a delicate balance between community and individual responsibility. Most significantly, while the series raises concerns about whether this Dream can be achieved, what it ultimately delivers is an unwavering and reassuring optimism for an American Dream that never quite materialized.

Nostalgia for Compassion: *The Office*

It's this boring regular-ness that makes The Office *so indispensable. It's not simply that the show occupies the familiar mundane, but also that it depicts a cast of characters trying to build their lives despite the obvious crappiness of their world—one where God has to be found in a Chili's, because Chili's is as good as it gets.*

Saraiya 2019

I just don't want my employees thinking that their jobs depend on performance. I mean what sort of place is that to call home.

"Business Ethics"

If *Friends* optimistically celebrates the potential for a successful balance of a gratifying career and a fulfilling personal life, *The Office* insinuates that although this distinction is no longer meaningful, the happiness and contentment promised by the American Dream is, nevertheless, still achievable. Despite *The Office*'s apparent cynicism, the show maintains a sense of hopefulness as viewers watch the characters use their disappointing work experiences to shape a loving and loyal community that, in some ways, mirrors John Winthrop's 1630 image of the "city upon a hill" in which we "delight in each other, make others' condition our own, rejoice together, mourn together, labor and suffer together, always having before our eyes our commission and community in the work, our community as members of the same body" (Cullen 2006, 23). The US remake of a short-lived but critically acclaimed British series (*The Office*, BBC 2001–3), the NBC series (2005–13) centers on the regional sales office for the Dunder Mifflin Paper Company located in Scranton, Pennsylvania. Famously, the show was shot as a mockumentary, diegetically explained as a documentary being made about a contemporary US workplace.[6] Most of the series takes place in the office, with occasional work activities in outside locations and infrequent looks at the characters' home lives, primarily as they intersect with work events.

The *Office* is more difficult to understand in relation to nostalgia as it was still releasing new episodes when it began airing in syndication in 2009. *The Office* didn't have the most auspicious start on NBC and its ability to sell in aftermarkets was not as certain as was *Friends*'. *The Office* was given a six-episode first season in 2005, doing well with critics but not with audiences (Schneider 2009, 16). The show was still renewed for a second season during which its ratings climbed, particularly with the desirable audience of 35- to 54-year-olds with household incomes over $100,000 (Griffin 156). The nature of the series' fans prompted NBCUniversal (the company that both produced the show and aired original episodes) to include it among the first twelve series it released on iTunes for Apple's new video iPods in early 2006 (Griffin 2008, 156). *The Office*, whose audience was described by showrunner Greg Daniels as "very young, and tech savvy and affluent" (Schneider 2009, 16), regularly appeared within the top 10 iTunes downloads (Griffin 2008, 156) and "accounted for one-third of all the NBCU downloads on iTunes" (NBC: iPod Boosts Prime Time 2006). NBCUniversal anticipated that "the iTunes halo effect could have far-reaching consequences" (NBC: iPod Boosts Prime Time 2006). Frederick Huntsberry, the president of NBCU Television Distribution, credited an increase in ratings for new episodes of the series to iTunes bringing "fresh eyeballs to the network" (NBC: iPod Boosts Prime Time 2006). Furthermore, iTunes downloads demonstrated the repeatability of *The Office* as many viewers bought episodes they had already watched on NBC, suggesting a promising future in the syndication market (NBC: iPod Boosts Prime Time 2006).

Over time *The Office* grew into an important asset for NBCUniversal. Not only did the series help the company make a mark on the iTunes store but it also spawned one of the most successful short-form web series in the summer of 2006.[7] And, in 2007, NBC also used *The Office* to experiment with what it called "newpeats" in which two half-hour episodes were reedited and combined with unused footage to create "new" hour-long episodes in an attempt to increase viewership for reruns and "keep the program's rabid fan base from moving on" (Barnes 2007).[8] Within this context, *The Office* became the number one show in its time period for "men and adults aged 18–34" (Pursell 2006).

NBCUniversal surprised the industry by putting *The Office* on the syndication market in 2007, at the end of only its second season, with what was considered a high asking price (Benson, "The Office Set" 2007). Several reasons were given for why the series might have been released to second cycle so early in its run, including that the show was about the change to a more competitive time slot and the network was concerned its ratings (and thus its worth) would decline (Benson, "The Office Set" 2007). Additionally, there were rumors (which turned out to be true) that GE was getting ready to sell NBCU and wanted to increase its value with the sale (Benson, "The Office Set" 2007). Concerns, however, were raised by industry insiders that *The Office*, despite its appeal to the elusive young, male viewer, would not do well in syndication. The large Tribune broadcast station group declined to bid for the series, the prominent Fox station group low-balled NBCU, and TBS suggested that the company come back to the cable network with a more reasonable offer (Benson, "The Office Set" 2007). NBCUniversal quashed apprehensions with an innovative arrangement announced in 2007 with TBS, which was looking to reinforce its "Very Funny" brand discussed above, with replacements for *Seinfeld* and *Friends*, both of which had declining ratings (Dempsey, "Stations Aren't Laughing" 2007, 15). The unusual, exclusive deal, starting in fall 2007, gave the cable network the right to air two episodes a week in prime time for two years before broadcast stations (and TBS) could air the more usual five episodes a week in fall 2009. TBS paid approximately $650,000/episode for this package that included streaming rights starting in 2009 (Dempsey, "Stations Aren't Laughing" 2007, 15). John Dempsey and Josef Adalian wrote in *Variety* that "the arrangement could make 'The Office' less attractive to some station buyers" but NBCUniversal thought it was worth it to get the strong TBS deal and the extra exposure for new episodes on NBC (2007, 40). In 2007, Fox bought the series for its owned and operated stations to begin airing in fall 2009 for approximately $500,000–750,000/episode (Benson, "'Office,' 'Earl'" 2007), and by fall 2009 *The Office* was sold to enough stations to reach 98 percent of US viewers (Schneider 2009, 16). Andrew Krukowski reported that, in the end, the broadcast and cable sales brought "the off-network haul for 'Office's' initial syndication run—including barter and local-station sales—to about $3 million an episode, in line with the distributor's original projections" (2008).

Ultimately, the decision to put *The Office* on the market in 2007 rather than 2008, when the full force of the economic downturn was in play, was potentially advantageous. The larger outlets—like TBS and the Fox stations— may have been willing to spend larger amounts of money in 2007 than they could allocate in 2008; and, as the show was sold to smaller station groups and individual stations around the country, it benefited from the reduced number of first-run syndication shows that were being stalled due to the recession. As discussed above, in the wake of the 2007 Writers Strike, there were fewer off-network comedies available for syndication and "despite the limited number of offerings in 2009, off-net is expected to grow in popularity as stations need to fill programming hours as cost-effectively as possible" (Krukowski 2008). In 2009, Michael Schneider wrote that *The Office* was "the biggest franchise to come out of the conglom since NBC and Universal first merged in 2004. Between DVD, international sales and now off-net (which garnered more than $3 million per episode for NBCU), 'The Office' has easily netted hundreds of millions of dollars for the Peacock" (2009, 14). *The Office*, then, opportunely straddled the Great Recession in ways that appealed to television companies and audiences.

Although not as successful in broadcast syndication as *Friends*, *The Office* did well particularly with young viewers and the second cycle expanded its availability on cable, premiering on, for example, Comedy Central in 2017; Cozi TV, Nick at Nite, and The Paramount Network in 2019; and Freeform in 2022. According to a Comedy Central press release, a marathon of *The Office* in 2018 "delivered big gains in multiple key demographics, outperformed time-period benchmarks and similar holiday marathons, and reached the network's highest primetime rating since September, 27 2017. . . . Adults 18–49 and the key Men 18–34 rating increased 71% and 23%, respectively, against total-day year-ago numbers" (Comedy Central 2018). *The Office* maintained its pull for younger audiences. In 2019, when it was heralded as the most streamed show on Netflix, NBCU's new streaming service Peacock, paid $500 million for rights to the series (Low 2019, 126), with NBCUniversal's CEO Steven Burke calling it a "tentpole" property that is "very important to us" (Hayes 2019).

As mentioned above, the nostalgic appeal of *The Office* in the post-Recession period is more difficult to untangle as it's not only a more recent show but also one that was still releasing new episodes in the 2010s. Furthermore, *The Office* is lauded for its innovative format and content, accolades that tend to distance it from nostalgia, which is generally associated with the past, not the cutting edge. As a faux documentary—what Brett Mills termed comedy verité (2004)— *The Office* plays with viewers' expectations of and knowledge about television docudrama, differentiating the show from legacy sitcoms in several ways. Instead of setting up audiences in idealized viewing positions through proscenium staging and multi-camera coverage, *The Office* relies on documentary techniques, appearing to "reveal" information. Often, as one character is speaking, the shaky, handheld camera will either pan or cut to reaction shots to demonstrate how other characters feel about what's being said. And characters' direct address to the camera, mimicking the confessional interviews in reality TV, provide a great deal of information that either explains or challenges previously seen material. Unlike with *Friends*, nostalgia is not sparked by the familiar comfort of the sitcom format. Rather, the show's formal experimentation with comedy verité distinguishes it from other comedies and allows it to use stylistic elements to foreground an ironical stance by setting up contradictions between what characters say and do when they know they are being filmed and what they say and do when they think they are not being watched.

The Office repeatedly deploys irony to critique the "corporate capitalist order" (Detweiler 736), drawing attention to the stifling nature of the meaningless work done under the direction of an incompetent boss. Sonia Saraiya writes,

> Other tv shows offer wish-fulfillment or a fantasy of a different life: *Friends*, in particular, presented a vision of exciting, young New York. *The Office*, meanwhile, offered an aesthetically challenged, humdrum existence—drab carpets, faux-wood interiors, glossy fake plants, and the oppressive, omnipresent fluorescence of a mass-produced life. *The Office* takes place amongst the detritus of late capitalism. (2019)

One of the most profound indictments of the work environment is seen in the third season episode "The Convict," in which the office staff discovers that one of their co-workers had been in prison. After hearing about life in prison—with outdoor time, art and business classes, and free time—the staff, invoking comparisons between prison and corporate office work, somewhat jokingly assert that it "kind of sounds like prison is better than Dunder Mifflin." The series particularly highlights the elimination of any semblance of a work/life balance, demonstrating that although the characters don't enjoy their jobs, "work dominates their lives" (Detweiler 2012, 739). Furthermore, while work appears to rule these characters' lives (at least in part because that is all the documentary crew shoots, and, therefore, all that we see), and despite all the attempts made by regional manager Michael Scott to mold the office into a family, as will be discussed below, "it is clear that, at some level, business at Dunder Mifflin is still business as usual in the sense that generating profit trumps all other considerations" (Kocela 2009, 165). When disgruntled warehouse workers threaten to unionize, Jan, an executive from New York, quickly shuts it down, simply stating that if they unionize everyone will get fired; there's little funny about this speech, except when she suggests that any further questions be directed to Michael who is shown hiding behind a janitorial supply cart ("Boys and Girls").

The use of humor, primarily irony, to draw attention to the inadequacies of the neoliberal workplace, may, on the surface, distance *The Office* from any nostalgic potential. As Linda Hutcheon and Mario J. Valdés explain, "unlike the knowingess of irony—a mark of the fall from innocence, if ever there was one—nostalgia is, in this way, a 'prelapsarian' and indeed utopian" (2000, 21). In highlighting contradictions or troubles within society, irony may lead to restorative nostalgia in an attempt to seek solutions in a "better" past, but there is little room to generate nostalgia for the time being portrayed within the series, the way that *Friends* leads some viewers to romanticize the 1990s. *The Office*, then, is potentially disconnected from nostalgic impulses by its ironic reflections on the inadequacies of the depicted work environment. Nevertheless, *The Office* both rejects and embraces elements of the traditional American Dream in ways that evoke nostalgia. In the new millennium, the world began to shift as "in 2005 the first Facebook users were just signing up for their accounts; the iPhone was still two years away. The disrupted, networked world was imminent, and *The Office* positioned itself on the precipice: The world doesn't need paper anymore, but Dunder Mifflin was still trying to sell it" (Saraiya 2019). In *The Office*, technological encroachment on one's time was limited, and a secure (if frustrating) job was still realistic. If "nostalgia affectively links between the times before and after a perceived change" (Menke 2017, 629), then in the 2010s, *The Office* connected viewers to a work world (and in some cases to their own selves) before the exponential growth of social media, the Great Recession, and the sense of resignation that accompanied both. The series allows irony and nostalgia to coexist, encouraging viewers to consider the depicted workplace with both derision and longing.

Moreover, although *The Office* addresses some of the frustrations found within the neoliberal workplace, the series, created before the Great Recession, still reflects an optimism that bolsters, even as it redefines the American Dream. Ultimately, happiness and contentment in *The Office* is disassociated not from work but from *achievement* at work. In a confessional interview in the series' last episode, Jim says, "even if I didn't love every minute of it, everything I have I owe to this job. This stupid, wonderful, boring, amazing job" ("Finale Part 2"). In *The Office*, the American Dream is grounded in employment, but for the personal connections and empowerment it enables rather than the opportunities it offers for career satisfaction and professional accomplishments.

The balance of innovation and tradition in both the series' form and content made *The Office* more palatable to broadcast television viewers, and created the potential for a nostalgic affect that embraced a hopeful if reconfigured vision of the American Dream. Certainly, the mockumentary format differentiates it from more traditional sitcoms. However, Nina Metz, lays out several ways that *The Office* aligns with legacy television (2019). For example, unlike more contemporary, complex comedies that often produce around 8 to 13 episodes a season, most of the nine seasons of *The Office* featured over 20 episodes, and the run of the series includes 201 episodes. This substantial number presents a great deal of variety for viewers engaging with the series through syndication. Additionally, although there are loose narrative threads that create a timeline for the show (romantic relationships, side characters who come and go, or even the presence/absence of Michael who leaves the show after the seventh season), most episodes can be appreciated on their own without knowing much backstory. Metz also notes that the accessible slapstick humor, the ability to watch without paying full attention, and the static nature of the characters all contribute to successful syndication runs by allowing for an easy enjoyment of the repeat episodes in any order (2019). And, Mills, in his discussion of the British version of *The Office*, touches on ways that the series, like its US remake, "conforms to the expected characteristics of sitcom" by using a primary single setting, featuring recurring characters, and highlighting discreet narrative problems within individual episodes (2004, 69). As Saraiya writes about the show's continued popularity in 2019:

> *The Office* debuted just as TV was about to morph into something new; it remained successful by adroitly balancing the two worlds it was straddling. On the one hand, it had the familiar friendly qualities of a broadcast sitcom: predictable structure, short running times, pratfalls. On the other, it was an experimental series for the modern world; its single-camera format ditched the laugh track and broke the fourth wall, adding a pleasantly disconcerting undercurrent of bleak irony to the hijinks. (2019)

Novel qualities of form existed alongside elements of the traditional sitcom, inviting viewers of *The Office* to enjoy something a little bit different while still preserving a familiarity that could feed nostalgic comfort. On top of this, in true sitcom form, the series ends with narrative events (Dwight's wedding and the airing of the documentary) that allow for a satisfying conclusion in which characters achieve their goals and find happiness. As with *Friends*, knowing this while rewatching the series contributes to the sense of control and enjoyment viewers can have as they screen earlier episodes in which characters face troubles or frustrations.

Similarly, the ideological interrogation promised by the show's ironic depiction of office work and corporate capitalism is undercut in several ways that were, if not utopian, then reaffirming. While the series demonstrates some of the stresses put on white-collar workers, these harsh realities rarely impact the main characters. From the very first episode, threats of consolidation and downsizing loom over the office, eventually leading to mergers. Although there are redundancies, the characters to whom we are attached keep their jobs (and some new characters are even introduced). Additionally, while the series addresses the impact of computer technologies on Dunder Mifflin's business model, this is managed without impact to our main characters who continue to make sales and get promoted. At times, even the bureaucratic absurdities connected with corporate culture are seen to be beneficial for the characters. After being promoted from office receptionist to salesperson, Pam discovers that she isn't good at, nor does she enjoy, sales. On a whim, she identifies herself to an outside salesperson as the office administrator and then proceeds to work the system to create this position while trying to prevent anyone from figuring out that this role never really existed ("Counseling"). Pam pulls this off, creating the ideal job for herself and setting her own salary almost without detection because of the convoluted, bureaucratic functioning of the company. In a sense, Pam models the self-reliance and self-starter attitude idealized within the American Dream as she uses corporate confusion to enable her own upward mobility.

More than anything else, *The Office*'s sentimental and compassionate representation of the office cohort, allows for an idealistic vision of the US workplace and the ability to find happiness there. In the show's first season, *The Office* borrows heavily from the original British version, which was often described as a bit harsher in its depiction of the characters and labor. Tara Brabazon writes that in the British series, "*The Office* demonstrates the consequences and fears of downsizing. The destruction of job security, when matched with the technological 'innovations' of pagers, cell phones and email, means that work colonizes the rest of life" (Brabazon 2005, 107). The British series, however, only ran for two seasons and was not expected to develop characters for the long term; it also was created within the BBC system which offers a very different set of sociocultural and industrial parameters. Imagined ideas about what US viewers expect and want from TV comedies led to changes in the remake's tone, altering it to be more hopeful (Beeden and de Bruin 2010, 10; Kocela 2009, 162). Even as the US series acknowledges that "hegemonic corporate structures are inherently ridiculous" (Detweiler 2012, 740), it purports that "a compassionate solidarity among workers . . . trumps irony as an instrument for combating corporate banality and oppression" (Detweiler 2012, 743). Over the course of the show, the characters are fashioned into a strong community who care for one another, undercutting the message that working at Dunder Mifflin is a terrible, soul crushing job. Jim, for instance, is set up from the start of the series as the "sympathetic ironic guide for viewers" (Detweiler 2012, 129); but,

Eric Detweiler writes, his "ironic stance is only the vehicle for delivering what is ultimately a sentimental perpetuation of American romantic ideals" (2012, 734). In the third episode of the series, Jim says during one of his confessionals that he doesn't want to move up within Dunder Mifflin because that would make this his career rather than just a job and, "If this were my career, I'd have to throw myself in front of a train" ("Health Care"). Repeat viewers know, however, that Jim comes to appreciate if not his work, then all that he has in his life because of his work. Despite being the ironic core of the series and claiming to hate his job, Jim frequently demonstrates a loyalty to his co-workers contributing to his perception as not only funny but also a "good" person who is worthy of success. For example, when Michael crashes a barbeque that Jim is having for his co-workers, Jim joins him in a karaoke duet of "Islands in the Stream" simply to keep Michael from being humiliated by singing alone ("Email Surveillance"). And, while Jim may pull pranks on Dwight on a regular basis, when Dwight claims to be slighted by a salesperson, he steps up to help Dwight get his revenge ("Counseling"). Viewers watching the series in syndication know that, while Jim finally plans to leave the company in the very last episode, he stays at Dunder Mifflin throughout the nine seasons moving up (and down) the corporate ladder if only to stay close to his love-interest-turned-wife, Pam. Viewers root for Jim to stay at this job that he, the audience, and the series recognize as "beneath" him, since staying at this job means that he eventually gets "everything."

Even more so, Michael is a contradictory character who raises questions about merit as the foundation of the American Dream. Depicted as a narcissistic, politically incorrect, incompetent manager, Michael is given more redeeming characteristics and workplace competence in the US version than the British to make him more "likeable." Showrunner Greg Daniels described Michael as a good salesperson who's not a good manager (Abele 2009, A1). While Michael's ability to manage is constrained by his narcissism, complete lack of social skills, and unending need to be liked, he is praised multiple times over the course of the series for increasing profits, maintaining clients, and cutting costs without firing staff (see, for example, "Pilot" and "The Job Part 2"). And, in contrast to his British counterpart, Michael's "attempts at comedy are designed not to garner respect and power from his employees but rather to entertain them, to create 'community' within the workplace" (Beeden and de Bruin 2010, 12). Throughout the series, we see Michael clumsily prioritize people over work, trying to shape his co-workers into a family whether or not they want this. While these efforts contribute to the show's commentary on the erasure of the work/life balance, they also demonstrate Michael's authentic belief that his subordinates are his friends/family. As a result, "although Scott's leadership is often absurd, and purposely comical, his leadership legacy is concern for others through the close relationship he maintained on the show" (Aust 2022, 72).[9] Significantly, we are expected to disregard Michael's frequent remarks that are racist, sexist, homophobic, body-shaming, and so on because we are supposed to see that he doesn't mean to be abusive; he's just blinded by his overwhelming need to be liked and admired by his work family. Frequently, Michael's elision of work and family is comical yet telling, as when he says, "I just don't want my employees thinking that their jobs depend on performance. I mean what sort of place is that to call home" ("Business Ethics").

In the more poignant episode "Business School," after serving as a guest speaker in one of Ryan's business classes, Michael is upset to learn that, out of earshot, Ryan introduced Michael by telling the class that Dunder Mifflin is an outdated company that would soon be obsolete. Trying to appease a truly agitated Michael, Ryan tells him, "it's not personal." Michael responds, "business is always personal. It's the most personal thing in the world," adding that a good manager inspires people, "and people will never go out of business." Later in this same episode, Michael demonstrates his dedication to his employees when he is one of the few co-workers to support Pam at her art show (Figure 10).

Figure 10 Michael admires Pam's drawing of Dunder Mifflin in "Business School." *The Office* © NBCUniversal 2005–13.

Pam's work had not received much (positive) attention, but Michael is enamored with her drawing of the Dunder Mifflin building, asking to buy it, telling her, "That is our building, and we sell paper. And I'm really proud of you." Pam hugs Michael, clearly appreciating his validation. Michael's loyalty to his staff, despite his frequent offensive and selfish behavior, engenders acts of support for Michael on the part of his subordinates. When Michael has problems with Jan, his former girlfriend (and current boss), the women in the office rally to help him, meeting with him regularly to prevent him from returning to the unhealthy relationship ("The Job Part 1"). After Michael meets a potential romantic partner but doesn't get her name, the staff stays late to keep him company ("Two Weeks"). And Pam leaves her job at Dunder Mifflin to work with Michael when he briefly starts his own competing paper company in season five.

In its depiction of a workplace where people matter more than business, *The Office* does offer a nostalgic vision of US work life in which a manager cares more about helping his employees than profits. Regardless of competence, co-workers accept and help one another, even if they do so with reluctance and passive-aggressive humor. Michael's continued creation of and absorption into the work family as well as Jim's sentimental choice to remain at Dunder Mifflin, recreate familiar and familial relationships within television comedies. If these people, who aggravate, offend, and, occasionally, physically harm each other, can—in the end—care for one another, then there's hope for happiness in the workplace, even if the work itself isn't rewarding. Regardless of its ironic edge, the series reinscribes nostalgic notions of work by not only offering post-Recession viewers images of people who *have* jobs but also people who, at the end of the day, choose to stay at their jobs because of the people. This sentiment is particularly reinforced in the series two-part finale, which is, not surprisingly for a series wrap-up, nostalgic about itself. As we see clips from past episodes, Dwight, arguably the show's least likable character, tells the interviewer in his final confessional:

> Do I get along with my co-workers? Well, first of all I don't have co-workers anymore; I have subordinates. So, have I gotten along with my subordinates? Let's see, my supplier relations rep Meredith Palmer is the only person I know who knows how to properly head bang to Motorhead. Oscar Martinez, my accountant, is now godfather to my son. Angela Schrute, my former accountant, is now my wife. My top salesman Jim Halpert was best man at my wedding and office administrator Pamela Beesly Halpert is my best friend. So, yes. I'd say I have gotten along with my subordinates. ("Finale Part 2")

Dwight, the character who takes his job most seriously and, as a result, has the most contentious relationship with his co-workers, has been accepted for who he is. And, although most of the characters on *The Office* may not find their work meaningful, unlike Chandler on *Friends*, they recognize the more contemporary limits on being free to "find your passion." Instead, they settle into secure jobs—and it's not that bad. They find camaraderie, love, and perhaps most nostalgic for post-Recession viewers, a steady and reliable paycheck.

The American Dream depicted in *The Office* is less utopian than that of *Friends* in which the characters find life partners and meaningful careers, yet it is no less optimistic. Instead, it realigns the American Dream to reflect the joy that comes from simply knowing that you've put in an honest day of work (even if there are some hijinks and little personal fulfillment) surrounded by people who, like family, you may find exasperating, but who ultimately support you. *The Office* doesn't suggest any kind of subversion of the capitalist order but rather promotes the idea that fulfillment comes from its acceptance. *The Office*, Detweiler writes, demonstrates "that surviving the oppressive banality and inanity of corporate capitalism is primarily an existential, affective matter—an issue of how one positions oneself in relation to the economic system, not a matter of challenging the capitalist order via political action" (2012, 740). The key to the American Dream, the path to happiness and success, the merit necessary to succeed, is based on one's attitude. In this way, the nostalgia that drew viewers to *The Office* after the recession, and that continues to appeal to audiences, rethinks the idea of merit as the basis for the American Dream, maintaining that effort and acceptance are good enough to justify security.

Nevertheless, despite their disdain for the work at Dunder Mifflin, most of the characters in *The Office* endeavor to actually do their jobs. Even Jim demonstrates a "commitment to the job," actively pursuing sales and promotions (Beeden and de Bruin 2010, 13). In fact, both he and Pam, for social and romantic reasons and until the very last episode, eschew more meaningful (though perhaps less lucrative) opportunities to stay at Dunder Mifflin. In the first episode, Pam acknowledges in a confessional interview, "I don't think it's many little girls' dream to be a receptionist" ("Pilot"). But even as she pursues art commissions through later seasons, she remains at Dunder Mifflin. And Jim repeatedly gives up opportunities for advancement both within and outside of the company to work with Pam (see, for example, "The Job Part 2"). Jim grows to be a good employee, even if he does stir up trouble on occasion, and he has his eye on making sales and earning money. The security of the American Dream, the show suggests, resides in the willingness to be a good "company man," even if one does so with a healthy dose of cynicism. Christopher Kocela writes, "the arc of Jim's character development implies that cynical detachment now serves, in fact, to suture subjects more tightly to the ideologies from which they claim a critical distance. . . . Jim looks to the camera and shrugs instead of objecting to the behavior he finds offensive in the workplace" (2009, 167). This attitude of detached acceptance helps steer Jim toward the American Dream as he is willing to put up with all the frustrations of work in order to maintain his personal relationships.

The character of Ryan perhaps best reflects how the American Dream is modified in *The Office*. A wunderkind who starts the series as a temp, he works his way up eventually to a management position at the corporate office in New York. Ryan demonstrates the desire for promotion and has the skills to adapt to different positions; he is the ideal neoliberal employee. This "go getter" attitude, however, turns out to be a façade as Ryan is convicted of defrauding Dunder Mifflin shareholders while addicted to drugs. Ryan ends his time at Dunder Mifflin back in Scranton doing unspecified work and being depicted as a fairly immoral and unkind person. When we last see him in the series finale, Ryan runs off with another man's wife while abandoning the baby he was caring for (whose mother left him with Ryan). In the end, the character who was perhaps most aligned with the American Dream ideal of upward mobility is a dissolute charlatan, and true happiness, the sustained American Dream, is achieved by those who find contentment in simply doing the jobs they were able to get and keep.

By questioning the importance of intellectual skill and competence and foregrounding compassion and acceptance, *The Office* espouses Victor Chen's morality of grace. As discussed in Chapter 3, Chen argues that younger people in the United States see "visible cracks in the national faith of meritocracy" and recognize the inequalities created by this cornerstone of the American Dream, particularly following the Great Recession (2021, 63). The morality of grace calls on society to reject the American Dream's focus on status and achievement, and even the more progressive concern with equalizing access to the Dream, and instead mobilize around the values of forgiveness, kindness, and compassion. While *The Office* doesn't do away with the idea of the American Dream, it does move closer to a conceptualization of "worthiness" that is grounded in benevolence rather than skill. Though day-to-day relationships in *The Office* may seem contentious, they are founded on a solid basis of care. In its "privileging of compassion over irony" (Detweiler 2012, 742), *The Office* foregrounds an American Dream reliant on the morality of grace rather than that of ability.[10] Unlike *Friends* this isn't a family of choice but a family that has been chosen for you, and the American Dream is found in taking what you're given and making do; carrying on with a recognition of the need for "caring for those left out of life's good fortune, whoever they may be" (Chen 2021, 69). *The Office* created a nostalgic space for the post-Recession viewers where they could imagine a work world that was based on the morality of grace, creating a hopefulness that we all deserve and can find happiness, an American Dream, regardless of the quality or meaningfulness of our work. Importantly, in the end, *The Office* doesn't ask for a rethinking of the neoliberal work environment to allow people to achieve their full potential, just an acceptance of its limitations and its potential for compassion.

Conclusion

This chapter demonstrates the ways that *Friends* and *The Office* offered viewers a nostalgic escape not just from the precarious nature of their worlds but also from the increasingly complex television ecosystem. Their continued appeal to viewers in syndication benefited players within the television industry also facing tough economic times. Production companies, broadcast stations, cable networks, and eventually streaming platforms all had to stake out space in a shifting industry. The ability to draw on existing content allowed production companies to continue to make money from preexisting television libraries. For distribution platforms, existing content not only filled time but appealed to viewers overwhelmed by television content and the world around them.

The rerun culture of the 2010s intersected easily with the rise of nostalgia that worked as a cultural balm for the anxiety that pervaded post-Recession society. The industry provided constant opportunities for endless rewatching that fostered a melancholic relationship with older television series that kept viewers watching without critiquing and without moving on. Television viewers could escape into programming of the past that they imbued with affective nostalgia, taking them back to a time when things seemed (though probably weren't really) less complicated and frightening. Reruns also offered a sense of power and control to viewers who already knew what would happen and were therefore not on the "edge of their seats." Television comedies especially offered an ease of viewing that supplied both laughs and a sense of security.

Friends and *The Office* emerged in the post-Recession years as two totemic television series that became touchstones for multiple generations. Generation X, Millennials, and later Gen Z viewers found comfort in these series, putting them on constant replay through different platforms ranging from cable to DVD to Netflix.[11] As sitcoms, these shows took a particular approach to the representation of their characters, their troubles, and their resolutions. Both these series fostered relationships around family/community and work that intersected with ideas about the American Dream and perpetuated them beyond their contemporaneous moments. *Friends* and *The Office* questioned the Dream's attainability, but in the end, reinforced the hegemonic ideas that hold out hope for the happiness and contentment promised by the American Dream embedded within the existing capitalist system.

Notes

1   Television, in particular, may satisfy the nostalgic longing for a return to established practices of the past since so much television viewing is often ritualistic (Niemeyer and Wentz 2014, 133).

2   Interestingly, as will be discussed, the cable network TBS started to pay for exclusive rerun rights to some sitcoms, such as *The Office*, airing them before they became available to local stations.

3   Importantly, *Friends'* initial release to the syndication market coincided with the end of the Prime Time Access Rule, which forbade broadcast stations in the top 50 markets from airing off-network programming during "access time" from 7:00–8:00 p.m. EST. Because this rule was discontinued, *Friends* was seen as an ideal series for these stations to program during this fringe time (Freeman, Syndication, 1996, 9). This time slot, with its high viewership, was expected to increase advertising sales for the series (Freeman, "New Best 'Friends'" 1996, 4).

4   After the first season, the opening also includes clips from episodes.

5   Moreover, the series reaffirms the whiteness of the romantic relationships as Ross's Black girlfriend Charlie, a character with whom he seems uniquely compatible, is written off the show (with her leaving him for an ex-boyfriend), allowing Ross to ultimately reunite with Rachel.

6   Writers for the show later said that the original reason for the documentary was to look at how people in the workplace handled the suicide of one of their co-workers, a character named Tim mentioned in the episode "Performance Review" (Hedash 2019).

7 The web series, ten 2-minute episodes titled *The Accountants* released on NBC.com, was at the heart of the 2007 Writers Strike as the webisodes were promoted to the public as a series, but the writers were paid (or not paid) as if they were promotions (Dawson 2011, 214). Payment for writers for web content was one of essential issues contested during this strike.

8 These newpeats, which were released as regular episodes on the series' DVDs, caused some confusion when the original episodes were streamed on Netflix and viewers, expecting the same episodes as those on the DVD, were surprised by different content.

9 Despite this, Philip Aust's use of Michael Scott's character to demonstrate the qualities of an "authentic leader" in the *Journal of Leadership Studies* still seems questionable (2022).

10 Despite his incompetence Kevin, for example, is only fired in the last episode when Dwight asks the office staff to provide a reason for his retention that has to do with his merit at work and no one can answer. This creates a wedge between Kevin and Dwight, which is resolved when Dwight reassures Kevin that he only fired him because he wasn't good at his job. This placates Kevin, who has no problem being seen as incompetent but didn't like the idea of being fired by Dwight for personal reasons.

11 Some recent chatter on the internet has suggested that perhaps younger members of Gen Z and Alphas are less forgiving of these series' jokes about race, ethnicity, gender, sexuality, body image, and so on.

Conclusion

Holding on to the Dream: Everything Changes

Developing a critical media industries analysis of television requires an exploration of its economic ecosystem, the sociopolitical context in which it's created, and the resulting cultural content. *TV's American Dream* moves toward this goal by examining how the US television industry operated within a specified social and economic framework and the television programming that was created in this moment. It investigates how television reflected and refracted ideas about the American Dream after the Great Recession in reaction to pressures from changes both within the television industry and the larger US socioeconomic environment.

The Great Recession of the early 2000s was a moment when many cracks within the system became apparent. The foundational values of the American Dream—freedom, equality, meritocracy, optimism, social responsibility, individual agency, materialism, and happiness—were imbued with uncertainty. The discourses through which these anxieties were negotiated made their way into popular culture finding salience during the slow recovery from the financial meltdown. At the same time, due to shifts in the industry, television content faced increased competition, found new distribution windows, and contended with changing audience expectations. The strategies discussed in the previous pages—the production of popular tentpole franchises, the rebranding of cable networks, the creation of authentic signature comedies, and the reliance on nostalgic second-cycle television—demonstrate a few of the ways that television attempted to appeal to audiences grappling with personal and national trauma.

What makes television so exciting as a medium of study is that it's very difficult to predict where it's headed. The intervening years between those examined in *TV's American Dream* and the time of its completion (2024) have only solidified the growing primacy of streaming platforms, which both proliferated and still failed to find solid financial footing. Content of all kinds has increasingly moved to streaming platforms, transforming how audiences experience programming such as signature comedies and tentpole franchises. The shift to streaming television has also changed how viewers understand television brands. Developing a solid brand is complicated and yet necessary for platforms that are increasingly subsumed under conglomerate streaming sites. The growing importance of streaming distribution windows also provided impetus for yet another WGA strike (2023) as writers continue to grapple with the work demands, compensation reductions, and technological shifts within a fluctuating industrial environment. The Millennial audience, once seen as the most important of all audiences, is older now and growing less desirable. Reaching young viewers means hailing Gen Z, a generation that is as likely (if not more so) to watch a video on a social media platform than a TV program. Instead of looking to older sitcoms for nostalgic comfort, many of my Gen Z students now rewatch reality shows like *Dance Moms* (Lifetime, 2011–19), which live in perpetuity online.

Like the series discussed in the previous chapter, these shows speak to young adults about more recent social tensions around the American Dream. While immediate and dire financial concerns may have subsided for some, wealth inequality persists, sustaining conversations about the fairness of the US economic system. Ideas about inequality have been shaped by the increase in student loan debt, the rise of Black Lives Matter and #MeToo movements, contention around immigration and asylum, and growing legislation around reproductive and LGBTQ+ rights. Movements that question the equity of the US financial and social systems have found support in younger Americans but have also spurred backlashes that generate political and social anxieties. Apprehensions about US democracy are fueled by crises within the political system, particularly the January 6 insurrection, an unending questioning of the 2020 election results, and the sustained prominence of Donald Trump's populist movement. On top of these and other sociocultural and economic worries, global crises such as the Covid-19 pandemic, environmental destruction, and international wars incite fear and discord, which, as with all contemporary disputes, have been exacerbated by divisive social media exchanges. Before the United States could recover from the Great Recession, new traumas amassed. Questions about the equity of the American Dream and the opportunities for upward mobility for those with merit (and the unfair definition of merit) remain. Disagreements about the definition of the Dream and who should have access to it thrive in the contemporary toxic and divided partisan culture.

Yet, the influence of the American Dream endures. Books, popular articles, and scholarly research interrogate the functions and promises of the Dream.

And, television continues, and will continue, to act as a forum in which these anxieties play out. Television programming carries on informing and adjusting to insecurities about who is American, who deserves the American Dream, and what one can hope for or expect from this Dream. More contemporary series like *Ozark* (Netflix, 2017–22), *Succession* (HBO, 2018–23), and *Reservation Dogs* (FX, 2021–3), for example, contribute to an understanding of today's American Dream on television, particularly as they ask questions about the significance of family in achieving this Dream. These concerns are being addressed in different ways as we move through the 2020s than they were in the post-Recession 2010s, and they will, undoubtedly be dealt with in yet other ways in the ensuing years. Examining television's depiction of the American Dream, or really any myth or belief that undergirds our culture, as a reflection of and a reaction to industrial and social shifts recognizes popular media as a force intertwined with our understanding of society and our place within it.

Works Cited

Aaron's, Inc. 2014. "The American Dream—Redefined, but Still Viable for Many." *PR Newswire,* June 9. Accessed September 13, 2023. https://www.prnewswire.com/news-releases/the-american-dream--redefined-but-still-viable-for-many-262374991.html.

Abele, Robert. 2009. "Adjust and Conquer." *Variety,* May 14: A1, A4.

Adalian, Josef. 2015. "How Did a Show Like Mr. Robot End up on USA?" *New York,* August 27. Accessed September 13, 2023. http://www.vulture.com/2015/08/mr-robot-how-did-it-end-up-on-usa.html.

Adams, James Truslow. 1931. *The Epic of America.* New York: Little Brown.

Adams, Sam. 2024. "Why Suits was the Most Streamed Show of 2023." *Slate,* January 30. Accessed May 21, 2024. https://slate.com/culture/2024/01/suits-show-netflix-most-streamed-tv-procedurals.html.

Advertising Age Cable Guide. 2008. "Hallmark Channel." C52.

Albarran-Torres, Cesar. 2021. *Global Trafficking Networks on Film and Television.* London: Routledge.

Albiniak, Paige. 2004. "Quit Crying, Friends." *Broadcsting & Cable,* January 19: 1, 48.

Albiniak, Paige. 2007. "Diversity for the Fun of It: NBC Looks for Minority Talent to Help Create Sitcoms." *Broadcasting & Cable,* September 17: 26.

Albiniak, Paige. 2008. "Does that Rerun Fit the Brand?" *Broadcasting & Cable,* May 19: 20.

Albiniak, Paige. 2008. "The Sweet Sound of Laughter." *Broadcasting & Cable,* January 14: 30.

Albiniak, Paige. 2009. "Off-Net Exclusivity May be Dead." *Broadcasting & Cable,* March 23: 13.

Albiniak, Paige. 2013. "Established Comedies Prove Oldies But Goodies." *Broadcasting & Cable,* December 2: 20.

Albiniak, Paige. 2015. "Distribution: Hulu Antes Up." *Broadcasting & Cable,* May 11: 15.

Alloway, Meredith. 2014. "Catching Up with Daredevil Showrunner Steven S. DeKnight." *Paste Magazine,* September 12. Accessed March 18, 2020. www.pastemagazine.com /tv/daredevil/catching-up-with-daredevil-showrunner-steven-s-dek/.

Anderson, James. 2021. "Some Say Occupy Wall Street Did Nothing. It Changed Us More Than We Think." *Time,* November 14. Accessed September 13, 2023. https://time.com/6117696/occupy-wall-street-10-years-later/.

Archer, John. 2014. "The Resilience of Myth: The Politics of the American Dream." *Traditional Dwellings and Settlements Review* 25 (2): 7–21.

Arnade, Chris. 2015. "Who Still Believes in the American Dream?" *The Atlantic,* September 23. Accessed September 13, 2023. https://www.theatlantic.com/business/ archive/2015/09/american-dreams-portraits/405907/.

Arvidsson, Adam. 2005. "Brands: A Critical Perspective." *Journal of Consumer Culture* 5 (2): 235–58.

Atwater, Deborah. 2007. "Barack Obama; The Rhetoric of Hope and the American Dream." *Journal of Black Studies* 38 (2): 121–9.

Ault, Susanne. 2015. "Cable's Rerun Binge." *Variety,* July 22: 31–3.

Aust, Philip. 2022. "Michael Scott and Authentic Leadership: What We Learn About Leadership from The Office." *Journal of Leadership Studies* 15 (4): 63–77.

Baer, Don, and Mark Penn. 2015. "The American Dream: Personal Optimists, National Pessimists." *The Atlantic,* July 1. Accessed September 13, 2023. https://www.theatlantic .com/national/archive/2015/07/aspen-ideas-american-dream-survey/397274/.

Bakare, Lanre. 2016. "The Writer's of FX's Atlanta." *The Guardian,* November 2: Web.

Banet-Weiser, Sarah. 2014. "'We Are All Workers': Economic Crisis, Masculinity, and the American Working Class." In *Gendering the Recession: Media and Culture in the Age of Austerity,* edited by Diane Negra and Yvonne Tasker, 81–106. Durham, NC: Duke University Press.

Bank of America/USA Today. 2015. "Better Money Habits Millennial Report." *Better Money Habits,* Spring. Accessed June 5, 2020. https://about.bankofamerica.com/ assets/pdf/bmh-millennials-report-spring-2015.pdf.

Barnes, Brooks. 2007. "NBC Remixes 'The Office'; Reruns Become 'Newpeats.'" *The Wall Street Journal,* March 9: B1.

Barney, Lee. 2016. "Two-Thirds of Americans Believe 'The American Dream' Is Attainable." *Plan Advisor,* April 26. Accessed September 13, 2023. https://www .planadviser.com/two-thirds-of-americans-believe-the-american-dream-is -attainable/.

Bauder, David. 2015. "Switch to Netflix Means New World for Tina Fey's Comedy." *Chicago Daily Herald,* January 9: Web.

Baugher, Lacy. 2020. "Marvel Television is Gone, and Fans are Losing Something Important With It." *Syfy.com,* January 14. Accessed April 20, 2020. www.syfy.com /syfywire/marvel-television-is-gone-and-fans-are-losing-something-important -with-it.

Baysinger, Tim. 2015. "USA Leaves 'Blue Skies' Behind." *Broadcasting & Cable,* April 13: 22.

Baysinger, Tim. 2015. "With Netflix, Marvel Bets on 'Daredevil.'" *Broadcasting & Cable,* April 6: 6–8.

Beckelhimer, Lisa. 2020. "Fail and Religion v. Secular Morality: The Sanitization of Evangelical Christian Messaging on the Hallmark Channel." In *The Hallmark*

Channel: Essays on Faith, Race and Feminism, edited by Emily Newman and Emily Witsell, 50–66. Jefferson, NC: MacFarland & Co.

Beeden, Alexandra, and Joost de Bruin. 2010. "The Office: Articulations of National Identity in Television Format Adaptation." *Television and New Media* 11 (1): 3–19.

Benson, Jim. 2007. "'Office,' 'Earl' Syndication Deals." *Broadcasting & Cable*, June 25.

Benson, Jim. 2007. "The Office Set for 2009 Syndication." *Broadcasting & Cable,* June 4. Accessed July 11, 2022. https://www.nexttv.com/news/office-set-2009-syndication -82874.

Berkshire, Geoff. 2015. "Fresh Voices Find Audiences." *Variety*, June 10: 23–8.

Berry, David. 2015. "Cult Classic: Tina Fey's New Netflix Comedy is the Very Best Kind of Weird." *National Post (Canada)*, March 10: B1.

Bianco, Robert. 2016. "'Atlanta' and 'Queen Sugar': Sweet Relief." *USA Today*, September 6: 1D.

Blair, Iain. 2009. "10 Comics to Watch: Donald Glover." *Variety*, July 21: A12, A14.

Blumberg, Arnold. 2016. "The Deal of the First Marvel Television Universe." In *Marvel Comics into Film: Essays on Adaptations Since the 1940s*, edited by Matthew McEniry, Robert Moses Peaslee and Robert Weinter, 118–28. Jefferson, NC: McFarland and Co.

Boesveld, Sarah. 2012. "Trying to Revive the American Dream." *National Post (f/k/a The Financial Post) (Canada)*, September 1: A22.

Bolton, Matthew, Emily Welty, Meghana Nayak, and Christopher Malone. 2013. "We Had a Front Row Seat to a Downtown Revolution." In *Occupying Political Science: The Occupy Wall Street Movement from New York to the World*, edited by Emily Welty, Meghana Nakay, and Christopher Malone, 1–24. New York: Palgrave Macmillan.

Bond, Paul. 2015. "Netflix Ends Quarter with More than 59 Million Subscribers." *Hollywood Reporter*, April 15.

Bookman, Samantha. 2014. "Netflix Turns to Original Content, Innovative Formats to Continue Growth." *Fierce Online Video,* June 24. Accessed March 18, 2020. NexisUni.

Bore, Inger-Lise Kalviknes. 2017. *Screen Comedy and Online Audiences.* London: Routledge.

Boym, Svetlana. 2001. *The Futue of Nostalgia.* New York: Basic Books.

Brabazon, Tara. 2005. "'What Have You Ever Done on the Telly?' The Office, (Post) Reality Television and (Post) Work." *International Journal of Cultural Studies* 8 (1): 101–17.

Broadnax, Jamie. 2018. "Representation Matters." *Variety*, June 11: 33–4.

Brooker, Will. 2013. "We Could be Heroes." In *What is a Superhero*, edited by Robin S. Rosenberg and Peter M. Coogan, 11–17. Oxford: Oxford University Press.

Browne, Rembert. 2016. "Donald Glover's Community." *Vulture (New York Magazine)*, August 22. Accessed July 29, 2023. https://www.vulture.com/2016/08/donald-glover -atlanta.html.

Bryant, Andy, and Charlie Mawer. 2016. *The TV Brand Builders*. London: Kogan Page.

Bush, Melanie, and Roderick Bush. 2015. *Tensions in the American Dream: Rhetoric, Reverie, or Reality*. Philadelphia: Temple University Press.

Caldwell, John. 2006. "Critical Industrial Practice: Branding, Repurposing, and the Migratory Patterns of Industrial Texts." *Television and New Media* 7: 99–134.

Castells, Manuel, João Caraça, and Gustavo Cardoso. 2012. "The Cultures of the Economic Crisis: An Introduction." In *Aftermath: The Cultures of the Economic Crisis*, edited by Manuel Castells, João Caraça, and Gustavo Cardoso, 1–14. Oxford: Oxford University Press.

Cervantes, Richard, Elia Koutantos, Martha Cristo, Rosa Gonzalez-Guarda, Diego Fuentes, and Nancy Gutierrez. 2021. "Optimism and the American Dream: Latino Perspectives on Opportunities and Challenges Toward Reaching Personal and Family Goals." *Hispanic Journal of Behavioral Sciences* 43 (3): 135–54.

Chaney, Jen, Gazelle Emami, and Matt Z. Seitz. 2016. "Mr. Robot Creator Sam Esmail on How He Handles Criticism of the Show." *Vulture,* September 23. Accessed May 21, 2024. https://www.vulture.com/2016/09/mr-robot-sam-esmail-on-how-he-takes -show-criticism.html.

Chen, Victor Tan. 2021. "The Mirage of Meritocracy and the Morality of Grace." In *The Routledge Handbook on the American Dream*, Vol. 1, edited by Robert C. Hauhart and Mitja Sardoc, 58–72. Milton: Taylor and Francis.

Clake, Jenna. 2021. "Rat Phones, Alligators, Lemon Pepper Wet: The New Absurd of Atlanta." In *Television Series as Literature*, edited by R. Winckler and V. Huertas-Martin, 167–83. Springer Nature Singapore.

Cobb, Shelley, and Hannah Hamad. 2018. "Friends: 'The Last One.'" In *Television Finales: From Howdy Doody to Girls*, edited by Douglas L. Howard and David Bianculli, 123–8. Syracuse: Syracuse University Press.

Cobb, Shelley, Neil Ewen, and Hannah Hamad. 2018. "Friends Reconsidered: Cultural Politics, Intergenerationality, and Afterlives." *Television and New Media* 19 (8): 683–91.

Cochran, Tanya R., and Meghan K. Winchell. 2017. "When Fans Know Best: Oliciters Right the Ship." In *Arrow and Superhero Television: Essays on Themes and Characters of the Series*, edited by James Iaccino, Corey Barker and Myc Wiatrowski, 191–208. Jefferson, NC: McFarland.

Comedy Central. 2018. "'The Office' Marathon Delivers Big Gains for Comedy Central with Total-Day Rating Up 71% Against Year-Ago." *Futon Critic,* January 16. Accessed July 11, 2022. http://www.thefutoncritic.com/ratings/2018/01/16/the-office -marathon-delivers-big-gains-for-comedy-central-with-total-day-rating-up-71 -percent-against-year-ago-271301/20180116comedycentral01/.

Cornet, Roth. 2015. "Daredevil: How the Netflix Series Will Change the Marvel Cinematic University." *IGN,* April 8. Accessed 3 July, 2020. https://www.ign.com /articles/2015/04/09/daredevil-how-the-netflix-series-will-change-the-marvel -cinematic-universe.

Cullen, Jim. 2006. *The American Dream: A Short History of an Idea that Shaped a Nation.* Oxford: Oxford University Press.

Cullen, Jim. 2017. "Twilight's Gleaming: The American Dream and the Ends of Republics." In *The American Dream in the 21st Century,* edited by Peter Bruck and Eernst K. Sprachen, 17–26. Philadelphia: Temple University Press.

Cutler, Jacqueline. 2013. "'Cedar Cove' Review: 'A Modern Version of 'Andy Griffith.'" *Newsday (New York),* July 18. Accessed September 13, 2023. https://www.newsday .com/entertainment/tv/cedar-cove-review-a-modern-version-of-andy-griffith -c29440.

D'Antonio, William. 2011. "Religion and the American Dream: A Catholic Reflection in a Generational Context." In *The American Dream in the 21st Century,* edited by Sandra Hanson and John White, 117–40. Philadelphia: Temple University Press.

Dantzler, Perry. 2017. "Reading the Body, Deciphering the Text: Arrow's Multiliteracies, Superheroics and Merging Multimodalities." In *Arrow and Superhero Television. Essays on Themes and Characters of the Series,* edited by Cory Barker, James Iaccino and Myc Wiatrowski, 27–45. Jefferson, NC: McFarland.

Davidson, Lauren. 2014. "US Emerges from Recession but Minus the American Dream." *The Daily Telegraph (London),* October 7: 5.

Dawson, Max. 2011. "Television's Aesthetic of Efficiency: Convergence Television and the Digital Short." In *Television as Digital Media,* edited by James Bennett and Niki Strange, 204–29. Chapel Hill: Duke University Press.

De Groote, Michael. 2013. "Optimism and American Dream Surviving Pragmatism, Survey Shows." *Deseret Morning News (Salt Lake City),* May 22. Accessed September 13, 2023. https://www.deseret.com/2013/5/23/20452640/optimism-and-american -dream-surviving-pragmatism-survey-shows.

De Tocqueville, Alexis. 2003. *Democracy in America.* London: Penguin Books.

Demby, Gene. 2014. "Young People Want Equality But Struggle To Discuss Bias." *Code Switch,* May 15. Accessed July 20, 2020. https://www.npr.org/sections/codeswitch /2014/05/15/312532393/young-people-want-equality-but-struggle-to-discuss-bias.

Dempsey, John. 1998. "Cablers Strike Up the Brand." *Variety,* June 22: 1.

Dempsey, John. 2004. "Hallmark Ponies Up $30 Mil for 'Walker.'" *Variety,* June 9: 2.

Dempsey, John. 2005. "Buddy System: Warner's 'Friends' to TBS, Nick." *Variety,* July 12: 2, 8.

Dempsey, John. 2005. "Hallmark Valentine: Cabler Touts 40% Gain in Upfront Ad Sales." *Variety,* March 23: 4.

Dempsey, John. 2007. "Comedy Cavalcade Helps TBS Get Last Laff on Rivals." *Variety,* November 12–18: 17, 19.

Dempsey, John. 2007. "Stations Aren't Laughing at Turner Comedy Buys." *Variety,* July/ August 30–5: 15, 16.

Dempsey, John. 2007. "Syndie's Sitcom Slump Socks Stations." *Variety,* June 18–24: 17, 19.

Dempsey, John. 2008. "Hallmark in 'Golden' Age." *Variety*, March 26: 5.

Dempsey, John. 2008. "Looking for Laffs." *Variety*, September 22–8: 18, 20.

Dempsey, John, and Josef Adalian. 2007. "'Office' Reports for Work at TBS." *Variety*, June 22: 1, 40.

DeSilver, Drew. 2013. "5 Reasons Americans Have the Economic Blahs." *Pew Research Center*, July 25. Accessed July 2022. https://www.pewresearch.org/fact-tank/2013/07/25/5-reasons-americans-have-the-economic-blahs/.

Detweiler, Eric. 2012. "'I Was Just Doing a Little Joke There': Irony and the Paradoxes of the Sitcom in The Office." *The Journal of Popular Culture* 45 (4): 727–48.

Dimock, Michael. 2017. "Defining Generations: Where Millennials End and Generation Z Begins." *Pew Research Center*, January 17. Accessed June 5, 2020. https://www.pewresearch.org/fact-tank/2019/01/17/where-millennials-end-and-generation-z-begins/.

Dittmer, Jason. 2013. *Captain American and the Nationalist Superhero: Metaphors, Narratives, and Geopolitics*. Philadelphia: Temple University Press.

Downey, Kevin. 2004. "Fans Know What They Like, Repeatedly." *Broadcasting & Cable*, December 6: 29.

Dunleavy, Trisha. 2018. *Complex Serial Drama and Multiplatform Television*. Milton: Routledge.

Eco, Umberto. 2005. "The Myth of Superman." In *Arguing Comics*, edited by Jeet Heer and Kent Worcester, 146–64. Jackson: University of Mississippi Press.

Edgerton, Gary, and Kyle Nicholas. 2005. "I Want my Niche TV: Genre as a Networking Strategy in the Digital Era." In *Thinking Outside the Box: A Contemporary Genre Reader*, edited by Gary Edgerton and Brian Rose, 247–67. Lexington: Univeristy of Kentucky Press.

Ehrenreich, Barbara. 2005. *Bait and Switch: The (Futile) Pursuit of the American Dream*. New York: Metropolitan Books.

Elber, Lynn. 2016. "Netflix Driving Force in Glut of Scripted Shows." *Richmond Times Dispatch (Virginia)*, August 11: 11F.

Ellis, Christopher. 2017. "Social Class, Meritocracy, and the Geography of the 'American Dream.'" *The Forum: A Journal of Applied Research in Contemporary Politics* 15 (1): 51–70.

England, Robert Stowe. 2016. "Millennials Recast the American Dream." *Mortgage Banking*, July: 34–43.

Ewen, Neil. 2018. "'If I Don't Input Those Numbers . . . It Doesn't Make Much of a Difference': Insulated Precarity and Gendered Labor in Friends." *Television and New Media* 19 (8): 724–40.

Ewen, Neil. 2020. "'Talk to Each Other Like It's 1995': Mapping Nostalgia for the 1990s in Contemporary Media Culture." *Television and New Media* 21 (6): 574–80.

Fisher, Walter R. 1973. "Reaffirmation and Subversion of the American Dream." *Quarterly Journal of Speech* 59 (2): 160–7.

Flint, Joe, and Amol Sharma. 2019. "Netflix Fights to Keep Its Most Watched Shows: 'Friends' and 'The Office." *The Wall Street Journal,* April 24. Accessed July 8, 2022. https://www.wsj.com/articles/netflix-battles-rivals-for-its-most-watched-shows -friends-and-the-office-11556120136?shareToken=stb3190ef1056940f1bc366ef2c 370ca99.

Fox, Charity. 2019. "Flashback to the Bunker: Reframing Echoes of Captivity in Unbreakable Kimmy Schmidt." *Nano: New American Notes Online* 14. https:// nanocrit.com/issues/issue14/Flashback-to-the-Bunker-Reframing-Echoes-of -Captivity-in-Unbreakable-Kimmy-Schmidt.

Frankel, Daniel. 2001. "Friends Shopped Market-by-Market." *MediaWeek*, June 11: 12.

Frankel, Daniel. 2015. "NBCU Research Chief: Change in Millennial Viewing Behavior is 'Stunning." *Stream TV Insider,* February 17. Accessed September 13, 2023. https:// www.streamtvinsider.com/cable/nbcu-research-chief-change-millennial-viewing -behavior-stunning.

Freeman, Michael. 1996. "New Best 'Friends." *Media Week*, April 15: 4.

Freeman, Michael. 1996. "Syndication." *MediaWeek*, March 18: 9.

Friedlander, Whitney. 2017. "Actors Thrive on Double Duty." *Variety*, August 3: 21.

Friedman, Lauren. 2016. "Why Nostalgia Marketing Works So Well With Millennials, And How Your Brand Can Benefit." *Forbes,* August 2. Accessed October 4, 2023. forbes.com/sites/laurenfriedman/2016/08/02/why-nostalgia-marketing-works-so -well-with-millennials-and-how-your- brand-can-benefit.

Friedman, Milton. 1962. *Capitalism and Freedom.* Chicago, IL: University of Chicago Press.

Frizell, Sam. 2014. "The New American Dream Is Living in a City, Not Owning a House in the Suburbs." *Time.com,* April 25. Accessed June 5, 2020. https://time.com/72281/ american-housing/.

Frow, John. 2002. "Signature and Brand." In *High-Pop: Making Culture into Popular Entertainment*, edited by Jim Collins, 56–74. Maiden, MA: Blackwell Publishing.

Fry, Richard, and Rakesh Kochhar. 2014. "America's Wealth Gap Between Middle-Income and Upper-Income Families is Widest on Record." *Pew Research Center,* December 17. Accessed September 30, 2023. https://www.pewresearch.org/short -reads/2014/12/17/wealth-gap-upper-middle-income/.

Gates, Racquel. 2018. *Double Negative: The Black Image and Popular Culture.* Durham, NC: Duke University Press.

Genzlinger, Neil. 2013. "Dialing Down the Adrenaline in a Town with a Laid-Back Judge." *The New York Times*, July 20: C3.

Gillette, Felix. 2009. "Hallmark TV Chief Henry Schleiff On His Network's Programming: 'It's Very Formulaic. That's Our Brand." *Observer,* March 25. Accessed September 13, 2023. https://observer.com/2009/03/hallmark-tv-chief -henry-schleiff-on-his-networks-programming-its-very-formulaic-thats-our -brand/.

Glaser, Marc. 2015. "Marvel's Merchandising Plan for 'Avengers: Age of Ultron': Make the Big Bigger." *Variety*, March 15 .

Goldberg, Lesley. 2013. "AMC Rebrands with New Logo, Tagline." *The Hollywood Reporter*, April 1. Accessed September 13, 2023. https://www.hollywoodreporter .com/tv/tv-news/amc-rebrands-new-logo-tagline-431997/.

Goldberg, Lesley. 2016. "FX Chief on Network's 18 Emmy Wins: 'We Made the Right Sacrifices.'" *Hollywood Reporter*, September 21. Accessed July 28, 2023. https://www .hollywoodreporter.com/news/general-news/fx-chief-networks-18-emmy-931222/.

Gomes, Lee. 2004. "Web TV is Changing the Way Programming is Watched and Sold." *Wall Street Journal*, May 10: B1.

Goodman, Laurie S., and Christopher Mayer. 2018. "Homeownership and the American Dream." *Journal of Economic Perspectives* (American Economic Association) 32 (1): 31–58.

Goodman, Tim. 2016. "Atlanta." *The Hollywood Reporter*, September 2: 63.

Graham, Carol. 2017. *Happiness for All? Unequal Hopes and Lives in Pursuit of the American Dream*. Princeton, NJ: Princeton University Press.

Grant, Drew. 2016. "We're Hopefully Woke': Brian Tyree Henry Atlanta Race Playing Paperboi." *New York Observer*, September 6: Web.

Gray, Herman. 1989. "Television, Black Americans, and the American Dream." *Critical Studies in Mass Communication* 6: 376–86.

Green, Mark Anthony. 2023. "Inside Donald Glover's New Creative Playground." *GQ.com*, April 4. Accessed July 29, 2023. https://www.gq.com/story/donald-glover-global -creativity-awards-cover-2023.

Griffin, Jeffrey. 2008. "The Americanization of The Office: A Comparison of the Offbeat NBC Sitcom and Its British Predecessor." *Journal of Popular Film and Television* 35 (4): 154–63.

Grossman, Ben. 2011. "Why the $1B CW-Netflix Deal Should Catch Your Attention." *Broadcasting & Cable*, October 17: 30.

"Groundbreaking Study Reveals Significant Media Generation Gap in the Use of New TV Technology, Buying Power and Brand Loyalty." 2008. *PR Newswire*. March 26. Accessed July 31, 2023. link.gale.com/apps/doc/A177054357/PPNU?u=uarizona_ main&sid=bookmark-PPNU&xid=c09fa487.

Guerrero, Lisa. 2020. *Crazy Funny: Popular Black Satire and the Method of Madness*. New York: Routledge.

Haggins, Bambi. 1999. "There's No Place like Home: The American Dream, African American Identity, and the Situation Comedy." *The Velvet Light Trap* 43: 23–36.

Hahn, Kate. 2012. "Buzz-Seeking Cablers Make Mark by the Hour." *Variety*, June 13: 16, 26.

Haley, Kathy. 2004. "Defining a Brand: Original Programming Will Advance an Agenda that Includes a New Branding Campaign and More Promotion." *Broadcasting and Cable*, April 5: 12A.

"Hallmark Channel Captures 'The Heart of TV' with New Tagline and Brand Image." 2012. *Business Wire,* August 22. Accessed September 13, 2023. https://www .businesswire.com/news/home/20120822006162/en/Hallmark-Channel-Captures-%E2%80%9CThe-Heart-of-TV%E2%80%9D-with-New-Tagline-and-Brand-Image.

"Hallmark Channel Rebrand." n.d. *Art of Channel Branding.* Accessed September 13, 2013. https://artofchannelbranding.com/2015/11/18/40/.

Halloway, Daniel. 2014. "Diversity in Primetime." *Broadcasting & Cable*, February 17: 6.

Halpin, John, and Karl Agne. 2009. *State of American Political Ideology, 2009.* Center for American Progress.

Hamad, Hannah. 2018. "The One with the Feminist Critique: Revisiting Millennial Postfeminism with Friends." *Television and New Media*, 692–707.

Hanson, Sandra. 2011. "Whose Dream? Gender and the American Dream." In *The American Dream in the 21st Century*, edited by Sandra Hanson and John White, 77–103. Philadelphia: Temple University Press.

Harmetz, Al Jean. 1987. "Figuring Out the Fates of 'Cop II' and 'Ishtar.'" *The New York Times,* June 4: C21.

Hassler-Forest, Dan. 2012. *Capitalist Superheroes: Caped Crusaders in the Neoliberal Age.* Lanham: John Hunt Publishing.

Havas, Julia, and Maria Sulimma. 2020. "Through the Gaps of My Fingers: Genre, Femininity, and Cringe Aesthetics in Dramedy Television." *Television and New Media* (SAGE Publications Inc.) 21 (1): 75–94.

Havas, Julia, and Tanya Horeck. 2022. "Netflix Feminism: Binge-Watching Rape Culture in Unbreakable Kimmy Schmidt and Unbelievable." In *Binge-Watching and Contemporary Television Research*, edited by Mareike Jenner, 250–73. Edinburgh: Edinburgh University Press.

Havens, Timothy. 2018. "Netflix: Streaming Channel Brands as Global Meaning Systems." In *From Networks to Netflix: A Guide to Changing Channels*, edited by Derek Johnson, 321–31. New York: Routledge.

Hayes, Dade. 2019. "Comcast Brass Update NBCUniversal Streaming Service Launch Timing, Address 'Office' Deal." *Deadline,* July 25. Accessed July 11, 2022. https:// deadline.com/2019/07/comcast-brass-update-nbcuniversal-streaming-service -launch-timing-address-office-deal-1202653435/.

Hedash, Kara. 2019. "The Office: The Dark Reason Why Dunder Mifflin was being Filmed." *Screen Rant,* July 25. Accessed July 11, 2022. https://screenrant.com/office -series-documentary-filmed-reason-dunder-mifflin-suicide/.

Heldenfels, Rich. 2012. "Heldenfiles: The CW New Schedule Plans." *HeldenFiles Online,* May 17. Accessed April 14, 2020. https://advance-lexis-com.ezproxy1.library.arizona .edu/api/document?collection=news&id=urn:contentItem:55NF-4121-JBF5-T09N-00000-00&context=1516831.

Hertz, Joshua. n.d. "USA: 'We the Bold' Rebrand." *joshuahertz.com.* Accessed September 13, 2023. https://joshuahertz.com/USA-WE-THE-BOLD-Rebrand.

Hills, Matt. 2007. "From the Box in the Corner to the Box Set on the Shelf: TVIII and the Cultural/Textual Valorisations of DVD." *New Review of FIlm and Television Studies* 5 (1): 41–60.

Hinckley, David. 2015. "Freedom for Fey: Move from NBC to Netflix Alters her Sitcom 'Schmidt." *Daily News (New York)*, February 16: 29.

Hochschild, Jennifer. 1996. *Facing up to the American Dream: Race, Class, and the Soul of the Nation.* Princeton, NJ: Princeton University Press. http://ebookcentral .proquest.com/lib/uaz/detail.action?docID=581607.

Hogan, Monica. 2001. "Hallmark Crowns Channel's Rebranding Plan." *Multichannel News*, July 16: 48.

Holdsworth, Amy. 2011. *Television, Memory and Nostalgia.* New York: Palgrave Mamillan.

Holloway, Daniel. 2014. "The CW's Pale-Pattern Boldness." *Broadcasting & Cable*, October 27: 12–15.

Holt, Douglas, and Douglas Cameron. 2010. *Cultural Strategy: Using Innovative Ideologies to Build Breakthrough Brands.* Oxford: Oxford University Press.

Hughes, Akilah. 2016. "FX's 'Atlanta' Depicts a Truth of Black Experience Unseen on TV." *New York Observer*, September 7: Web.

Hughes, Jason. 2014. "'Daredevil' Netflix Series Designed to be One 'Very Large Movie." *The Wrap*, May 13. Accessed March 18, 2020. TheWrap.com.

Hughes, Sarah. 2014. "Are Television Superhero Dramas Just Marketing Tools?" *The Independent (UK)*, September 16.

Hunt, Darnell. 2015. "Hollywood Story: Diversity, Writing and the End of Television as We Know It." In *The Sage Handbook of Television Studies*, edited by Manuel Alvarado, Milly Buonanno, Herman Gray and Toby Miller. Sage. https://doi.org/10 .4135/9781473910423.

Hunt, Darnell. 2017. *Race in the Writer's Room: How Hollywood Whitewashes the Stories that Shape America.* Color of Change Hollywood, https://hollywood .colorofchange.org/wp-content/uploads/2019/03/COC_Hollywood_Race _Report.pdf.

Hunt, Lee, interview by Barbara Selznick. 2023. August 15.

Hurwitz, Heather. 2020. *Are We the 99%? The Occupy Movement, Feminism and Intersectionality.* Philadelphia: Temple University Press.

Hutcheon, Linda, and Mario J. Valdes. 2000. "Irony, Nostalgia, and the Postmodern: A Dialogue." *Poligrafías* 3 (5): 18–41.

Ibrahim, Shamira. 2022. "Donald Glover Doesn't Know What To Do With Black Women." *Buzz Feed News,* November 10. Accessed July 29, 2023. https://www .buzzfeednews.com/article/shamiraibrahim/atlanta-season-four-donald-glover -black-women.

Innis, Leslie, and Joe Feagin. 1995. "The Cosby Show: The View from the Black Middle Class." *Journal of Black Studies* 25 (6): 692–711.

Itzkoff, Dave. 2014. "Netflix Snags New Series Created by Tina Fey and Robert Carlock." *Arts Beat, New York Times Blog,* November 21. Accessed July 28, 2023. https://archive.nytimes.com/artsbeat.blogs.nytimes.com/2014/11/21/netflix-series-tina-fey-robert-carlock/.

Itzkoff, Dave. 2015. "Netflix Builds its Own Superteam." *The New York Times,* April 7: C1.

Itzkoff, Dave. 2015. "Sprung from a Cult to Stream on TV." *The New York Times,* February 22: AR1.

Jaramillo, Deborah. 2002. "The Family Racket: AOL Time Warner, HBO, The Sopranos, and the Construction of a Quality Brand." *Journal of Communication Inquiry* 26 (1): 59–75.

Jayson, Sharon. 2009. "The Recession Generation." *USA Today,* June 24: 1A.

Jenner, Mareike. 2018. *Netflix and the Re-invention of Television.* Cham: Springer International.

Jillson, Calvin C. 2016. *The American Dream: In History, Politics, and Fiction.* Lawrence, KS: The University Press of Kansas.

Johnson, Derek. 2015. "Party Like It's 1999: Another Wave of Network Nostalgia." *Flow,* April 21. Accessed July 8, 2022. https://www.flowjournal.org/2015/04/party-like-it%E2%80%99s-1999/.

Joseph, Charles. 2018. "The CW Arrowverse and Myth-Making, or the Commodification of Transmedia Franchising." *International Journal of TV Serial Narratives,* 27–46.

Jost, John, and Orsolya Hunyady. 2003. "The Psychology of System Justification and the Pallative Function of Ideology." *European Review of Social Psychology* 13 (1): 111–53.

Jurgensen, John. 2015. "'Marvel's Daredevil': The Breakable Superheroes of Netflix." *Wall Street Journal,* April 10: D1.

Jurgensen, John. 2016. "Donald Glover's Hot 'Atlanta.'" *The Wall Street Journal,* September 30: D5.

Kadlec, Dan. 2014. "Millennials Put Their Surprising Stamp on the American Dream." *Time.com,* February 10. Accessed June 5, 2020. https://time.com/5074/millennials-put-their-surprising-stamp-on-the-american-dream/.

Kamp, David. 2009. "Rethinking the American Dream." *Vanity Fair,* March 5. Accessed July 2022. https://www.vanityfair.com/culture/2009/04/american-dream200904.

Katz, A. J. 2015. "They're Not Afraid Of the Dark." *Broadcasting & Cable,* March 9: 12–14.

Keightley, Emily, and Michael Pickering. 2014. "Retrotyping and the Marketing of Nostalgia." In *Media and Nostalgia,* edited by Katharina Niemeyer, 83–94. New York: Palgrave Macmillan.

Keller, Jared. 2015. "What Makes Americans So Optimistic?" *The Atlantic,* March 25. Accessed September 13, 2023. https://www.theatlantic.com/politics/archive/2015/03/the-american-ethic-and-the-spirit-of-optimism/388538/.

Kellner, Douglas. 2009. "Media Industries, Political Economy, and Media/Cultural Studies: An Articulation." In *Media Industries: History, Theory, and Method*, edited by Jennifer Holt and Alisa Perren, 95–107. Malden, MA: Wiley-Blackwell.

Kiefer, Brittaney. 2012. "CEO Q&A: Bill Abbott, Crown Media Family Networks." *PR Week,* August 1. Accessed September 13, 2023. https://www.prweek.com/article /1278488/ceo-q-a-bill-abbott-crown-media-family-networks-extended.

Kimmage, Michael. 2011. "The Politics of the American Dream, 1980 to 2008." In *The American Dream in the 21st Century*, edited by Sandra L. Hanson and John Kenneth White, 27–39. Philadelphia: Temply University Press.

Klinger, Barbara. 2006. *Beyond the Multiplex: Cinema, New Technologies, and the Home.* Berkeley: University of California.

Knox, Simone, and Kai Hanno Schwind. 2019. *Friends: A Reading of the Sitcom.* Cham: Palgrave Macmillan.

Kocela, Christopher. 2009. "Cynics Encouraged to Apply: The Office as Reality Viewer Training." *Journal of Popular FIlm and Television* 37 (4): 161–8.

Kompare, Derek. 2006. *Rerun Nation.* London: Taylor and Francis.

Kostidakis, Perry. 2016. "Donald Glover's 'Atlanta' is the Highlight of Fall TV." *FS View and Florida Flambeau (Florida State University)*, August 28: Arts 1.

Kozan, Saliha, Ellen Gutowski, and David Blustein. 2020. "A Qualitative Exploration of Women's Work Aspirations and Beliefs on Meritocracy." *Journal of Counseling Psychology* 67 (2): 195–207.

Krukoswki, Andrew. 2008. "'Office,' 'L&O: SVU' Headed to Fall '09." *TV Week,* December 14. Accessed July 11, 2022. https://www.tvweek.com/in-depth/2008/12/ office-lo-svu-headed-to-fall-0/.

Kulikowski, Lauri. 2014. "Netflix Ups Betting on Original Content." *TheStreet.com,* February 21. Accessed March 18, 2020. TheStreet.com.

Lackner, Chris. 2015. "Romance Feels Like the Longest Ride." *Windsor Star (Ontario),* April 6: A9.

Ladenburg, Kenneth. 2015. "Illuminating Whiteness and Racial Prejudice through Humor in It's Always Sunny in Philadelphia's 'The Gang Gets Racist.'" *Journal of Popular Culture* 48 (5): 859–77.

Lafayette, Jon. 2012. "Hallmark Channel Building a Home for Integrations." *Broadcasting & Cable*, March 19: 4.

Lafayette, Jon. 2014. "The CW's Ads Selling in a 'Flash.'" *Broadcasting & Cable*, October 27: 16.

Lagerwey, Jorie, Julia Leyda, and Diane Negra. 2016. "Female-Centered TV in an Age of Precarity." *Genders* 1 (2): Web.

Landau, Neil. 2018. *TV Writing On Demand: Creating Great Content in the Digital Era.* New York: Routledge.

Lausch, Kayti. 2021. "'Tune in to the Affirmative': The Family Channel and the Politics of Positive Programming." *Television and New Media* 22 (6): 616–32.

Learmonth, Michael. 2011. "Netflix Looks Toward Original Content, Competition with HBO Go." *AdAge,* December 6. Accessed May 4, 2020. https://adage.com/article/digital/netflix-original-content-competes-hbo/231411.

Lee, Mike. 2012. "Saving the American Dream." *Mike Leet U.S. Senator for Utah,* May 16. Accessed September 13, 2023. https://www.lee.senate.gov/2012/5/saving-the-american-dream.

Levin, Gary. 2015. "Netflix Has Big Plans for 2015 Originals." *USAToday.com,* January 8. Accessed July 28, 2023. https://www.usatoday.com/story/life/tv/2015/01/06/netflix-2015-lineup/21308665/.

Levinson, Julie. 2012. *The American Success Myth on Film.* New York: Palgrave.

Lima, Cecilia Almeida, Diego Gouveia Moreira, and Janaina Costa Calazans. 2015. "Netflix and the Maintenance of Television Genres Out of the Flow." *Matrizes* 9 (2): 237–55.

Lippman, Walter. 1914. *Drift and Mastery: An Attempt to Diagnose the Current Unrest.* New York: M. Kennerley.

Lipsitz, George. 1990. *Time Passages: Collective Memory and American Popular Culture.* Minneapolis: University of Minnesota Press.

Lisanti, Tony. 2013. "Avengers: The Tentpole Approach." *License: The Source for Licensing and Retail Intelligence,* June. Accessed May 6, 2020. www.licensemag.com.

Littleton, Cynthia. 2015. "FX Gives Series Order to Donald Glover Comedy 'Atlanta.'" *Variety.com,* October 15. Accessed July 28, 2023. https://variety.com/2015/tv/news/donald-glover-fx-community-atlanta-series-1201618952/.

Littleton, Cynthia. 2016. "Donald Glover Celebrates 'Absurdity of the World' in FX's 'Atlanta.'" *Variety.com,* January 16. Accessed July 29, 2023. https://variety.com/2016/tv/news/donald-glover-atlanta-fx-comedy-series-1201681620/.

Littleton, Cynthia. 2016. "USA Network Revamps Brand Image, Tagline for 'Mr. Robot' Era." *Variety,* April 14. Accessed September 13, 2023. https://variety.com/2016/tv/news/mr-robot-usa-network-brand-tagline-refresh-1201752745/.

Lizardi, Ryan. 2015. *Mediated Nostalgia: Indvidual Memory and Contemporary Mass Media.* Lanham: Lexington Books.

Lizardi, Ryan. 2018. "Mourning and Melancholia: Conflicting Approaches to Reviving Gilmore Girls One Season at a Time." *Television and New Media* 19 (4): 379–95.

Loofbourow, Lili. 2015. "Girls' Club." *The New York Times Magazine,* January 16: 20–1.

Lotz, Amanda D. 2007. *The Television Will be Revolutionized.* New York: New York University Press.

Lotz, Amanda D. 2018. *We Now Disrupt this Broadcast: How Cable Transformed Television and the Internet Revolutionized it All.* Cambridge: MIT Press.

Low, Elaine. 2019. "Reruns Raise Mega Millions from Streamers." *Variety,* December 4: 126.

Lowenthal, David. 1985. *The Past is a Foreign Country.* Cambridge: Cambridge University Press.

loyalkaspar. n.d. "USA Brand Identity." *loyalkaspar.* Accessed September 13, 2023. https://www.loyalkaspar.com/usa.

Lund, Jeb. 2019. "Hallmark's Christmas Movies are Part of a Culture War their Viewers are Losing." *The Washington Post,* December 23. Accessed September 13, 2023. https://www.washingtonpost.com/outlook/2019/12/23/hallmarks-christmas-movies -are-part-culture-war-their-viewers-are-losing/.

Lyall, Sarah. 2016. "Viewing Habits of the Complex Millennial." *The New York Times,* May 16: B1.

Lynch, Jason. 2015. "The Not-So-Funny State of TV Comedy." *Adweek.com,* Feburary 16. Accessed July 28, 2023. https://www.adweek.com/convergent-tv/not-so-funny -state-tv-comedy-162976/.

Lynch, Jason. 2016. "How Risk-Taking Catapulted FX's John Landgraf to TV Executive of the Year." *Adweek.com,* November 28.

Mallick, Heather. 2015. "The Growing Childishness of American Adults." *The Toronto Star,* April 8: A19.

Malone, Michael. 2014. "The Loneliest Stations in the Nation." *Broadcasting & Cable,* October 27: 17.

Maly, Michael, Heather Dalmage, and Nancy Michaels. 2012. "The End of the Idylic World: Nostalgia Narratives, Race, and the Construction of White Powerlessness." *Critical Sociology* 39 (5): 757–79.

Mandese, Joe. 1999. "'Friends' Vaults into Top-Priced Syndie Spot." *Advertising Age,* January 18. Accessed July 8, 2022. https://adage.com/article/news/friends-vaults-top -priced-syndie-spot-sitcom-breaks-a-record-net-season/63812.

Mangan, Ben. 2011. "Does Occupy Wall Street Have the 'X-Factor'?" *HuffPost,* October 20. Accessed September 13, 2023. https://www.huffpost.com/entry/occupy-wall -street-x-factor_b_1016159.

Marcus, Daniel. 2004. *Happy Days and Wonder Years; The Fifties and the Sixties in Contemporary Cultural Politics.* New Brunswick, NJ: Rutgers University Press.

Marian, Cate. 2016. "USA Network Revamps Brand with 'We the Bold' Tagline." *Promax,* April 14. Accessed September 13, 2023. https://brief.promax.org/article/usa -network-revamps-brand-with-we-the-bold-tagline.

Martin, Ed. 2014. "The CW President Mark Pedowitz on 'The Vampire Diaries,' 'The 100' and More." *Media Village,* January 22. Accessed April 13, 2020. www .mediavillage.com /article/the-cw-president-mark-pedowitz-on-the-vampire-diari es-the-100-and-more-ed-martin/.

McCall, Leslie. 2013. *The Underserving Rich: American Beliefs about Inequality, Opportunity, and Redistribution.* New York: Cambridge University Press.

McCarthy, Tyler. 2014. "'Marvel's Daredevil' Upcoming Netflix Series Just Cast Its Villain." *The Huffington Post,* June 11. Accessed March 18, 2020. huffingtonpost.com.

McClay, Wilfred. 2016. "A Distant Elite: How Meritocracy Went Wrong." *The Hedgehog Review* 18 (2): 36–49.

McDonald, Kevin. 2016. "From Online Video Store to Global Internet TV Network." In *The Netflix Effect: Technology and Entertainment in the 21st Century*, edited by Kevin McDonald and Daniel Smith-Rowsey, 203–18. New York: Bloomsbury.

McDowell, Walter, and Alan Batten. 2005. *Branding TV: Principles and Practices.* Burlington: Focal Press.

McGee, Rex. 1979. "TVs Fall Offensive: The Tent-Pole Strategy." *American Film*, September 1: 26–31.

McLean, Thomas J. 2012. "Comedies Old and New Enjoy Bounce in Syndie Marketplace." *Variety*, January 23–9: 20.

McNamee, Stephen J., and Robert K. Miller. 2018. *The Meritocracy Myth.* New York: Rowman and Littlefield.

McSweeney, Terence. 2018. *Avengers Assemble: Critical Perspectives on the Marvel Cinematic Universite.* London: Wallflower Press.

Menke, Manuel. 2017. "Seeking Comfort in Past Media: Modeling Media Nostalgia as a Way of Coping With Media Change." *International Journal of Communication* 11: 626–46.

Metz, Nina. 2019. "'The Office' is Netflix's Most Popular Show, Even Though it was Made For and Originally Aired on an Old-School Broadcast Network." *Chicago Tribune,* July 3. Accessed July 11, 2022. https://www.chicagotribune.com/ entertainment/tv/ct-mov-netflix-the-office-0705-20190703-fjlo4pkt5jb7llpo2ai xl7o2pe-story.html.

Metz, Walter. 2018. "A Hallmark of the Classical Holiday Cinema, or Meeting Two Christmas Queens." *Film Criticism* 42 (4). https://quod.lib.umich.edu/f/fc/13761232 .0042.410?view=text;rgn=main. https://quod.lib.umich.edu/f/fc/13761232.0042.410 ?view=text;rgn=main.

Miller, Dale, and Bill Merrilees. 2011. "Corporate Rebranding." In *Corporate Reputation Managing Opportunities and Threats*, edited by Ronald Burke, Graeme Martin, and Cary Cooper, 281–303. Burlington: Gower.

Mills, Brett. 2004. "Comedy Verite: Contemporary Sitcom Form." *Screen* 45 (1): 63–78.

Mills, Brett. 2009. *The Sitcom.* Edinburgh: Edinburgh University Press.

Mittell, Jason. 2015. *Complex TV: The Poetics of Contemporary Television Storytelling.* New York: New York University Press.

Mondal, Anshuman. 2018. "Taking Liberties? Free Speech, Multiculturalism and the Ethics of Satire." In *Comedy and the Politics of Representation*, edited by Helen Davies and Sarah Ilott, 25–41. London: Palgrave McMillan.

Monk-Payton, Brandy. 2024. "'I'm Trying to Make People Feel Black': Affective Authenticity in Atlanta." In *Watching While Black Rebooted*, edited by Beretta Smith-Shomade, 169–84. Ithaca, NY: Rutgers University Press.

Morgan, Danielle Fuentes. 2020. *Laughing to Keep from Dying: African American Satire in the Twenty-first Century.* Urbana: University of Illinois Press.

Morris, Emily. 2016. "Ranking 2015's Most Culturally Relevant Shows." *Multichannel News*, January 4: 31.

Morris, Wesley. 2016. "'Atlanta' Walks a Line Between Magic Realism and Keeping it Real." *The New York Times*, October 19: Web.

Morris, Wesley, and James Poniewozik. 2016. "Why 'Diverse' TV Matters: It's Better TV. Discuss." *The New York Times*, February 10: Web.

Moylan, Brian. 2015. "California Streaming: An Inside Look at the Netflix 'War Room.'" *The Guardian*, April 10.

Moylan, Brian. 2015. "Unbreakable Kimmy Schmidt." *The Guardian*, March 5: Web.

Mudhar, Raju. 2014. "Can Superheroes Save Prime Time TV?" *Waterloo Region Record*, June 25. Accessed October 8, 2023. https://www.therecord.com/things-to-do/can -superheroes-save-prime-time-tv/article_3ea7eb83-9809-5330-bb16-c09f741fc8fc .html.

"Multicultural Content Goes Multiplatform." 2016. *Multichannel News,* April 6: 13.

Murphy, James. 2015. "How Mr. Robot Killed the Centerpiece of Prestige Television: Capitalism." *Vanity Fair,* September 2. Accessed September 13, 2023. https://www .vanityfair.com/hollywood/2015/09/mr-robot-capitalism.

Murphy, Mike. 2015. "Biz Break." *San Jose Mercury News*, April 6.

Murray, John C. 2019. "The Consumer Has Been Added to Your Video Queue." In *Netflix Nostalgia: Streaming the Past on Demand*, edited by Kathryn Pallister, 57–74. Lexington: Lexington Books.

Murray, Mitch. 2017. "The Work of Art in the Age of the Superhero." *Science Fiction Film and Television* 10 (1): 27–51.

Murray, Simone. 2005. "Brand Loyalties: Rethinking Content within Global Corporate Media." *Media Culture and Society* 27 (3): 415–35.

Napoli, Philip. 2009. "Media Economics and the Study of Media Industries." In *Media Industries: History, Theory, and Method*, edited by Jennifer Holt and Alisa Perren, 161–70. Malden, MA: Wiley-Blackwell.

"NBC: iPod Boosts Prime Time." 2006. *TVWeek,* January 16. Accessed July 8, 2022. https://www.tvweek.com/in-depth/2006/01/nbc-ipod-boosts-prime-time-1/.

Newcomb, Horace, and Paul Hirsch. 1983. "Television as a Cultural Forum: Implications for Research." *Quarterly Review of Film Studies* 8 (3): 45–55.

Newman, Benjamin, Christopher Johnston, and Patrick Lown. 2015. "False Consciousness or Class Awareness? Local Income Inequality, Personal Economic Position, and Belief in American Meritocracy." *American Journal of Political Science* 59 (2): 326–40.

Newman, Emily, and Emily Witsell. 2020. "Introduction." In *The Hallmark Channel: Essays on Faith, Race and Feminism*, edited by Emily Newman and Emily Witsell, 1–14. Jefferson, NC: MacFarland & Co.

Newman, Michael Z., and Elana Levine. 2012. *Legitimating Television: Media Convergence and Cultural Status.* New York: Routledge.

Neylon, Cáit. 2022. "Irrational Exuberance: Cuteness as Affective Bubble in Crazy Ex-Girlfriend and Unbreakable Kimmy Schmidt." *Feminist Media Studies* (Routledge), 1–16.

Nielsen. 2014. *Millennials—Breaking the Myths.* The Nielsen Company.

Niemeyer, Katharina, and Daniela Wentz. 2014. "Nostalgia Is Not What It Used to Be: Serial Nostalgia and Nostalgic Television Series." In *Media and Nostalgia: Yearning for the Past, Present and Future*, edited by Katharine Niemeyer, 129–38. London: Palgrave Macmillan.

Nussbaum, Emily. 2015. "The Price is Right: What Advertising Does to TV." *The New Yorker,* October 5. Accessed September 13, 2023. https://www.newyorker.com/ magazine/2015/10/12/the-price-is-right-emily-nussbaum.

Obama, Barack. 2007. "Obama's November 7, 2007, Speech on the 'American Dream.'" *CNN.com,* November 7. Accessed September 13, 2023. www.cnn.com/2007/politics /12/21/obama.trans.americandream/.

Obama, Barack. 2013. "Remarks by the President on Economic Mobility." *The White House Office of the Press Secretary,* December 4. Accessed July 2022. https:// obamawhitehouse.archives.gov/the-press-office/2013/12/04/remarks-president -economic-mobility.

O'Connell, Mikey. 2015. "Tina Fey: What Netflix Move Means for 'Unbreakable Kimmy Schmidt." *HollywoodReporter.com,* January 7. Accessed July 28, 2023. https://www .hollywoodreporter.com/tv/tv-news/tina-fey-what-netflix-move-761584/.

Oh, David. 2020. "'Opting out of That': White Feminism's Policing and Disavowal of Anti-Racist Critique in The Unbreakable Kimmy Schmidt." *Critical Studies in Mass Communication* 37 (1): 58–70.

O'Donnell, Jennifer Lee. 2021. "Groomed for Capitalism: Biopower and the Self-Care, Self-Improvement Rituals of Adolescence in Bo Burnham's Eighth Grade and Donald Glover's Atlanta." *Social Identities: Journal for the Study of Race, Nation and Culture* (Routledge) 27 (3): 307–25.

Otterson, Joe. 2017. "Donald Glover's 'Atlanta' to Stream on Hulu." *Variety.com,* May 3. Accessed July 28, 2023. https://variety.com/2017/tv/news/atlanta-donald-glover -hulu-1202407669/.

Owen, Rob. 2013. "Debbie Macomber's 'Cedar Cove.'" *Pittsburgh Post-Gazette,* July 14: TV1.

Pagello, Federico. 2017. "The 'Origin Story' is the Only Story: Seriality and Temporality in Superhero Fiction from Comics to Post-Television." *Quarterly Review of Film and Video* 34 (8): 725–45.

Parmett, Helen Morgan. 2016. "It's HBO: Passionate Engagement, TV Branding, and Tourism in the Postbroadcast Era." *Communication and Critical/Cultural Studies* 13 (1): 3–22.

Parrot Analytics. 2021. *The Global Demand for Sitcoms.* July 1. Accessed July 8, 2022. https://www.parrotanalytics.com/insights/the-global-demand-for-sitcoms/.

Patrick, Stephanie. 2017. "Breaking Free?: Domesticity, Entrapment, and Postfeminism in Unbreakable Kimmy Schmidt." *The Journal of American Culture* 40 (3): 235–49.

Patrick, Stephanie. 2021. "You Get to Stop Him!: Gendered Violence and Interactive Witnessing in Netflix's Kimmy vs The Reverend." *Critical Studies in Television* 16 (1): 30–46.

Peabody Awards. 2016. *Atlanta*. Accessed July 28, 2023. https://peabodyawards.com/award-profile/atlanta/.

Pennington, Gail. 2015. "Ellie Kemper Makes Lemonade in 'Unbreakable Kimmy Schmidt'." *St. Louis Post-Dispatch*, March 6: G23.

Perdiago, Lisa. 2017. "'I Must Become Something Else': The Evolution of the CW's Arrow." In *Arrow and Superhero Television: Essays on Themes and Characters of the Series*, edited by Cory Barker, James Iaccino, and Myc Wiatroswki, 11–26. Jefferson, NC: McFarland.

Perrucci, Robert, and Carolyn Perrucci. 2009. *America at Risk: The Crisis of Hope, Trust, and Caring.* Lanham, MD: Rowman & Littlefield.

Peterson, Richard, and Roger Kern. 1996. "Changing Highbrow Taste: From Snob to Omnivore." *American Sociological Review* 61 (5): 900–7.

Petrashko, Paige. 2016. "Donald Glover's 'Atlanta' is a Triumphant Exploration of Racial Politics." *Daily Californian (University of California—Berkeley)*, September 12: Arts 1.

Pew Research Center. 2006. *Once Again, the Future Ain't What It Used to Be.* Social Trends Report, Pew Research Center, 1–14.

Pew Research Center. 2011. "Home Sweet Home. Still." *Pew Research Center,* April 12. Accessed July 29, 2023. https://www.pewresearch.org/social-trends/2011/04/12/home-sweet-home-still/.

Pew Research Center. 2014. "Millennials in Adulthood." *Pew Research Center,* March 7. Accessed July 20, 2020. https://www.pewsocialtrends.org/2014/03/07/millennials-in-adulthood/.

Pineda, Antonio, and Jesus Jimenez-Varea. 2017. "'You have failed this city': Arrow, Left-Wing Vigilantism and the Modern Day Robin Hood." In *Arrow and Superhero Television: Essays on Themes and Characters of the Series*, edited by Cory Barker, James Iaccino, and Myc Wiatrowski, 150–66. Jefferson, NC: McFarland.

Platon, Adelle. 2016. "Actor Brian Tyree Henry Talks Atlanta Hip-Hop & Working with Donald Glover on FX Show 'Atlanta'." *Billboard.com,* September 1. Accessed July 29, 2023. https://www.billboard.com/music/rb-hip-hop/actor-brian-tyree-henry-donald-glover-atlanta-tv-7495405/.

Proctor, William. 2017. "'Bitches Ain't Gonna Hunt No Ghosts': Totemic Nostalgia, Toxic Fandom and the Ghostbusters Platonic." *Palabra-Clave* 20 (4): 1105–41.

Pursell, Chris. 2006. "'Office,' 'Family' Natpe Darlings." *Television Week*, December: 17–19.

Pustz, Matthew. 2006. "Spider-Man: Class Straddler as Superhero." In *Webslinger: Unauthorized Essays on Your Friendly Neighborhood Spider-man*, edited by Gerry Conway and Leah Wilson, 73–86. Dallas: BenBella Books.

"Q2 2013 Crown Media Holding Inc. Earnings Conference Call." 2013. *Fair Disclosure Wire,* July 1.

Radosinska, Jana. 2017. "New Trends in Production and Distribution of Episodic Television Drama: Brand Marvel-Netflix in the Post-Television Era." *Communication Today* 8 (1): 4–29.

Redfearn, Dominique. 2016. "Donald Glover's 'Atlanta' Already Renewed for Second Season." *Billboard,* September 20. Accessed July 28, 2023. https://www.billboard .com/music/music-news/fx-atlanta-renewed-second-season-donald-glover -7517943/.

Reid, Michael D. 2012. "Hatley Castle Home to the Arrow." *Canwest News Service,* March 12. Accessed April 14, 2020. https://advance-lexis-com.ezproxy1.library .arizona.edu/api/document?collection=news&id=urn:contentItem:555G-T991- JDK3-93C0-00000-00&context=1516831.

Reisman, Abraham. 2016. "Greg Berlanti Knows the Secret to Superhero TV." *New York,* September 5.

"Report Details Anxiety Over 'American Dream.'" 2007. *Voice of America,* July 26. Accessed September 13, 2023. https://www.voanews.com/a/a-13-2007-07-26-voa27 /404331.html.

Rhone, Nedra. 2016. "'Atlanta' to Finally Premiere." *The Atlanta Journal-Constitution,* June 30: 2D.

Robinson, MJ. 2017. *Television on Demand.* New York: Bloomsbury.

Roemer, John. 2018. "Equality of Opportunity." In *Meritocracy and Economic Inequality,* edited by Kenneth Arrow, Samuel Bowles, and Steven Durlauf, 17–32. Princeton, NJ: Princeton University Press.

Rose, Lacey. 2012. "Upfronts 2012: CW Peddles Bold Programming, Fan Favorites and the Power of Netflix." *HollywoodReporter.com,* May 17. Accessed April 14, 2020. https://www.hollywoodreporter.com/news/upfronts-2012-cw-ringer-gossip-girl -netflix-326170.

Rosenberg, Alyssa. 2015. "A Sardonic Comedy with Bite." *Ottawa Citizen,* March 14: F8.

Rosenberg, Alyssa. 2015. "Daredevil the Wrong Hero for Out Times?" *Edmonton Journal (Alberta),* April 18: D2.

Rossiter, John, and Steve Bellman. 2012. "Emotional Branding Pays Off." *Journal of Advertising Research* 52 (3): 291–6.

Roy, Subhadip, and Soumya Sarkar. 2015. "To Brand or to Rebrand: Investigating the Effects of Rebranding on Brand Equity and Consumer Attitudes." *Journal of Brand Management* 22 (4): 340–60.

Rudin, April, and Catherine McBreen. 2017. "The Psychology of Millennials." In *Financial Behavior: Players, Services, Products, and Markets,* edited by H. Kent Baker,

Greg Filbeck, and Victor Ricciardi, 241–62. Oxford: Oxford University Press. DOI:1 0.1093/acprof:oso/9780190269999.003.0014.

Sacks, Ethan. 2015. "Devil in the Night." *Daily News (NY)*, April 5: 3.

Samuel, Lawrence R. 2012. *The American Dream: A Cultural History*. Syracuse: Syracuse University Press.

Sandell, Jillian. 1998. "I'll Be There For You: Friends and the Fantasy of Alternative Families." *American Studies* 39 (2): 141–55.

Sands, Zach. 2018. *Film Comedy and the American Dream*. London: Routledge.

Saraiya, Sonia. 2019. "Why is Gen Z So Obsessed with The Office." *Vanity Fair*, April 26. Accessed July 11, 2022. https://www.vanityfair.com/hollywood/2019/04/billie-eilish -the-office-gen-z-netflix.

Scepanski, Philip. 2021. *Tragedy Plus Time: National Trauma and Television Comedy*. Austin: University of Texas Press.

Schafer, Lee. 2015. "American Dream Now is Just to Hold On." *Star Tribune (Minneapolis MN)*, May 24: 1D.

Schneider, Michael. 2009. "'Office' Clocks in to Syndie on Upswing." *Variety*, September 28/October 4: 14, 16.

Schoon, Ingrid, and Jeylan Mortimer. 2017. "Youth and the Great Recession: Are Values, Achievement Orientation and Outlook to the Future Affected?" *International Journal of Psychology* 52 (1): 1–8.

Scott, Janny, and David Leonhardt. 2005. "Shadowy Lines That Still Divide." *The New York Times*, May 15. Accessed July 7, 2022. https://www.nytimes.com/2005/05/15/us /class/shadowy-lines-that-still-divide.html.

Seale, Jack. 2015. "Unbreakable Kimmy Schmidt." *The Guardian*, March 10: Web.

Sedikides, Constantine, and Tim Wildschut. 2018. "Finding Meaning in Nostalgia." *Review of General Psychology* 22 (1): 48–61.

Selznick, Barbara. 2009. "Branding the Future: Syfy in the Post-network Era." *Science Fiction Film and Television* 2 (2): 177–204.

Selznick, Barbara. 2018. "Freeform: Shaking Off the Family Brand within a Conglomerate Family." In *From Networks to Netflix: A Guide to Changing Channels*, edited by Derek Johnson, 219–28. New York: Routledge.

Sen, Armatya. 2000. "Merit and Justice." In *Meritocracy and Economic Inequality*, edited by Kenneth Arrow, Samuel Bowles, and Steven Durlauf, 5–16. Princeton, NJ: Princeton University Press.

Serazio, Michael. 2013. "Selling (Digital) Millennials: The Social Construction and Technological Bias of a Consumer Generation." *Television and New Media* 16 (7): 599–615.

Setiaki, Tsamarah Augustina, and Herlin Destari. 2019. "Unbreakable Dong Nguyen: Reaffirming Asian-American Masculinity in the Series Unbreakable Kimmy Schmidt." *International Review of Humanities Studies* 4 (1): 104–13. www.irhs.ui .ac.id.

Shapiro, Ari. 2012. "American Dream Faces Harsh New Reality." *NPR,* May 29. Accessed September 13, 2023. https://www.npr.org/2012/05/29/153513153/american-dream -faces-harsh-new-reality.

Shapiro, Stephen. 2016. "Realignment and Televisual Intellect: The Telepraxis of Class Alliancesin Contemporary Subscription Television Drama." In *Class Divisions in Serial Television,* edited by Sieglinde Lemke and Wibke Schniedermann, 177–205. London: Palgrave MacMillan.

Shaviro, Steven. 2012. "Post-Continuity: Full Text from My Talk." *The Pinocchio Theory,* March 26. Accessed July 28, 2023. http://www.shaviro.com/Blog/?p=1034.

Sheridan, Patricia. 2012. "Marie Osmond." *Pittsburgh Post-Gazette*, October 1: C1.

Siegemund-Broka, Austin. 2014. "CBS Execs Talk Plans to Increase Diversity." *The Hollywood Reporter*, November 7: Web.

Sinha, Jill W. 2017. "Millennials and Social Capital: Explorations in Re-Inventing the American Dream." In *Social Capital and Community Well-Being*, edited by Alva G. Greenberg, Thomas P. Gullotta, and Martin Bloom, 13–31. Cham: Spring International.

Skovmand, Michael. 2008. "The Culture of Post-Narcissism Post-teenage, Pre-midlife Singles Culture in Seinfeld, Friends, and Ally—Seinfeld in Particular." In *Television and Criticism*, edited by Solange Davin and Rhona Jackson, 205–13. Bristol: Intellect.

Slattery, Laura. 2015. "Netflix Steps Up Release of Original in Pursh for Must Have Status." *The Irish Times*, February 12: 8.

Smith, Anthony. 2018. "Pursuing 'Generation Snowflake': Mr. Robot and the USA Network's Mission for Millennials." *Television and New Media* 20 (5): 443–59.

Smith, Hedrick. 2012. *Who Stole the American Dream?* New York: Random House.

Smith, Nigel. 2016. "FX Takes Major Steps to Improve Diversity in 'Racially Biased' TV System." *The Guardian*. August 9.

Smith, Sarah. 2015. "Netflix's 'Daredevil' Takes Superhero Origin Story to New Heights." *Kansas City Star*, April 8: A10.

Spangler, Todd. 2014. ""Disney to Spend $200 Million on Marvel Series for Netflix Set to Film in NY." *Variety.com,* February 26. Accessed May 6, 2020. Variety.com.

Sperb, Jason. 2021. "Clearing Up the Haze: Toward a Definition of the 'Nostalgia Film' Genre." In *Was It Yesterday? Nostalgia in Contemporary Film and Television*, edited by Matthew Leggatt, 15–33. Albany: State University of New York.

Stamps, David L. 2017. "The Social Construction of the African American Family on Broadcast Television: A Comparative Analysis of The Cosby Show and Blackish." *Howard Journal of Communications* 28 (4): 405–20.

Stanhope, Kate. 2016. "Donald Glover Previews His FX Comedy 'Atlanta': "'Twin Peaks' With Rappers"." *TheHollywoodReporter.com,* January 16. Accessed July 29, 2023. https://www.hollywoodreporter.com/tv/tv-news/donald-glover-previews-his-fx -comedy-atlanta-twin-peaks-rappers-856412/.

Stanley, T. L. 2012. "CW's 'Arrow' Aiming for More Realistic Hero." *Daily Press (Newport News, Virginia)*, September 21: C10.

Stein, Louisa Ellen. 2015. *Millennial Fandom: Television Audiences in the Transmedia Age.* Iowa City: University of Iowa Press.

Stephan, Matthias. 2019. "Branding Netflix with Nostalgia: Totemic Nostalgia, Adaptation, and the Postmodern Turn." In *Netflix Nostalgia: Streaming the Past on Demand*, edited by Kathryn Pallister, 25–39. Lexington: Lexington Books.

Stephen, Bijan. 2018. "Atlanta Dreaming." *Dissent*, 7–10.

Sternbergh, Adam. 2019. "Is Friends Still the Most Popular Show on TV?" *Vulture*, September 17. Accessed July 8, 2022. https://www.vulture.com/2016/03/20 -somethings-streaming-friends-c-v-r.html.

Steuver, Hank. 2016. "Glover Return to TV with Hypnotic 'Atlanta'." *Chicago Daily Herald*, September 5: 12.

Stevenson, Billy. 2020. "Cedar Cove and the Spaces of Hallmark." In *The Hallmark Channel: Essays on Faith, Race and Feminism*, edited by Emily Newman and Emily Witsell, 174–88. Jefferson, NC: MacFarland & Company.

Stevenson, Billy. 2021. "Television After Complexity: Crazy Ex-Girlfriend and the Late 2010s." In *Perspectives on Crazy Ex-Girlfriend: Nuanced Postnetwork Television*, edited by Amanda Konkle and Charles Burnetts, 78–91. Syracuse: Syracuse University Press.

"Streaming Service Bent on Raising the Dead." 2014. *Broadcasting & Cable*, December 8: 44.

Sung, Yongjun, and Namkee Park. 2011. "The Dimensions of Cable Television Network Personality: Implications for Media Brand Management." *International Journal on Media Management* 13 (1): 87–105.

Sutton, Kelsey. 2019. "You Gotta Have Friends." *AdWeek*, October 21: 21–2.

Thielman, Sam. 2014. "This Fall DC Gets Its TV On." *Adweek*, September 22: 10.

Thomas, Rob. 2015. "Netflix's 'Daredevil' Might Just Be the 'The Wire' of Superhero Shows." *Capital Times (Madison)*, April 15: 33.

Thomas, Rodney A. 2017. "'What, O.J. and Charles Manson Weren's Available?: DC Comics, the CW's Arrow and the Quest for Racial Diversity." In *Arrow and Superhero Television: Essays on Themes and Characters of the Series*, edited by James Iaccino, Cory Barker, and Myc Wiatrowski, 167–76. Jefferson, NC: McFarland.

Thompson, Craig, Aric Rindfleisch, and Zeynep Arsel. 2006. "Emotional Branding and the Strategic Value of the Doppelgänger Brand Image." *Journal of Marketing* 70: 50–64.

Truitt, Brian. 2012. "'Arrow' Targets the Small Screen." *USA Today*, October 9: 1D.

Truitt, Brian. 2015. "In 'Daredevil,' Darkness if Visible; Netflix Series Brings Grit of a Crime Drama to Marvel's World." *USA Today*, April 7: 3D.

Truitt, Brian. 2017. "You Won't Believe What Shows Lead Viewers to Watch Netflix's Marvel Series." *USA Today*, August 22.

Tucker, Terrence. 2018. *Furiously Funny: Comic Rage from Ralph Ellison to Chris Rock.* Gainesville: University Press of Florida.

Tueth, Michael V. 2000. "Fun City: TV's Urban Situation Comedies of the 1990s." *Journal of Popular Film and Television* 28 (3): 98–107.

Tueth, Michael V. 2016. "Breaking and Entering: Transgressive Comedy on Television." In *The Sitcom Reader*, edited by Laura Linder and Mary Dalton, 247–58. Albany: State University of New York Press.

Turchiano, Danielle. 2019. "How Hallmark Built a 'Brand Experience' Around 'Countdown to Christmas.'" *Variety,* November 15. Accessed September 13, 2023. https://variety.com/2019/tv/features/hallmark-countdown-to-christmas-10th -anniversary-candace-cameron-bure-ron-oliver-interview-1203399216/.

Turnock, Robert. 2007. *Television and Consumer Culture: Britain and the Transformation of Modernity.* London: I.B. Tauris.

Tyler, Lisa. 2020. "'Embrace the Community': Hallmark Channel Movies and Childhood Nostalgia." In *The Hallmark Channel: Essays on Faith, Race and Feminism*, edited by Emily Newman and Emily Witsell, 17–31. Jackson, NC: MacFarland & Co.

Tyson, Alec. 2016. "Americans' Views of Job Availability Among Most Positive in Last 15 Years." *Pew Research Center,* April 1. Accessed July 8, 2022. https://www .pewresearch.org/fact-tank/2016/04/01/americans-views-of-job-availability-among -most-positive-in-last-15-years/.

Uchitelle, Louis. 2010. "American Dream is Elusive for New Generation." *The New York Times,* July 7: A1.

Umstead, R. Thomas. 2012. "Hallmark Lures Women Back." *Multichannel News,* October 8: 14.

Umstead, R. Thomas. 2013. "Holiday Movies Give Hallmark a Ratings Lift." *Multichannel News,* December 9: 16.

Umstead, R. Thomas. 2016. "FX's 'Atlanta' Draws 3 Million Viewers in Premiere." *Multichannel News,* September 13. Accessed July 28, 2023. https://www.nexttv.com/ news/fx-s-atlanta-draws-3-million-viewers-premiere-407713.

Varghese, Daniel. 2016. "Why Glover's Atlanta is Essential TV." *The Georgetown Voice (Georgetown University),* September 12: 1.

Vernon, Matthew, and Daniel Gustafson. 2020. "A World on Fire: Seeing Beyond the Discrimination Paradim in Marvel's Daredevil." *Journal of Graphic Novels and Comics* 11 (2): 144–66.

Wallenstein, Andrew. 2015. "Netflix Ratings Revealed: New Data Sheds Light on Original Series' Audience Levels." *Variety,* April 28. Accessed May 6, 2020. Variety.com.

Warner, Kristen. 2015. *The Cultural Politics of Colorblind TV Casting.* London: Routledge.

Wayne, Michael. 2017. "Netflix, Amazon, and Branded Television Content in Subscription Video On-Demand Portals." *Media, Culture and Society* 40 (5): 725–41.

Weinstein, Shelli. 2015. "Netflix, AMC, Sony Execs Talk 'New Era of Television.'" *Variety .com,* February 10. Accessed July 28, 2023. https://variety.com/2015/biz/news/netflix -amc-sony-execs-talk-new-era-of-television-the-way-we-keep-score-has-changed -1201429984/.

White, John. 2011. "The Presidency and the Making of the American Dream." In *The American Dream in the 21st Century*, edited by Sandra Hanson and John White, 41–58. Philadelphia: Temple University Press.

White, John, and Sandra Hanson. 2011. "The Making and Persistence of the American Dream." In *The American Dream in the 21st Century*, edited by Sandra Hanson and John White, 1–16. Philadelphia: Temple University Press.

Whitney, Daisy. 2002. "Cable's Bossy Branding: Nets Employ New Taglines, Palettes to Recast Image." *Electronic Media*, July 15: 23.

Wiegand, David. 2015. "'Kimmy' is No Lemon, But She's Funny on Her Own." *Pittsburgh Post-Gazette*, March 6: A9.

Williams, Bob. 2017. *The Privileges of Wealth: Rising Inequality and the Growing Racial Divide*. London: Routledge.

"Worth Watching, Driven by Demand." 2015. *Broadcasting & Cable,* January 5: 1.

Xu, Yilan, Carrie Johnson, Suzanne Bartholomae, Barbara O'Neill, and Michael Gutter. 2015. "Homeownership Among Millennials: The Deferred American Dream?" *Family and Consumer Sciences Research Journal* 44 (2): 201–12.

Zimmer, Ben. 2015. "From Stage to Screen, the Rise of 'Tentpoles.'" *Wall Street Journal On-line,* May 15. Accessed February 2020. ProQuest.

Zinoman, Jason. 2015. "More Plot than Jokes. Can These Be Sitcoms?" *The New York Times*, March 26: C1.

Index

Abbott, Bill 71, 72, 75, 77, 78, 89, 91 n.13
Adams, James Truslow 53 n.3
  The Epic of America 1, 17
Agent Carter (2015–16) 39, 41, 54 n.9
Agents of S.H.I.E.L.D (2013–20) 38, 39,
  41, 54 n.9
Amazon Prime Video 11, 42, 100, 101
American Dream, *see also* meritocracy
  for Black Americans 5, 62, 63, 96–7,
    105, 114, 121–31, 133 n.5, 174
  community/social responsibility 4,
    5, 8, 9, 14–19, 21, 22, 33, 35, 46–8,
    51–3, 59, 75, 76, 79, 89, 154, 156,
    157, 164, 171, 173
  equality/fairness 4–9, 13, 14, 18–19,
    22, 33, 35, 62, 63, 83–4, 93, 94,
    96–8, 104, 106, 111, 114, 117, 121,
    129, 173, 174
  freedom/agency 1–3, 5, 6, 9, 13, 14,
    16–22, 24, 25, 28–37, 45–7, 50,
    52–3, 57, 58, 93, 99, 110, 113, 117,
    118, 121, 125, 129–32, 138, 168, 173
  and the Great Recession 6–10
  history of 1–10
  hope within 1, 8, 13, 20, 31, 57,
    58–65, 69, 75, 79, 80–2, 84, 86,
    88–90, 96, 118, 131, 135, 136, 144,
    148, 156, 157, 162, 170, 171, 175
  (*see* optimism for)
  individualism/individual
    responsibility 2–6, 8, 9, 14, 16–19,
    21, 22, 32, 35, 46, 52, 53, 53 n.3, 57–
    60, 62, 75, 76, 95, 98, 104, 115–18,
    121, 130, 151, 154, 156, 173
  and Millennials 20–2, 44–5
  nostalgia for 136–9
  optimism for 8, 9, 14, 20, 57–68,
    75–6, 79, 82–4, 86, 88–90, 93, 115,
    118, 131, 135, 136, 138–9, 141, 151,
    153–4, 156, 162, 173
  for women 5, 55 n.12, 63, 75, 96, 97,
    116–19

Arrow (2012–20) 14, 16, 23–37, 39,
  44, 45, 49, 51, 52, 54 n.9, 54 n.10,
  55 nn.14, 16, 81, 95, 106, 126
Atlanta (2016–22) 14, 94, 99, 108,
  119–32

Banet-Weiser, Sarah 29, 141
Black Lives Matter movement 62, 105,
  123, 174
brand/branding 66
  brand identity 67, 75
  Cultural Innovation Theory
    of 67–9, 79
  The CW 35, 41, 52
  FX Network 119–21
  Hallmark Channel 69–79, 89, 135
  Netflix 44, 45, 52, 110
  rebranding 14, 68–9, 75, 88, 173, 174
  TBS 146, 159
  in television industry 23, 27, 42,
    33 n.10, 53, 57, 65–9, 94, 100,
    102, 139
  television (re)brand, audiences
    for 65–9
  USA Network 80–90, 91 n.7
cable television 10–14, 23, 26, 57,
  66–8, 71, 81, 90 n.3, 100–2, 105,
  142–3, 146, 170–1, 173, *see also* FX
  Network; Hallmark Channel; HBO;
  TBS; USA Network
capitalism 30, 53 n.2, 55 n.11, 83, 117,
  161, 163, 168
  neoliberal capitalism 6, 19, 53 n.2,
    60, 76, 94, 116–18, 121, 131, 132,
    155, 161, 162, 169, 170
CBS 25, 26, 54–5 n.10, 132 n.1
Cedar Cove (2013–15) 78–9
Chen, Victor Tan 95, 97, 99, 108,
  169, 170
class, *see* socioeconomic class
Colony (2016–18) 84–6, 88

colorblindness   22, 33, 52, 62, 97, 103, 106, 122, 129, 149
comedy   93–4, 103, *see also* television comedies
  transgressive comedy   105–6, 123
consumerism, *see* materialism
critical media industries studies   12–14, 173
Cullen, Jim   1, 8, 17–19, 34, 58–9, 96, 141, 157
Cultural Innovation Theory   67–9, 79
The CW   22–9, 33, 35, 36, 39, 52, 53, 54 n.8, 55 n.10, *see also* Warner Bros.

Daredevil (2015–18)   14, 16, 23, 36–52, 55 nn.17, 19, 81, 95, 100, 110, 126
DC Entertainment   14, 24–7, 35, 39, 52, 54 nn.8–10, *see also* Arrow (2012–20)
Disney   38, 41, 56 n.18, 101, 113

Eco, Umberto   16–17

Fey, Tina   94, 109, 110, 119
Financial Interest and Syndication Rules   142
The Flash (2014–23)   25, 27, 39, 54 n.9, 55 n.16
Friends (1994–2004)   14, 122, 136, 143–57, 159, 161–3, 168, 170–1 n.3
FX Network   72, 81, 88, 94, 102, 119–21, 127

Gen X   146, 150, 156
Gen Z   75, 89, 91 n.8, 171, 172 n.11, 174
Glover, Donald   94, 119, 121–7, 130, 132 n.1
Grace   95, 108, 114–15, 118, 127, 131, 169–70
Great Depression   1, 2, 4, 63, 136
Great Recession   1–3, 6–10, 12, 15, 29, 97, 160
  housing crisis   7, 15, 20, 60–1, 93, 97, 98, 135
  impact on television   68, 71, 105, 106, 109, 116, 131, 143, 144, 147, 148, 150, 156, 172, 173

impact on values   57, 59–61, 64, 65, 68, 93, 95, 98, 99, 105, 129, 135, 169, 173
insecurity caused by   13, 93, 116, 123, 135–8, 141, 147, 156, 170
Millennials   9, 15, 16, 22, 136, 139, 156
recovery phase of   7, 9, 12, 13, 23, 59, 61–2, 68, 79, 99, 127, 129, 135–6, 138, 145, 147, 150, 173, 174
Guerrero, Lisa   121, 123, 128, 130

Haggins, Bambi   10, 99, 122
Hallmark Channel   14, 57, 68–79, 89, 91 n.13, 135, 155
HBO   40, 42, 66, 68, 69, 101
HBO Max   147, 148
Home & Family (2012–21)   77–8, 91 n.6
home
  in *Atlanta*   123, 129–30
  homeownership   5, 7, 18, 45, 60, 62, 73, 98–9
  the housing crisis   7, 15, 20, 60–1, 93, 97, 98, 135
  Millennials   20, 21, 62
  security of   78, 79, 98, 99
  in *Unbreakable Kimmy Schmidt*   117–18
Hulu   28, 42, 75, 89, 100, 101, 121, 142
Hunt, Lee   72, 75, 77, 80

Kimmage, Michael   95, 97–8, 138
Klinger, Barbara   137, 139, 140, 149
Kompare, Derek   135, 141, 146

Lizardi, Ryan   139–41, 143
Loofbourow, Lili   107–8
Lotz, Amanda   11, 91 n.7, 142–3

Marvel   14, 19, 25, 36–44, 52, 54 n.9, 55 n.17, 56 n.18, *see also* Daredevil
materialism   1, 4, 5, 8–9, 16–18, 20–1, 29, 31, 35, 37, 45, 52, 60, 65, 75, 104, 116, 132, 173
meritocracy/merit   2, 4, 7–9, 14, 16, 17, 19, 22, 29–30, 35, 45, 57, 59, 76, 83, 93–9, 106, 108, 111, 113–14, 116–18, 121, 123, 127, 129, 131–2, 135, 138, 154, 165, 168–9, 172 n.10, 173, 174

Millennial(s) 9
  homeownership 20, 21, 62
  nostalgia 141, 148, 149, 170
  in post-Recession period 9, 15, 22,
    136, 140, 154
  redefining the American Dream
    20-2, 44-5
  as television audience 12, 15, 22-4,
    26, 28, 41, 50, 52, 69, 70, 75, 88,
    90, 91 n.9, 100, 102-3, 136, 139,
    174
  television for 81-2, 84, 86
  USA Network audience 80-9
  values and concerns 22, 27, 31, 33,
    37, 39, 44, 52, 53, 62, 63, 81-2, 86,
    90, 103
Mills, Brett 104, 160, 163
Mr. Robot (2015-19) 83-4, 86, 88

NBC 38, 109-10, 119, 145-6, 157-9,
    172 n.7, *see also Friends; The Office;
    Unbreakable Kimmy Schmidt*
NBCUniversal 80-2, 90, 101, 132 n.1,
    158-60, *see also* USA Network
neoliberalism, *see* capitalism
Netflix 11, 22, 28, 36, 38-9, 41-5, 49,
    51, 52, 54 n.9, 56 n.18, 67, 75, 89,
    90, 91 n.8, 94, 100-1, 109, 110,
    112, 133 n.4, 142, 143, 147, 160,
    171, 172 n.8; *see also Daredevil;
    The Office; Unbreakable Kimmy
    Schmidt*
nostalgia
  affective 139, 140, 144, 149, 170
  American Dream, safety in 136-9
  business of 70, 141-4
  Millennials 141, 148, 149, 171
  reflective 137
  regressive 136, 137, 140, 141
  restorative 137, 149, 161-2
  for television 75, 135, 138-41, 170
  totemic 139, 140, 144, 146, 171
nuclear families 55 n.11, 104, 151-2

Obama, Barack 8, 9, 18, 20, 61, 63,
    64, 123
Occupy Wall Street movement 7, 24, 28,
    63, 83, 93, 105

Odyssey Channel 69-70, 91 n.4
The Office (2005-13) 14, 111, 136, 147,
    157-71, 171 n.2
over-the-top (OTT) television, *see*
    streaming television

Patrick, Stephanie 106, 115, 117, 118
postcomplex television 106-7, 124,
    129, 131
Puritans 2-4, 58-9

Queen of the South (2016-21) 86-8

rerun culture 135-7, 140, 143, 170,
    see also second-cycle television;
    syndication
Roosevelt, Franklin Delano 4-5, 18, 19

second-cycle television 14, 42, 67,
    132, 141-3, 145, 146, 158, 160,
    173, *see also* rerun culture;
    syndication
Seinfeld (1989-98) 143, 144, 146, 148,
    152, 159
Shapiro, Stephen 21, 44, 98
sitcoms 99, 104-6, 111, 118, 122, 136,
    143-4, 146-8, 150, 151, 156, 160,
    162-3, 171, 171 n.2, 174, *see also*
    television comedy
socioeconomic class/status 2, 5, 44,
    63, 96-9
  lower 5, 7, 24, 32, 36, 44, 96, 119,
    122, 128
  middle 5, 7, 8, 21, 35, 36, 44, 46, 48,
    49, 51-2, 60-1, 63, 64, 75, 79, 93,
    94, 110, 118, 122
  mobility 1, 2, 5, 8, 37, 46, 57-62, 65,
    138, 164, 169, 174
  upper 7, 8, 21, 22, 30, 32, 34, 35,
    44-7, 49, 52, 91 n.9, 114, 129
  working 7, 21, 22, 29, 44-6, 48-52,
    63, 64, 97, 104, 128
Stevenson, Billy 78-9, 106-7
streaming television 10-12, 15, 23, 28,
    42, 67, 81, 90, 100-1, 140, 142-3,
    147, 160, 170, 173-4
Suits (2011-19) 81, 84, 86, 87, 90,
    91 n.8

superhero narratives   14–19, *see also*
    Arrow; *Daredevil*
syndication   10, 136, 141–6, 148, 150,
    157–60, 163, 170, 171 nn.2, 3, *see*
    also rerun culture; second-cycle
    television

TBS   145, 146, 159, 171 n.2
television comedy   14, 94, 99, 104–7,
    118, 132, *see also Atlanta*; *Friends*;
    The Office; *Unbreakable Kimmy*
    Schmidt; *sitcoms*
  as prestige television   101–2
  sitcoms   104–6, 143, 147, 156
  transgressive comedy   103, 105–8,
    113, 123, 132
  trauma in   105, 109, 113, 119

tentpole television   14, 16, 22–5, 28, 35,
    39, 41, 42, 44, 52, 53 nn.5, 6, 100,
    106, 160, 173–4
30 Rock (2006–13)   94, 109, 110, 119

Unbreakable Kimmy Schmidt
    (2015–20)   94, 99, 108–19,
    121, 129, 131–2
USA Network   14, 57, 68, 72, 80–90

Warner, Kristen   22, 33, 97, 129
Warner Bros.   25–6, 54 n.10, 144–6, *see*
    also CW; *Friends*
Winthrop, John   4, 157
Writers Guild of America Strike
    2007–8   10, 143, 147, 159, 172 n.7
    2023   174

www.ingramcontent.com/pod-product-compliance
Lightning Source LLC
Chambersburg PA
CBHW050155070225
21491CB00003B/10